Thomas Abthorpe Cooper

Thomas Abthorpe Cooper

*Father of the American Stage,
1775–1849*

F. ARANT MAGINNES

McFarland & Company, Inc., Publishers
Jefferson, North Carolina, and London

LIBRARY OF CONGRESS CATALOGUING-IN-PUBLICATION DATA

Maginnes, F. Arant, 1936–
    Thomas Abthorpe Cooper : father of the American stage, 1775–1849 / F. Arant Maginnes.
        p.   cm.
    Includes bibliographical references and index.

    ISBN-13: 978-0-7864-1935-7
    softcover : 50# alkaline paper ∞

    1. Cooper, Thomas Abthorpe, 1776–1849. 2. Actors—United States—Biography. I. Title.
    PN2287.C595M34   2004
    792.02'8'092—dc22   2004010968

British Library cataloguing data are available

©2004 F. Arant Maginnes. All rights reserved

No part of this book may be reproduced or transmitted in any form or by any means, electronic or mechanical, including photocopying or recording, or by any information storage and retrieval system, without permission in writing from the publisher.

Front cover: Oil portrait of Cooper as Hamlet, by Thomas Sully (courtesy Louis Cooper Rutland, Fitzpatrick, Alabama)

Manufactured in the United States of America

McFarland & Company, Inc., Publishers
    Box 611, Jefferson, North Carolina 28640
    www.mcfarlandpub.com

To the two hundredth anniversary of the
opening of the city of Washington

"Thou art not, as impostors say,
A shadow soon to pass away
A superstition and a name
Echoing from the cave of Fame."

"The Mask of Anarchy" LIV,
—*Percy Bysshe Shelley*

Acknowledgments

Cooper's large family endeared him to the American public. I remember his great-great-granddaughter, the late Elizabeth Tyler Coleman, with affection and gratitude, for her professional advice in suggesting this subject to me, and for her trust in giving me her notes on the Cooper family, as well as permission to quote from the superlative collection she gathered of Cooper and Tyler family letters. These letters together with the diary of the Coopers' eldest daughter, Mary Grace, comprise the "Elizabeth Tyler Coleman Papers," preserved in the W. S. Hoole Special Collections Library at the University of Alabama.

I would like to thank the late Lord Abinger, of Castle Hedingham, Halstead Essex, for his generosity in granting me permission to read and quote from the Cooper letters and references in his definitive collection of the Godwin and Shelley papers on deposit in the Bodleian Library at Oxford University, and give special thanks to the staff of the Bodleian, especially Dr. Bruce Barker-Benfield for his informative and thoughtful assistance.

I would like to express particular gratitude to Mr. Louis Cooper Rutland, great-great grandson of Cooper's eldest daughter Mary Grace and her husband Frederic Sebastian Raoul, for granting his permission, and his and his wife's gracious assistance, for the reproduction of the Thomas Sully portrait of Cooper he owns for this book. I am also grateful to Mr. Rutland's mother, the late Rose Raoul Rutland, for sharing the *Bible* Frederic Raoul gave Mary Grace as a wedding present; the family record handwritten in the frontispiece is a significant primary source of information on Cooper's children by his first wife, Joanna Johnstone; as well as his second wife, Mary Fairlie, her family, and their descendants.

My thanks to several other direct descendants of the Cooper and Fairlie families who gave me specific assistance and generous offerings of their family records: Fairlie Shattuck Benson, Adele Bibb Colvin, Priscilla Crommelin, Mary Goodwyn, Caroline W. Hill, Lucia Nelson,

Fairlie Maxwell Pasfield, Adèle Griffin Sands, and Nelle Cubbedge Walker.

I would like to express my very special gratitude to Dr. Don B. Wilmeth, Professor of Theatre and English at Brown University, for the strong direction and support he gave me, my mainstay on the road to publication. My thanks as well to Professor Arthur H. Ballet, Department of Theatre Arts, University of Minnesota, advisor for my Ph.D. dissertation on Cooper; Professor Betty T. Bennett, American University, and Professor Philip H. Highfill, Jr., George Washington University, for their support; Professors Stephen M. Archer, Gresdna Doty, Julian Mates, and Bruce McConachie for their gifts of knowledge and information; and Professor Sarah Woolfolk Wiggins, University of Alabama, for her generous support and assistance.

I express particular thanks to the George Washington University Gelman Library staff: Glenn Canner of Inter-Library Loan; Catherine Hamer; and Wendell Kellar; to my excellent research assistants at George Washington, Motrja Paluch and Siobhan Starrs; and to Imad Aldean Ahmad for his timely computer support. I am also very grateful to the Washington Research Library Consortium, which gave me access to other area libraries: in particular, American University, where I spent a great deal of time; also Catholic University; Gallaudet University; George Mason University; Georgetown University, Marymount University; and University of the District of Columbia. Special gratitude to The Folger Shakespeare Library for their generosity in granting me an extended readership for the course of my work, Georgianna Ziegler; Channing Pollock Theatre Collection, Howard University, Arthuree Wright, Steven Yoon; District of Columbia Historical Society, Gail Rudman; Library of Congress for both their collection and their excellent responsiveness to queries; Martin Luther King Memorial Library; Bethesda-Chevy Chase Regional Library; Enoch Pratt Free Library, Baltimore; Maryland Historical Society, Jeannine Disviscour, Mary E. Herbert; Boston Public Library; Harvard Theatre Collection, Annette Fern, Kathleen Coleman; Carl H. Pforzheimer Library; New York Public Library; Hampden-Booth Theatre Library, Raymond Wemmlinger; American Philosophical Society; Free Library of Philadelphia, Geraldine Duclow; Library Company of Philadelphia; Margaret R. Grundy Memorial Library, Bristol, Pennsylvania, Mary Jane Mannherz; Pennsylvania Historical Society; Van Pelt-Dietrich Library Center, University of Pennsylvania; Charleston Historical Society; Hoole Special Collections Library, University of Alabama, Jessica Lacher-Feldman; New Orleans Public Library, Mary White; Tulane University Library; Richmond Historical Society; British

Library Newspaper Library; Royal Academy of Arts, Patricia Eaton; Theatre Museum, London, Margaret Benton, Janet Birkett.

I would like to express particular gratitude to the Bristol Cultural and Historical Foundation in Bristol, Pennsylvania, where Cooper had his homes: Charlotte Landreth-Melville, Harold and Carol Mitchener, Helen M. Younglove; with a very special tribute to the late Paul Ferguson, for his dedication to the American arts, to his wife Carol for continuing the strong interest they expressed in this book from the beginning, and to both of them for their generosity in sharing their research on Cooper and correspondence with Washington Irving that is featured here.

I gratefully remember my mother and father, Letitia McNeel and Douglas Arant, for their inspiration and assistance in the early part of my work on Cooper; and give special thanks to my son David Tyler Maginnes for his faith and help in the search; to all the other good relatives and friends who have sustained their interest in this project through the years; and to Goodwyn for his patience.

My dearest love and gratitude I reserve for my husband, David Russell Maginnes, who offered me unfailing support throughout all the years of research and writing, as well as his keen professional knowledge and assistance.

Contents

Acknowledgments vii
List of Illustrations xiii
Preface 1
Introduction 5

Part I
The Rise to Fame, 1775–1803

One—"This Wild Immeasurably Spread"—1800 9
Two—British-Born—1775–88 21
Three—"Aut Caesar aut Nihil"—1788–92 25
Four—"The Die Is Cast"—1792–93 34
Five—"My Fortune Smiles" 42
    An Irish Benefit—1793   42
    "A Wretched Set of Mummers"—1794   48
Six—"A Young Gentleman" 55
    Mr. Holcroft—1795   55
    First Appearance—1795–96   59
Seven—*The Wheel of Fortune*—1796–98 71
Eight—The New House 84
    The Park Debut—1798   84
    André—1799   87
    New Successes—1799   89
Nine—"Fame Is My Deity" 92
    New York City—1799–1800   92
    Philadelphia—1800–01   98
Ten—Rising Returns—1801–03 102

Part II
The American Star, 1803–1849

Eleven—An American Indeed 111
    Drury Lane—1803   111
    The Provinces—1803–04   116

Twelve—The United States' Star 122
    New York and Philadelphia—1804–05   122
    Boston—1805–06   125
    The South—1806–07   131

Thirteen—Yankee Ingenuity 137
    Itinerant Star—1807–10   137
    "This Glorious Son of York"—1810   145
    "A Hearty Welcome"—1811–12   150

Fourteen—The American Roscius—1812–19 156

Fifteen—A Rival 165
    A New Vogue—1819–20   165
    "A Triumph to Cooper"—1820–21   171

Sixteen—A New Venue—1820–25 175

Seventeen—Turning Tide 181
    An American Tragedian—1825–28   181
    Success and Sorrow—1828–33   189

Eighteen—"The Father of the American Stage"—1833–36 196

Epilogue 1835–49 203
Chapter Notes 207
Bibliography 221
Index 229

List of Illustrations

Mr. Cooper as Pierre	16
Playbill for the United States' Theatre, September 5, 1800	19
Mr. Cooper as Barnwell	51
Mrs. Merry as Alzira	52
Sketch of Thomas Holcroft and William Godwin	53
Playbill for Mr. Cooper's London Debut	60
Mr. Cooper as Pericles	67
Old Holliday Street Theatre	73
Portrait of Mr. Cooper as Hamlet attributed to Rembrandt Peale	79
Interior of the Park Theatre	82
Engraving of Mr. Cooper by C. H. Meyer	120
Engraving of Mr. Cooper by S. Harris	129
Engraving of Mr. Cooper as Hamlet by Edwin	143
George Frederick Cooke as Iago	152
Portrait of Mrs. Thomas A. Cooper by William Dunlap	158
The Cooper Home in Bristol	164
Mr. Cooper as Leon	166
Mr. Cooper as Macbeth	170
Portrait of Mr. Cooper by John Wesley Jarvis	173
Miss Priscilla Cooper as Helena	200
Portrait of Mr. Cooper by Gilbert Stuart	205

Preface

Thomas Abthorpe Cooper was the first actor to rise to fame in the new American nation. He became the first great star of the American stage. Beginning in 1797, with the next century in view, for more than thirty years he performed in theatres throughout the newly established United States; *Cooper* was a household name in the first half of the nineteenth century. Yet this primary American artist was largely forgotten once his acting powers declined and other stars took his place onstage.

Cooper died at his home in Bristol, Pennsylvania, in 1849. In 1854, his contemporary, Charles Durang, began writing a series of articles on the Philadelphia stage for the *Sunday Dispatch*. Of Cooper he observed, "Mr. Cooper's memory has been strangely neglected by his admiring contemporaries and friends." He went on to assert, "Professional accomplishments, requiring cultivated intellect and the blandishments of the gentleman, should have their just claims to position in society allowed—the respect due to the artiste, and the sympathies of the world accorded—for the player pictures sympathy, pathos, good manners, and all the charities of religion, in the form of poetry. If these be the player's functions, and his career is marked by morality and good citizenship, surely his memory deserves a record."[1] To fill the void, Durang suggested the erection of a monument, perhaps a statue of Cooper as a noble Roman; famously graced with perfection of form and feature, Cooper had repeatedly been described by theatre critics as an ideal subject for the sculptor. Despite Durang's impetus, however, no monument was erected.

George P. Morris, the editor of a New York weekly, *The Home Journal*, asked another of Cooper's contemporaries, Dr. John Beaufain Irving of Charleston, to write about the actor. An intimate friend of Cooper's, Irving responded with "Reminiscences of a Tragedian. Thomas A. Cooper: His Life, Social and Professional, in Charleston, South Carolina," which appeared in the *Journal* in a series of installments over a six-month period in 1857–58. Irving expressed the hope that his account would inspire

Cooper's friends in other cities to write similar records in order to accumulate a substantial memoir, but at that time no others came forward.

At the outset of the Civil War, Priscilla, the daughter who had acted with Cooper on the stage, was forced to flee with her husband, Robert Tyler, from Cooper's hometown of Bristol, Pennsylvania, where they had been living; son of U.S. President John Tyler of Virginia, Tyler was a Southern sympathizer with political ambition. The Tylers had to leave most of their effects in Bristol where they were confiscated. After the War, they joined her older sister in Alabama and never returned to live in Bristol, where Cooper's life had been established. Instead, his legacy seemed to vanish.

Cooper's successor on the stage was the first native-born star, Edwin Forrest, and America's youthful pride tended to subsume Cooper's reputation in Forrest's. Moreover, at the end of the Civil War, the *Booth* name would replace all others in American theatrical memory, because on Good Friday, April 14, 1865, Junius Brutus Booth's son, the young actor John Wilkes Booth, assassinated President Abraham Lincoln at Ford's Theatre in Washington. The Booth family, and actors in general, suffered demonization thereafter. John's brother, the gifted Edwin Booth, went into retirement after the tragedy, but he had to resume his stage career because of his family's financial necessity. Upon his return at the Winter Garden Theatre in New York, January 3, 1866, he found himself an instant celebrity, not just for his indisputable talent, but also for his brother's infamy; many people who had never attended the theatre before packed the house that night to see *Booth*. He went on to a brilliant career thereafter, but one city he declined ever to play again—the City of Washington, where Cooper had been the original star.

In 1888 for the Dunlap Society Joseph Norton Ireland wrote *A Memoir of the Professional Life of Thomas Abthorpe Cooper*. It was not until the mid-twentieth century, however, that scholars began to study American theatre history in earnest, and then Cooper became a subject of interest. In 1954 Lael Jay Woodbury began by devoting a portion of his Ph.D. dissertation on acting styles to Cooper. In 1955 Elizabeth Coleman wrote a biography of Cooper's daughter Priscilla, *Priscilla Cooper Tyler and the American Scene 1816–1889*, which provides a picture of Cooper's personal life with his family, as well as his theatrical touring with Priscilla. For his master's thesis in 1968, James Bearden compiled "A Tabulation of the Stage Performances of Thomas Abthorpe Cooper." Then in 1970 Ireland's *Memoir* was reissued.

In 1971 I completed my doctoral dissertation, "A Biography of the Actor Thomas Abthorpe Cooper," based in part on Cooper's letters to

William Godwin in the *Abinger Papers* at Oxford University and Cooper family letters in the *Elizabeth Tyler Coleman Papers* at the University of Alabama, for both of which the project gained the first permission rights granted. In 1972 Harold Jordan offered his dissertation, "Thomas Cooper: A Biographical Chronology"; and Nancy C. Schulte, a master's thesis, "The Acting Style of Thomas Abthorpe Cooper." In 1996 Geddeth Smith published a biography of Cooper, *Thomas Abthorpe Cooper America's Premier Tragedian*. With a useful "Chronology of the Repertoire," it emphasizes contextual history with the episodes of Cooper's life through his retirement years. I express my deep respect and gratitude to all those who have contributed to the Cooper canon, as well as for the distinguished work of the many other scholars in whose work I have found both information and insight, all cited in the Bibliography and Notes.

Coming in a new century, this book represents a departure from the compilations of the life in previous accounts, my own and others. It has a newly focused perspective by which detail is pared away to get closer to the true person and the people with whom he was most closely involved. It is designed to define the significance of a figure whose career is viewed as central to the foundation of American cultural life. To this effect new research has yielded additional primary sources. With interest in the project, the Cultural and Historical Foundation of Bristol, Pa., where Cooper maintained two homes, has granted first publication rights to Washington Irving's London correspondence with Cooper in their possession, which helps to illuminate the American–British theatrical rivalry which Cooper's career embodied. An essay on acting written by Cooper's mentor, the playwright Thomas Holcroft, forms the basis for a delineation of the development of his individual acting style, followed throughout the book. A manuscript record in private hands in Alabama corrects previous assumptions concerning certain facts of Cooper's family life. With careful respect for the sources, this book also corrects textual inaccuracies in previous accounts.

Cooper's guardian, William Godwin, trained him in his own trade, the writing profession, so while it was Godwin's friend, the actor/playwright Thomas Holcroft, whose profession he ultimately espoused, he also learned to write extremely well. In 1838 he told his son James, "I am making preparations for publishing my life—& that will require quietude and locality."[2] If he indeed wrote his book, it has never been found, but his early letters to Godwin, preserved in the *Abinger* archive in the Bodleian Library at Oxford University, constitute a partial autobiography, written with cultivated style and flair, though in haste, amid the heat of performance and ceaseless travel. These letters, written during Cooper's developmental years, are the chief primary source for Part I of this book. They give the reader a direct experience of his life and also provide invaluable accounts of the early theatre in America and England. And here, where the original is long removed in time, he is allowed to speak, sometimes at length, for himself.

The other central primary sources are newspaper and journal reviews of Cooper's performances, and personal accounts written by his contemporaries. The bulk of the reviews are American and reflect, despite ongoing prejudice in favor of the British, how cultivated the early American theatrical critics were and, like the audiences they described, how clearly cognizant of Cooper's excellence, as well as his significance to the cultural standards of their emergent nation. This book features extended quotations from these sources, in both the text and chapter notes, concerning his most notable portrayals—Macbeth, Hamlet, Othello, Coriolanus, Mark Antony, as well as Iago—since the story of an artist is primarily in his art.

The two contemporaries whose accounts of Cooper are most significant, in addition to Charles Durang, are the New York manager William Dunlap, who published his *Diary* and *History of the American Theatre*; and William Wood, actor/manager of the Chestnut Street Theatre, who was four years younger than Cooper and outlived him by twelve years to publish his *Personal Recollections of the Stage* in 1855. Wood said of Cooper, "No actor in our country ever had so long and so admired a career.... . The simple length of his service gives him a place and prominence which distinguishes him from other actors." He devoted a section of his book to Cooper, the only figure so honored.[3]

The concentration of this book is on the influence of Cooper's London upbringing, his rise to fame, and his formation and development of the role of independent touring star in America. Beyond the story of an individual life, the idea is to reveal a pattern to reflect the form and substance of his career and its relationship to the British culture from which it grew. The intent is to clarify the position which Cooper holds in the foundation of the American cultural dynamic. To reawaken the splendor of his contribution in the public mind, this book begins with his participation as a young man in the opening of the new American Capital, the City of Washington, in 1800.

Introduction

The shaping moment in the life of the British boy, Thomas Cooper, who became the first star of the American stage, was the death of his father out in India when he was eleven. The subsequent loss by shipwreck of papers documenting Dr. Cooper's property caused his family financial ruin; Mrs. Cooper had to go to Holland to take a position as a housekeeper, leaving her children to live with friends and relatives in England. Thomas was placed in the London household of his mother's cousin, the radical philosopher William Godwin.

Godwin determined to train his young charge for the writing profession, which he himself had espoused after turning away from the Christian ministry, but he also exposed the boy to the theatre, through his friendship with the playwright Thomas Holcroft. In response to the heady world of Godwin's circle, which included the fascinating poet, Samuel Taylor Coleridge, and the actress-playwright, Elizabeth Inchbald, young Cooper channeled his instincts and feelings into an intense desire for fame. Moreover, Godwin's and Holcroft's involvement in radical politics during the Revolutionary Age sparked an ardor for the ideals of liberty and equality in the boy which attuned him to the opportunities offered by the New World. With an excellent mind, a musical voice and ideal physique, he was well suited for the role he was destined to play.

At age sixteen, preparing to leave Godwin's household and strike out on his own, Cooper announced that he was bound for France to join the Republican Army. Godwin and Holcroft quickly arranged him an apprenticeship in the theatre instead, and for the next three years he learned his profession by acting in Britain's provincial theatres. At the young age of nineteen he appeared in an extraordinary debut in London at the Theatre Royal, Covent Garden, to notable success, but tainted by his political connections in a reactionary era in Britain, soon left for America and a position as the leading young actor in the Philadelphia Company.

In 1800, although he had already begun his rapid rise to prominence in the new nation, Cooper was still unaware of his destiny as the American star when he played the leading roles in the United States' Theatre to celebrate the opening of the unfinished American capital in Washington. He had broken his contract with the stock company in Philadelphia in order to play in New York, and shortly thereafter had also broken his contract in New York, thereby freeing himself to tour all of the existing states as an independent star. He would travel about replacing local actors, playing the well-known Shakespearean roles in the grand classical manner, also offering a wide repertoire of other plays, both tragedy and comedy, fulfilling the public's desire for myth and romance.

Wearing a cloak trimmed in gold lace and brandishing a pair of pistols for protection, Cooper drove his own team of horses from city to city, a familiar figure in the early American landscape. In the days before the steamship or railroad, he embodied the entrepreneurial spirit that the limitless nature of the young country invited, cutting a star track for others to follow. He solidified and extended his influence when he became the manager of the Park Theatre in New York, the first to import the major London stars, beginning with George Frederick Cooke.

Cooper's personal autocracy meant that he never feared the competition he brought to America, or those who came later. The grand insouciance of his public mystique; the fortune he made and carelessly dissipated, a figure of fate with a penchant for gambling; the wives he won from New York's first families; and his eight children—all served to advance his celebrity. The name *Cooper* became so identified with the American stage that in 1828, on a return tour of England, the British public rejected him as a renegade.

Part I

The Rise to Fame, 1775–1803

One

"This Wild Immeasurably Spread"—1800

In May of 1800 the Capital of the United States officially moved from Philadelphia to Washington, the city planned by George Washington on a site of ten square miles he had chosen at the confluence of the Potomac and Anacostia Rivers. In November, when First Lady Abigail Adams arrived to take up residence in the President's House, she confessed it "a beautiful spot," but also spoke with chagrin in her letter to her daughter of "this wilderness city."[1] A mere scattering of houses relieved the general terrain of brush and uncleared bushes, and tree stumps marred many of the muddy streets, which were still unpaved. The one other monumental Federal structure on the horizon was the northern house wing of the Capitol, all that was finished of the grand Palladian-style building, but a vast distance separated it from the President's House. This expanse may have prefigured the future dimension of a great nation as envisioned by the founders, but in 1800 it probably struck more than one of the early arrivers as absurd.

In the mid-city, on the north side of E Street between 7th and 8th Streets near the post office, was a large two-story building intended as a hotel. "Blodgett's Lottery Hotel," as it came to be known, had an attic, a basement, and a brick frontage of 120 feet, but the inside had never been finished, and the owner, Samuel Blodgett of New Hampshire, had devised the scheme of offering it as a lottery prize. During the summer of 1800 Thomas Wignell and the musician Alexander Reinagle, the managers of the Philadelphia Company resident at the Chestnut Street Theatre in Philadelphia, secured an agreement with the commissioners of the new Capital to set up a temporary theatre in the Hotel to celebrate the opening of the city. By that time, Blodgett, along with other speculators who had come there in order to make their fortunes, had departed, most of them bankrupt.

Wignell, who kept his company together all year to offset the losses which would occur when there was an outbreak of yellow fever, saw the Washington engagement both as an honor and as an opportunity to extend the summer season he generally offered in Annapolis and Alexandria. Although the government would not open in Washington officially until November 21, the six existing departments were already conducting their business in the city by July. In August the entire Philadelphia Company, between seventy and eighty actors and a twenty-piece orchestra, arrived and immediately began setting up a small theatre on the main floor of the hotel. With an audience section of 300 seats made of wooden planks, they claimed its significance by naming it grandly the *United States' Theatre*.

Mrs. Anne Brunton Merry was the new theatre's star attraction. With blue eyes and an aquiline nose, she was considered not only beautiful and charming, but also interesting, playing romantic roles with gentle intensity. As Anne Brunton, she had achieved stardom at an early age in London, but upon marrying the fashionably pedantic "della-cruscan" poet, Robert Merry, had given up the stage at his request. Despite his literary success, however, Merry became known as a political radical, and by 1795 was having difficulty making a living in England.

In October of that year, he went to see Thomas Cooper, the ward of a radical associate, the writer William Godwin, make his acting debut at Covent Garden, and was so favorably impressed that he wrote about it to his wife, who was out of London visiting her father at Bath: "'[A] most extraordinary lad of nineteen, named Cooper, said to be a ward of Godwin or Holcroft, has created much sensation by his admirable performance of Hamlet, but more of Macbeth[.]'" He urged her to return forthwith to see Cooper perform, which she did, and she was duly impressed as well.[2] The following year Wignell was in England recruiting a group of actors for his new theatre and offered Mrs. Merry a contract to star in America, which she signed with her husband's consent. Wignell then set about finding an actor to pair with her, and when a search of several months did not produce one, the Merrys suggested Cooper, who readily accepted the contract Wignell offered him.

Though only twenty years old when he landed in America, Thomas Cooper came determined to make his way in the new country immediately. After one season in Philadelphia, in August 1797 he and Mrs. Merry made highly lauded showcase appearances in New York. Thereafter, Cooper broke his contract with Wignell to make the most of the success he first fully garnered in New York, while Mrs. Merry remained with the Philadelphia Company. Wignell, however, filed and won a lawsuit against Cooper, thereby securing the talented young actor's return to the Philadelphia Company just in time for the Washington engagement.

One—"This Wild Immeasurably Spread"—1800

Cooper's youthful passion had filled him with heroic dreams, but in 1800 he did not yet realize he would live in the new country for the rest of his life, America's first rising star. In retrospect, however, it seems fitting that it was from the unfinished new American Capital, "the City of Washington," that he wrote a long letter back to William Godwin in London explaining the resolution of the contract suit: "I have compromised the business by agreeing to remain with them another year ... and paying L110 sterling—very much to their satisfaction, my services being more valuable than the penalty; and to my own, one year's servitude being preferable to imprisonment sine die."

In his letter Cooper unburdened himself, sharing some of the experiences that colored his early impressions of America. He had gone to live with Godwin, his mother's cousin, after his father's untimely death; from the age of eleven he had grown up under his care and influence during the very years when the philosopher was writing his definitive essay, *An Enquiry Concerning Political Justice*. Now in the United States, founded on Godwinian principles of liberty and equality, he referred to Godwin in his letter as "the father of my mind," but began his letter with a Miltonic image of hell in *Paradise Lost* to describe the new country:

> If I had lived a regular life since I have existed in this "wild immeasureably [*sic*] spread"—I should probably have kept a journal or such memorandums, as would have sufficed to call to my recollection variety of adventures that I have met with in my travels, by no means barren of amusement, nor altogether destitute of utility. But my misfortunes (whether originating in carelessness, passion, or bad judgment) have kept me so busy, so hurried in the means of opposing or forgetting them (I fear most frequently the latter) that I have never bestowed a thought as to what I shall have to say for myself at the dear moment of welcome return to my native country; or, what is of more importance, to the friends of my youth, the relations of my blood and the father of my mind. I have traversed over and over again, during long vacations a space of seven hundred miles in length and three hundred in breadth, without having possessed myself of any variety even of anecdote which I should think worthy repetition. I have seen great variety of men—(that is, have had a vastly extensive acquaintance) but no variety of minds. The same object engrosses the soul of every American, insatiable thirst of gain. They differ in their manners in the different parts, but their ultimatum is universal. I believe I may safely say I never was acquainted with four Americans who could converse decently or with common intelligence on any subject unless on contracted mercantile politics or the value of a ship or cargo. The fine arts or literature never were known to grow in this soil: when occasionally transplanted hither, they universally perish. Some foreigners of talents have become merchants and Americans; others

unable to adapt themselves to circumstances and languishing for want of due nourishment & culture have become drunkards & beasts—more than one melancholy instance of this latter fact I have witnessed. They are not even refined in their pleasures or elegant in debauchery—their tastes are gross, their manners vulgar & ostentatious; their enjoyments are depraved in conception, and filthy in execution. I know no one good or respectable quality they possess as a people (unless it be courage) and individually they are worse. Excessive vanity is their great national feature. Exceptional knavery their private characters. The merchants are almost universally cheats, because they are all speculators. They lend and borrow upon immense advantage, in hope of profiting immensely. Which hope is very, very frequently disappointed, and extensive ruin ensues.

The opening of the United States' Theatre was considerably delayed due to the misfortune the company had suffered on the road from Philadelphia when a driving rainstorm flooded their wagons. The rain ruined all the scenery they were transporting, as well as an artificial dome and adornments elaborately designed and painted for the audience section of the new enterprise. Upon their arrival in Washington, however, the leading citizens rallied around them to offer their interest and support. A young physician, Dr. William Thornton, who had created the winning design for the Capitol, was one of the three District Commissioners, and his wife kept a daily diary. On August 11 she recorded walking from her home over "to the Great Hotel" before tea to see how Mr. Wignell and his troupe were doing. She found them "fitting up one large room for the theatre & a few for dressing rooms[.]"[3] Some of the families of the laborers working on the Capitol were also staying there, and Christian Hines, a boy at the time, later recalled how he and some others hoisted themselves up through the basement, lifting the floorboards of the makeshift theatre to sneak in and watch.[4]

Finally, on Friday, August 22, Cooper, Mrs. Merry, and the rest of the Philadelphia Company gave the first theatrical performance in the new Capital.[5] They presented Thomas Otway's brilliant poetic tragedy, *Venice Preserv'd*, and a favorite farce (in two acts) called *The Spoil'd Child* [Dublin, 1792]. A thin audience, "about 130 people,"[6] the temporary stage and scant scenery, seem a fitting reflection of the incipient nature of the young Republic.

Wignell, a fine comic actor, with a slight stoop and large expressive blue eyes, spoke a Prologue written for the occasion by Mr. John Law; married to a granddaughter of Mrs. Washington, Law was a lively and enthusiastic Englishman who had come to the new city to speculate in real estate. The poetic piece began with a classical allusion, comparing the time it had taken to build Washington, "Ten tedious anxious years are past," to the length of time it had taken Greece to conquer Troy, and referred to the recent death of George Washington:

> Let other nations look to Greece and Rome,
> Columbia's bright examples are at home:
> Whate'er is great or good we find in one—
> All virtues join'd to form a *Washington*.
> ....
> Mourn not—but thankful that his life was spared
> So long, enjoy the blessings he prepared.

The conceit continued with a comparison of the building of new stage sets to the building of the new capital:

> The floods of late, which drown'd you many a horse,
> Have caused to us a much severer loss –
> Our groves, our temples, gone beyond repair,
> The gorgeous palaces it did not spare;
> The storm has swept our canvas almost bare.
> For this deficiency we'll soon atone –
> Would you could build as fast with brick and stone.
> ....
> If various tongues from building could disable,
> Your houses would of course be stopp'd like Babel:
> Dutch, Irish, German, French, *All* hither flee,
> To enjoy the sweets of Liberty.[7]

Fittingly for the Washington opening, *Venice Preserv'd* is a tale of political insurrection. First performed in London in 1682 after the collapse of the Whigs' Popish plot, the play held a place with Shakespeare on the London stage for over a century. With deeply impassioned ideals, love, and mixed loyalties, it offers starring roles with ample opportunity for varying interpretations and was performed by most of the great actors and actresses in London from Thomas Betterton to the Kembles, and was notably revived in the twentieth century by John Gielgud. Cooper played the role of Pierre, the leader of the conspiracy, motivated by a heroic code of honor as much as by political intention. Mrs. Merry acted Belvidera, and Wignell took the part of Pierre's friend and betrayer, Jaffier.

William Wood, who played Spinoza, one of the conspirators, observed of Cooper that he "possessed the advantage of a remarkably fine person. He was not quite six feet high, but his proportion and form was beautiful. He constantly recalled to those of us who saw his figure undressed, the remark of a quick observer in regard to another noble looking man of Philadelphia, now deceased, 'His figure was free from all imposture.'"[8] His first apprenticeship in the theatre had been with the tragedian John Philip Kemble's brother, Stephen Kemble, and their sister, the supremely gifted tragedienne Sarah Siddons. As his acting career developed, he assumed the classical style Kemble and Mrs. Siddons had made fashionable. With a clear musical voice, he would become its chief exponent in America.

The latter half of the eighteenth century had seen a revival of interest in classicism, inspired in part by excavations of the Roman city of Pompeii. In London beginning in 1768, the celebrated painter, Sir Joshua Reynolds, presented annual *Discourses* to the Royal Academy promoting his theory that art should not imitate but rather elevate nature, recognizing only the beautiful and noble aspects, the ideal. In the "theatrick art," he said, "every thing should be raised and enlarged beyond its natural state; ... Hence the deliberate and stately step, the studied grace of action, which seems to enlarge the dimensions of the Actor, and alone to fill the stage."[9] The art of elocution was also gaining attention, particularly through the performances of two well-known actors, Thomas Sheridan and John Walker, both of whom wrote dictionaries. Their efforts inspired the first focused initiative to study pronunciation and action in order to teach oral interpretation or reading aloud. These trends represented a distinct departure from the prevalent style of natural realism of the great actor/manager of Drury Lane Theatre, David Garrick. Garrick retired in 1776, opening the way for the new classical manner of acting, which John Philip Kemble introduced in his London debut at Drury Lane as Hamlet in 1783. Invoking an idealized sense of nobility and grace, the grand declamatory style that Kemble and Mrs. Siddons developed created a distinct vogue.

This brief period in the theatre would be supplanted by the romantic movement, which began to rise in the 1780s and peaked in the early decades of the new century. In September 1800, however, at the official opening of Washington, Cooper's noble form and style mirrored the Greco-Roman ideals reflected in the architectural style of the new Capital, giving a sense of the high purpose and republican virtues of equality and self-government that the founding fathers wished to promulgate. And as he began traveling throughout the existing states of the new nation, he would become a wildly popular star, the elevating grace of the representation, lingering in the public imagination, to be suggested as a model for copy not only for the stage, but the pulpit and bar as well.[10]

Typically, upon entering the stage, before speaking Cooper would take a balanced and elegant pose, delineating the passion of the hero he was portraying in a sculptural manner. After a lengthy pause, he would begin to speak, with precise articulation following the melodic thrust of the line, instead of the more ordinary conversational inflection. During the course of a play he seldom made use of direct crosses, sudden starts, or random pacing, relying instead on poses and frequent pauses to reflect nuances of the text. He would also use pantomimic gesture, such as pointing to his heart to depict love.[11]

The role of Pierre was perfectly suited to the classical style and remained a favorite in Cooper's repertoire. Although the play is set in Venice, he dressed, according to theatrical custom of the time, in a contemporary Empire-period military uniform. The drawing by C. R. Leslie [next page] delineates the moment of climax, when Pierre, in chains, confronts Jaffier with his betrayal:

> Yes, a most notorious villain—
> To see the sufferings of my fellow-creatures,
> And own myself a man; to see our senators
> Cheat the deluded people with a show of liberty,
> Which yet they ne'er must taste of.
> (*Venice Preserv'd*: Act One, Scene Two)

Wood said that the opening performance in Washington was "warmly received and applauded by an audience, more numerous, as well as splendid, than can be conceived from a population so slender and so scattered." He went on to note, "From the citizens of Washington the principal performers received the most gratifying attention and hospitality. Many of us commenced at this period acquaintances and friendships which have continued with unabated kindness through a long course of succeeding years."[12]

Cooper also met a British connection in Washington. Before he had left England, Godwin's future wife, Mary Wollstonecraft, author of *A Vindication of the Rights of Women*, had written him a letter of introduction to her youngest and favorite brother, Captain Charles Wollstonecraft; Mary had married Godwin soon thereafter, but had died only six months later, in giving birth to their daughter Mary, later Mary Shelley.* Wollstonecraft, who was serving in the U.S. Infantry stationed in Washington, happened to be quartered at Mrs. Finch's boarding house on Greenleaf Point where the Philadelphia Company was staying; meeting and conversing with him apparently prompted Cooper to add a note of sympathy in his letter to Godwin. His words reflect his ability to understand

---

*At age 16 Mary would elope with one of her father's disciples, romantic poet Percy Bysshe Shelley.

Cooper as Pierre. Engraving by J. O. Lewis, from a drawing by C. R. Leslie. Museum of the City of New York 47.86.11.

and identify with feelings, which would become a recognizable feature of his stage portrayals:

> At this distant period I can without apprehension of giving your mind accute [sic] anguish, condole with you on the decease of your wife. She was the individual who gave a new & more amiable character to a mind fixed in it's [sic] opinions by long habits to deep thought. Reasoning alone I am convinced would never have produced the effect. Your passions, your affection must have been deeply engaged. How happy she must have made you how exquisite miserable her loss. I had not her acquaintance but though unused to the melting mood, I was inexpressibly affected when I heard of her death. I loved her, for she was the means of happiness to him, whom I look upon as, at least among the first of human beings.

William Wood said of Wollstonecraft that his "lively and intelligent manner and conversation was strangely contrasted with his awkward, unprepossessing appearance." Wood also noticed, "During the many cheerful hours he passed with us I never heard a single disloyal or unkind remark, either from him, Cooper, or Mr. Merry, in regard to English politics." He went on to observe that they had all suffered from "their reputed ultra opinions," and commented, "So little is generally known of actors!"[13] Godwin and his close friend and political associate, the playwright Thomas Holcroft, had promoted Cooper's career in the theatre and had both strongly advised him against accepting Wignell's offer to go to America. However, Holcroft's arrest in 1794 by Pitt's government on the charge of treason, though he was exonerated, was undoubtedly a factor in Cooper's decision to leave England.

In response to Godwin's continuing interest, in his letter Cooper refuted his sponsors' prediction that going to America would destroy his career. He began, "I must now speak a little of myself. You certainly did injustice to the stability of my mind & character, my dear friend, & also Mr. Holcroft when you supposed that the transportation of my body to this world, was to be attended with the death of my mind, or at least was to put an end to progressive improvement. I have sometimes slept, it is true, but have frequently awoke to very considerable purpose." And went on to delineate his professional development in the four years he had been in America:

> I may say that I have constantly been improving in my profession: or if not unremittingly at least that every year has made important change for the better. I do not think that I am weak enough to be led into this idea merely by the commendation of fools or flatterers. Some accurate judges

there are whose opinions I have at various times heard directly & indirectly. And flatterers I stand in little danger from, for most men are my enemies.

Besides I consider my own judgment, even of myself, as very impartial and accurate. I have got rather more song, than I used to have while under the tuition of Holcroft, from being constantly associated in my profession with recitative speakers—but in respect to voice, discrimination, knowledge of character, ability to express passions, just intonation, ease and dignity of deportment &c I have acquired more, than in a period of four years, would be considered probable. In short I do not hesitate to say, that, assisted with the advantages which a London theatre afford, of time for preparation in respective characters, of dress, of rehearsals I should eclipse, (if a fair chance were open to me & a manager disposed to espouse my interests) every competition for dramatic reputation which England can produce. You will of course pardon this egotism and this assumption—Of myself, because you wish to be acquainted with me I must speak: And, speaking to you, I fear not to be called or thought a vain boaster *merely* because I state explicitly what I think. Do not imagine that I conceive myself arrived at the end of my journey. I have traveled far but much, very much farther I have to progress. I only think that I have got the start of those, who are journeying the same way. My personal appearance too is very considerably improved—except my face—which the badness of the climate, at intervals a debauched manner of life, and considerable care, has in measure deprived of its former prettiness. But even that has gained as much in character & expression as it has lost in other respects. Thus have I given you full, particular, & I believe true account of myself as far as relates to professional talents & expectations.

He concluded by assuring Godwin that he had a strong desire to return home: "What effect revisiting my dear native country may have on my mind I know not; but this I know that the hope of return is what alone nourishes my tree of existence; deprived of that I should cease to be. I would not decay in this soil, one blast should wither me." Nevertheless he countered, "But though hope exists, it shall not make me precipitate. I will never return without the certainty of a fair chance for reputation & honour & enjoyment. I ask but the chance. I am perfectly willing to trust to myself for the event."

Since the streets of the new Capital were muddy and ill-lit, most people ventured out to evening performances only when the weather was good. Attendance almost always fell far short of a full house, so the company was spending more than it was taking in. Despite the financial difficulties, however, Wood noted that Wignell played in the first performance

Opposite: From a playbill for the United States' Theatre, September 5, 1800. By permission of the Folger Shakespeare Library.

☞ The Public are respectfully informed, that for the remainder of the season the Doors of the Th[eatre] will be open at half past 5 and the curtain will rise at half past 6 o'clock precisely.

United States' Theatre,
CITY OF WASHINGTON.

On *Friday Evening*, Sept. 5th 1800,

Will be presented a TRAGEDY called

Romeo and Juliet.

Romeo,	Mr. *Cooper*.
Paris,	Mr. *Wood*.
Montague,	Mr. *L'Estrange*.
Capulet,	Mr. *Morris*.
Mercutio,	Mr. *Bernard*.
Benvolio,	Mr. *Wignell*.
Tibalt,	Mr. *Francis*.
Friar Lawrence,	Mr. *Warren*.
Balthazer,	Miss *Solomon*.
Apothecary,	Mr. *Milbourne*.
Peter,	Mr. *Blissett*.
Page,	Master *Harris*.
Juliet,	Mrs. *Merry*.
Lady Capulet,	Mrs. *Salmon*.
Nurse,	Mrs. *Francis*.

In Act I. A MASQUERADE, In which will be introduced the *Minuet de la Cour* and a *New Gavot* by Master Harris and Miss Arnold.
In Act V. A FUNERAL PROCESSION and SOLEMN DIRGE.
The *Vocal Parts* by Messrs. Darley, Francis, Blisset, Robins, Miss Arnold, Miss Solomon, Mrs. Warren, Mrs. Stuart, &c.

To which will be added, a FARCE (in two acts) called

The Village Lawyer.

Scout,	Mr. *Warren*.
Snarl,	Mr. *Francis*.
Charles,	Mr. *Hopkins*.
Justice Mittimus,	Mr. *Milbourne*.
Sheep-Face,	Mr. *Blisset*.
Kate,	Mrs. *Stuart*.
Mrs. Scout,	Mrs. *Francis*.

ADMITTANCE, One Dollar.
Places in the boxes to be taken at the Theatre from 10 to 2 o'clock on the days of Performance. Tickets to be had at the office in the Theatre, at Way & Groff's Printing-Office, and at M'Laughlin's tavern, George-town.
Days of Performance, Monday, Wednesday, Friday and Saturday.
On *Saturday next*, the COMEDY of the ROAD TO RUIN, with Harlequin Hurry Scurry; or, the Rural Rumpus.

City of Washington: Printed by Way & Groff, North E Street, near the General Post-Office.

of each new production they offered, continuing to consider it a distinct honor to be opening the first theatre in Washington, "at the foundation of what was properly entitled *The National Theatre*."[14]

The Wednesday after the premier performance, August 27, Cooper played Hamlet,[15] the role in which he had made his London debut at Covent Garden Theatre in 1795. Two nights later, August 29, he played Penruddock in Richard Cumberland's *The Wheel of Fortune*,[16] which he had performed for his American debut in Baltimore. Mrs. Thornton went to see the Cumberland play, but found it "very dull ... as good as a sermon[,]" and commented, "Mrs. Merry was sick & another was obliged to take the part she ought to have acted to do the piece justice."[17] On September 6 Thomas Holcroft's celebrated comedy, *The Road to Ruin*, was scheduled,[18] but when Mrs. Thornton found out Mrs. Merry was not to play that evening either, she changed her mind about going and apologized to the Laws.[19] She made no mention of the previous night's performance, Shakespeare's *Romeo and Juliet*, with Mrs. Merry as Juliet, her most celebrated role, to Cooper's Romeo.[20]

One play that filled the house in Washington that season was the September 17 performance of Richard Brinsley Sheridan's translation of the grand operatic tragedy of the Spaniards in Peru, *Pizarro*, by the German dramatist August von Kotzebue. A couple of days later, however, the company had to close their engagement early, playing Mrs. Morton's appropriately titled comedy, "A Cure for the Heartache," to a "very thin" house.[21] Nevertheless, in this abbreviated first season in the new capital city, Wignell's troupe had planted a valuable seed. Four years later, in 1804, Mr. Law succeeded in building a permanent theatre in Washington, the Washington Theatre at C and 11th Streets, and the Philadelphia Company played a regular season there until it burned in 1820.[22] Cooper himself would return to the Capital until the end of his career, when he took his daughter Priscilla to play there with him.

Two

British-Born—1775–88

Although many who have written about Thomas Cooper have said that he was born appropriately in the very year of American independence, 1776, in fact he was born on December 16, 1775, outside London at Harrow-on-the-Hill in Middlesex. Perhaps more fortuitous, his christening took place in the new year, on January 11, 1776, as noted in the registry of St. Mary's Church, which still sits at the top of the Harrow hill.[1]

Thomas' father, Dr. Thomas Cooper, had trained as a surgeon in his native Ireland. He had initially gone to England to finish his study in the London hospitals, but through his ready intelligence and considerable personal charm made many friends in London and decided to remain there to practice medicine. In 1771 he obtained an appointment to a lucrative position as inspecting surgeon of recruits for the East India Service and sailed to India in May of that year. His marriage to Grace Mary Rae probably took place after his return from that voyage.

Grace Mary and William Godwin's mother were first cousins. William's father, the Reverend John Godwin, had been a dissenting minister in the Puritan tradition, as opposed to the official Church of England. He died in 1772, and the following year Mrs. Godwin took William, who was intended for his father's profession, to London to arrange for his entry to the Dissenting Academy at Hoxton. Her young relatives, the Coopers, by then married and living in England, offered to take him in for the summer before he entered Hoxton, so he stayed with them near the seaside, at Stockbury and Gravesend in Kent.

It was a couple of years later that the Coopers had their first child, Thomas. Another son, John Robinson, was born the following year, and a daughter, Elizabeth Priscilla, soon after. Then, on October 28, 1781, when young Thomas was five, Dr. Cooper departed aboard the *Royal Bishop* on a second voyage to India. He landed in Bombay and was briefly attached to the army there. A handsome young man who enjoyed living well, he was said to have enjoyed the comradeship of officers higher placed than himself while remaining generous toward his recruits, showing particular attention to the young men from Ireland. In early 1783, deciding to remain in India, he moved to the wealthy center of Bengal to accept an appointment as surgeon to the factory at Bauleah, a position with "a fair and almost certain prospect ... of providing eligibly and respectibly for his family[.]"[2] Mrs. Cooper took the children out to see him there, but after they traveled back to England, presumably to make arrangements to join him, she received the shocking report of her husband's sudden death at Dacca, October 14, 1787.

Just two weeks before his death, on September 29, Dr. Cooper had signed a will leaving all of his effects "to my dear wife Grace Mary Cooper" and naming her as his executrix for his affairs in England.[3] However, for the purpose of expedition, upon his death all of his financial papers were sent by ship to his executors at Rangamutty, but the vessel was shipwrecked in the great storm that occurred at Bengal on November 2. The result was a significant misfortune for Grace Mary and the children, for in the catastrophe, his financial records, both of debts owed him, as well as those he himself had discharged, were lost. Moreover, just prior to his death, he had made a substantial investment in goods for the European trade, but in his absence, the sale was managed poorly, bringing in, after heavy duties, little more than half of the original cost.[4]

Most of Dr. Cooper's personal effects were sold at public auction in Calcutta on December 10. The rest were sent aboard the *Rodney* to the East India Company's warehouse in London to be consigned there, but what monies accrued from the sale of such items as his medicine box, his gold watch and chain, a pair of brass-barrelled pistols and six volumes of Alexander Pope, could in no measure offset the heavy financial losses; the Coopers were left destitute.[5]

When Godwin, by then a writer living in London, learned about the family's misfortune, he offered to repay their kindness to him during his college days by taking in young Thomas as his ward. Grace Mary necessarily accepted him and after placing her younger son Jack and daughter Betty with other relatives and friends, went off to Holland to take a job as a housekeeper.

By nature and as the eldest child, Thomas had assumed an independent spirit early, effectively separated from his father at the age of five when Dr. Cooper left for India. In joining Godwin's household, the boy was drawn forever away from the provincial and colonial milieu into which he had been born. Instead, at the most crucial stage of his growing up, his father's tragic death and the ensuing financial ruin impelled him into the midst of the radical intellectual circle in London during the Revolutionary period.

Godwin, of gentle but impoverished birth, had grown up in the remote Norfolk village of Guestwick. Dissenters from the English Church had established an independent congregation there during the time of Cromwell and the Puritan Commonwealth, by Godwin's day one of the last outposts of a harsh Calvinism which centered on sin, guilt, and fear. At the age of eleven he was sent to Norwich to live and study with the dissenting minister there, Samuel Newton, a distinguished scholar. In Norwich the democratic government of Newton's congregation, whereby power was shared equally by all, impressed Godwin and undoubtedly influenced him in his future political views. However, he was not prepared for the horror of being birched for the first time, a practice the Reverend engaged in regularly to instill the humility which his father felt was lacking. At the time the youth coped with the extremity of his situation by retreating into Newton's extensive library and his own imagination, beginning to write adventure stories. Later, the memory of the harsh treatment may have influenced his refusal, despite a quick temper, either to use or allow the birch in dealings with young Cooper, which were often fractious, or to condone any form of physical violence in political dissent in London.

When he was sixteen Godwin returned home to teach writing and arithmetic at his old school. It was the following year that he gained entry to Hoxton, one of the leading institutions of higher learning in Britain; dissenters from the Anglican faith were not allowed to enter the national universities. A prodigious student, at Hoxton he became known for the passion with which he argued in a single-minded search for truth, as well as for the dedication with which he pursued the broad curriculum: the classics, language, metaphysics, philosophy, Hebrew, logic, geometry, rhetoric, history, politics, etc.

Godwin remained firm in his Calvinism and Toryism while he was at Hoxton, but on leaving, with the range of his knowledge and thought, failed in four attempts to place himself in local parishes, his focused idealism finding no harbor with the farm laborers and artisans who made up the congregations. At that time he began to read the radical French philosophers of the Enlightenment: Baron d'Holbach's repudiation of religion in *Système de la Nature* (printed secretly in Holland under the name *M. Mirabaud*), Helvétius, and Rousseau. He soon abandoned Toryism for the Whig opposition, who were calling in Parliament for American independence. Responding to the new ideas of man's innate goodness and ultimate perfectibility, he also began an inexorable move away from the religion of his bitter upbringing, turning first to Unitarianism, and in 1792, to atheism.

Reason and Truth replaced God in Godwin's idea, but his roots in the moral purpose of dissenting thought led him to remain undeviating in his essential attitude and interest in the betterment of mankind. It was an age of educational experiment, so he decided to open a small educational seminary in a house in Surrey. He gratefully espoused the new idea that children are born spotless, their natural instincts to be cultivated through study of the classics, literature, and philosophy. The prospectus he wrote for the school, *An Account of the Seminary*, began, "The state of society is incontestibly artificial; the power of one man over another must be always derived from convention, or from conquest; by nature we are equal."[6] Here beginning the formulation of the radical thought that would take full form in his masterwork, *An Enquiry Concerning Political Justice*, the prospectus proved to be more philosophical than practical, and the school itself never materialized.

At age twenty-seven Godwin moved to London to take up writing as a profession. There he gathered a small circle of intellectuals around him: James Marshal, a friend from Hoxton; the playwright Thomas Holcroft; the scientist William Nicholson; and Joseph Fawcett, who became a celebrated poet and popular preacher. It was five years later, when he was thirty-two, that he took in young Tom Cooper. Though always on the edge of poverty himself, with little time to spare from the writing he depended on for a living, he approached the education of his bright young cousin with kind-hearted optimism, viewing it as an opportunity to try out his theories of education.

The summer of 1788, when Tom was twelve, he joined Godwin in the country at the riverside town of Guildford in Surrey. In August Godwin wrote a letter to Holcroft back in London; describing himself with his new charge as "'banished from human society, and condemned to eat grass with the beasts,'"[7] he welcomed Holcroft's offer to visit him for a day. That fall he took young Tom back to London with him, and on September 29, for the sake of economy, they moved into a lodging with James Marshal on Great Marylebone Street. Marshal would be part of Godwin's household throughout Tom's time with him; he too was earning his living as a writer, and though he would never rise beyond the hackwork with which he had started, would remain Godwin's devoted friend for life.

Without considering the boy's natural inclinations, Godwin made plans to educate him to become a writer like himself, since there was no money for a university education. It was probably that year that Godwin dropped the *Reverend* from his name.[8] But Cooper later recalled that when he first went to live with him, he still wore his black clerical dress "with a large cock'd hat, his hair friz'd at the sides & curl'd stiffly behind[.]"[9]

Three

"Aut Caesar aut Nihil"— 1788–92

At an early age Tom had taken the Latin phrase, "Aut Caesar aut nihil," for his personal motto. The story went that he was playing on the riverbank with a school friend, when one of them quoted the passage from *Julius Caesar*: "Darest thou Cassius, now leap in with me into this angry flood, and swim to yonder point?" jumping in with all his clothes on, as Cassius recalls he and Caesar had once done. The other met the challenge, and together they swam to the opposite shore, a good distance from where they had started.[1] With such a spirit, Tom would have seemed ready and able to accept the place Godwin offered him.

Indeed, had Godwin's practice as an educational tutor been equal to his theory, he and Tom might have proceeded in total comity. In his *Account of the Seminary*, claiming Rousseau as his major influence, Godwin had proceeded to set forth a truly enlightened plan for a youth's education, asserting, "The undesigning gaiety of youth has the strongest claim upon your humanity. There is not in the world a truer object of pity, than a child terrified at every glance, and watching, with anxious uncertainty, the caprices of a pedagogue. If he survive, the liberty of manhood is dearly bought by so many heart aches." Instead of the years of "rules heaped upon rules," he said basics of grammar should be dispensed in a fortnight, composition through subjects of the child's familiarity, and history as the story of "the hearts of men," not "mere external actions."[2]

Unfortunately, Godwin had taught only one pupil prior to Tom, a young man named Willis Webb who was easily led. The learned man found himself far less suited for dealing daily with the feelings of such a proud, sensitive boy as Tom proved to be, one who had not only lost his father, but seen his family reduced to poverty. Godwin had taught mathematics in Guestwick and proven himself excellent in geometry at Hoxton, so contrary to the enlightened ideas he had expressed in his writing, he found himself engaged in a persistent pedagogical determination to teach the boy geometry, which led to constant conflict. Tom would insist that he did not understand, and Godwin would lose his temper. Although he never struck the boy, he reduced him time and again to tears. Indeed the volatile mixture of male personalities in the household produced almost daily quarrels between the two of them, as well as between Tom and the characteristically mild-mannered Marshal, throughout the whole four years of their life together.

In directing the boy's character, however, Godwin proved somewhat more enlightened than he was with the lessons. When Tom first went to live with him, Grace Mary Cooper asked her cousin to promise he would see that her son went to church on Sundays. As Cooper later recalled to William Dunlap, the New York manager who wrote a history of the early American theatre, he soon began to linger in the park with friends instead, only pretending that he had gone to church. Eventually Godwin found out, and while he told Tom his mother's wishes, did away with the requirement, since he placed the highest value on truthfulness.[3] Instead, every Sunday afternoon he got in the habit of dining at Thomas Holcroft's and began taking Tom along. At these gatherings, which might include other writers, actors, and musicians, conversation would center on the theatre, as well as politics, providing Tom a signal influence, and later on, a mentor.

Eleven years older than Godwin, Holcroft was the son of a London shoemaker who had lost his business and taken to the roads as a peddler with his son in tow. At one point the young Holcroft was employed as a stable boy, but exposure to theatre at the country fairs eventually led him to join a group of strolling players, first as a prompter, later an actor. A remarkable man, though with a stringent personality laid to his itinerant early life, he was now in London having a popular success as a playwright, one of the very few men of that time who rose from the lower ranks into the cultured class.*

Assisted by his friends, Godwin spent a good amount of time and effort on his young ward, but necessarily remained preoccupied with his own writing and deeply involved in radical politics. The unfolding political events increased the dramatic intensity of the household. On July 14, 1789, the French mob stormed the Bastille in Paris, and that fall, on November 5 Godwin dined with fellow members of the Society for Commemorating

---

*To illustrate Holcroft's cleverness, the story is often told of him that in 1784 he went to Paris to get a copy of the new hit, Beaumarchais' Marriage of Figaro, to translate for the English stage, and when the French managers refused him a copy, he attended the performance every night for about a week, committing the play to memory and returning with it for Mr. Harris, who produced it at Covent Garden before Christmas.

the Glorious Revolution of 1688, who drafted an address of congratulation to the French National Assembly. Three days after the dinner, Holcroft's only son, a gifted youth of sixteen who had been given every attention and advantage, stole 40 pounds and a pair of pistols from his father's desk and ran away with a friend to board the *Fame* to sail to the West Indies. The youth had left a note threatening to kill himself if his father pursued him. Unbelieving, Holcroft, accompanied by Godwin, went to seek him. They caught up with the boy at the port of Deal, but when he heard his father approaching, he went below deck and as he had warned, shot himself. Holcroft was devastated and for a year afterward, hardly went out of his home. From that point on, Godwin became a more intimate friend of Holcroft's, visiting him almost every day.

The event had taken place before she was born, but Godwin's daughter, Mrs. Shelley, later commented from what she had heard: "'The youth was of an unfortunate disposition, and his conduct was very reprehensible, at the same time it is certain that Holcroft carried further than Godwin a certain unmitigated severity, ... conceived in language to humiliate and wound, a want of sympathy with the buoyant spirit of youth ... which tended to set still wider the distance too usually observed between father and child.'" She went on to point out a parallel with Godwin and Tom: "'Something of this Godwin detected in himself in his conduct towards Cooper. I mention this circumstance the more particularly, as it, several years afterwards, caused the breach between Holcroft and Godwin which was never healed until the death of the former.'"[4]

The suicide of Holcroft's son undoubtedly provided a strong caution to Godwin with regard to young Tom, who turned fourteen December 16. That January, 1790, he began keeping a daily record of their interactions, *Notes on Tom Cooper his studies and temper 1790–1*.[5] Godwin himself had a temper, but by nature and training he generally maintained a calm and dispassionate demeanor. In these *Notes* he described and analyzed problems he encountered, as well as mistakes he made, both in teaching the lessons, and also in determining to make the boy honest and willing to admit and make amends for wrong-doing; for in this he held to Helvétius' theory, that education is central to the development of character.[6]

In the entry for April 14 he admitted to himself that his recriminations toward Tom vis à vis his own charity in taking him into his home were antithetical to a caring relationship: "If ... a dependent can feel friendship for his benefactor, who every day takes care to tell him how much he is bound to his generosity, & on the slightest misunderstanding threatens, if he does not behave himself as he should, to turn him out of his house, ... saying, If I do not remain your friend, where can you find a hole to stow your miserable carcase? you know your relations are poor & cannot afford to keep to you, therefore reflect on your condition, & respect me more than you have hitherto done, whose generosity & condescension have deigned to take you into my [service]—If, I say, friendship can exist between either—"

Young Tom's sensitive feelings undoubtedly intensified when he saw the low estate to which his mother had come. By 1790 she was working back in London where heavy drinking was common at that time, and she was admittedly drinking too much. She wrote her daughter off at school to tell her she was quitting her present employer, describing him as "proud imperious ... morose, and penurious"—

> I have been shamefully humble, I blush when I think how I have degraded myself ... I shall have the means of support for a few weeks— & can perhaps get a lodging—half a bed at 18 week with Mrs. Kelly or some clean person—I can live cheap and low as any person, my appetite is very small at present, owing perhaps to the immense quantity of liquor I drink ...—a good bed on which I cannot sleep is not more comfortable than a hard one in a w^{te} wash garret—tho a garret is appropriated to me here—a hot joint of meat which my wretchedness deprives me of the power of tasting is no more pleasant to my sight than some broken & stale bread bought cheap at the Baker's which I have often done—& on which I have made with the additional luxury of an onion & a pint of small beer a hearty & a comfortable meal—

As for the prospect of dining at Godwin's, she went on proudly: "[I]f I at anytime should take a meal with them, it will be for the sake of their Society—& not their food—tho' we think so differently, that such society frequently repeated perhaps may not be desir'd by any party—... it is a disagreable reflection that we are thought to act speak & think in every instance wrong, by persons whom we love.... I have my prejudices—so has Mr. Godwin—& if two such persons as him & me have, Mr. G will not thank me for the conjunction, where shall we find an unprejudic'd Man or Woman?"[7]

Tom also began expressing his thoughts and feelings about his relationship with Godwin in writing; in this household of writers, climactic arguments often ended on paper. On one occasion he made a list of what Mrs. Shelley described as Godwin's "pointed and humiliating words" and left it open for his tutor to see:

| He called me | *foolish wretch*—in my presence |
| He said | *I had a wicked heart*—Ditto |

He would	*Thrash me*—Ditto. Does he think I would submit quietly?
I am called	*A Brute*—in my absence.
I am compared to	*A Viper*—Ditto
He went out	*Merely to avoid me*—Ditto

. . . .

I am	*A Tiger*—Ditto
I have	*A Black heart*—Ditto

No justice in it—Ditto
No proper feelings—Ditto
He has no enmity to my *person* Yet he hates me—I suppose he means by that that he does not think me very ugly....
He knew I must have heard
What does he think I am made of that I can bear it?[8]

Godwin wrote a letter of reply expressing his disinterested intentions:

MY DEAR BOY—...If I had seen this paper before last Tuesday what passed on that day would not have happened. But I am closely engaged in observing what passes through your mind & I observed a sullenness and obstinacy growing up in it....

...The love of independency, & dislike of unjust treatment is the source of a thousand virtues. If, while you are necessarily dependant [*sic*] on me, I treat you with heaviness and unkindness it is natural you should have a painful feeling of it.

But harshness and unkindness are relative. The appearance of them may be the fruits of the greatest kindness. In fact, can my conduct towards you spring from any but an ardent desire to be of service to you? I am poor, and with considerable labour maintain my little family; yet I am willing to spend my money upon your wants and pleasures. My time is of the utmost value to me; yet I bestow a large portion of it upon your improvement. Supposing I should be mistaken in any part of my conduct to you can it spring from anything but motives of kindness?

I ask for your confidence because without it I am persuaded that I cannot do you half the good I could with.... If I can contribute to make you virtuous & respectable hereafter, I donot [*sic*] care whether I then possess your friendship, I am contented you should hate me. I desire no gratitude & no return of favors, I only wish to do you good—W. Godwin.[9]

It would take time, however, for the boy to appreciate these sentiments. Meanwhile, life with Godwin was affording him a kaleidoscopic range of emotional experience to fuel his stage career, and in the not distant future he would become famous for portraying the deep and vehement passions onstage. Given the battle over the lessons, however, as a young actor he would not be a particularly "good book," apt to forget his lines when lacking motivation.

He resumed reading Latin with Godwin, this time Herodotus and Virgil, but again the conflicts began: "dispute about bantering his faults— he maintains that he did not banter them.—harmony, but with some remonstrance of inattention." Godwin confiscated a translation of the French novel *Gil Blas*, which he had "forbad him to procure," and "geometria lachrymans" continued. When Tom came home late from the Adelphi Society without apologizing, Godwin insisted he do so.

On October 17 Godwin wrote that he had chided Tom "for rudeness and impertinence to Mr. M____ [Marshal]—am heard with great sensibility—the rudeness was public in the mercer's shop." Despite his intervention, however, the conflict with Marshal continued on a rising scale. On October 28: "[Tom] Makes a good humoured jest on Mr. M [Marshal]—who is offended—I interfere—high words between them, Mr. M refusing to be silent, & talking of knock down blows & canes...[.]"

On November 3 Tom wrote Marshal a letter of apology:

> Sir,
> I am convinced that I was wrong in not immediately desisting from that from which you desired me desist; I therefore ask your pardon; & I shall endeavour to make amends for my misconduct by my future behaviour.
> We have lived, Sir, for some time in the same house, & I believe with a certain degree of friendship & good understanding. I am sorry that that friendship and good understanding has recieved [*sic*] such a shock as it has done to day. I was certainly wrong (as I have already [*sic*] in not complying with your desire; that noncompliance brought on high words; in course of which, you directly called me a liar, you called me so not by implication, you said: "You are a liar."
> I am glad that I have escaped doing that which your words naturally excited me to do[.]
> T. Cooper[10]

This was the same month that Edmund Burke harshly attacked the French Revolution and his former friends in *Reflections on the Revolution in France*. Descrying "literary caballers, and intriguing philosophers; with political theologians, and theological politicians, both at home and abroad[,]"[11] he foresaw the danger of the Revolution and wrote a firm affirmation of the British Constitution and social hierarchy. Godwin was shocked by Burke's changed attitude, though he too would be firmly opposed to the violence that ensued in France. Wounded, he became pettish with Tom, "Censure him for being out of hum [or] with me without reason—cause my not choosing to read before him Burke's pamphlet after he had pronounced it 'stupid stuff' a priori."

The boy had obviously gotten caught up in the political excitement, and Godwin's feelings were on edge. On December 1 he accused Tom of lying, comparing his reaction unfavorably to that of his friend George Dyson, who frequented Godwin's: "Tears for the supposed imputation of a lie—C. I will not bear it, you would not treat any body else thus.—G. ... from instruction to ignorance, from virtue to vice. You are as anxious to escape from opportunities of improvement, as your friend Dyson is obliged to be to obtain them." A young artist, Dyson had a particularly violent temper, and he and Tom would fight over such trivialities as books and who was or was not talking at dinner. They probably competed with one another for Godwin's attention, since Godwin took a great liking to Dyson, whom he even named, along with Holcroft, Coleridge, and Fawcett, as one of his "'four principal oral instructors,'" referring to the quality of their conversation.[12]

In one episode Godwin mortified Tom by making him cancel an engagement to go to a play with Dyson, because he had been late coming home that afternoon, making him go without dinner as well. On this occasion Godwin recognized, "I have made myself utterly contemptible to him ... it is to much purpose for me to express kindness for him, while I inflict upon him the torments of devils." The actual outcome of Godwin's strictness was that when Tom grew up, he became legendary for his fanatic punctuality, which stood him in good stead on the touring circuit in America.

On January 4, 1791, Godwin and Marshal with Tom moved to lodgings at Titchfield Street, a new beginning for a year when Godwin would sign a publishing contract in July, and in September begin writing *Political Justice*. At the end of January he began to summarize his faults in dealing with his pupil: "Do I not dwell too much in lectures? Am I not too minute in the discovery of faults? ... [A]t sixteen scholastic authority ought to cease: at that age I was an usher." Referring to the job he had taken as assistant to the schoolmaster in Guestwick, he came to the conclusion concerning his pupil, "He is too apprehensive of error, particularly geometrical error[.]"

In truth, Godwin's conscientious efforts to understand not only the boy, but his own faults in dealing with him, would assure his eventual success in achieving a mutual respect between them. He had established a regular habit of reading aloud to Tom after dinner in the evenings, novels such as Samuel Richardson's *Clarissa Harlowe*, and the works of Shakespeare. Also, viewing the study of foreign language as essential to the cultivation of the mind, in addition to the Latin, he managed to teach him some Greek, and Italian and French as well.[13]

Meanwhile, in March in response to Burke's pamphlet, Godwin, along with Holcroft, who had become a republican under Godwin's influence, helped arrange for the publication of Thomas Paine's *Rights of Man*. A paper war ensued, and the political climate for reformers worsened. On July 14 Godwin attended the annual dinner of the Society for Commemorating the Glorious Revolution to celebrate the second anniversary of the storming of the Bastille. In Birmingham, more darkly, rioters marched on the celebratory dinner there, and then on to the home of a Godwin associate, the well-known chemist Joseph Priestley, who had always advocated peaceable parliamentary reform; they burned down Priestley's house, destroying his library and distinguished laboratory and ran him out of town.

Tom's mother became concerned, for despite her gratitude and her feelings of kinship with Godwin, she was constantly worried about the influence he and Holcroft were having on Tom and his sister Betty,[14] who spent quite a bit of time at Godwin's even though she never lived there. Betty wrote Godwin, "my Mother ... told me if she found Paines rights of Man [*sic*] Mr. H. [Holcroft] gave me, she would burn it."[15] Working as a governess to a provincial family in Wales, she wished she were back in London and kept up a steady correspondence with Godwin and her brother Tom about politics, theories of education, Holcroft's plays, "the new actress," etc. To Godwin she confided, "I live and act in continual opposition to my judgement and my principles. In the first place, I attend church[.]" And as for politics: "Mrs. H. is a perfect perfect aristocrat.... If unask'd I should speak of the french [*sic*] nation, her remark would be that those people were certainly advocates for liberty & equality who had nothing to lose.... Nor would she have an idea that a young person, a woman, and above all a governess should ever meddle in politicks."[16]

In February Godwin had accused Tom of lying about letting his sister know that Holcroft was the author of the play "G. H."[*German Hotel*].* Honesty of character was essential to Godwin's tutelage. In arbitrating the most recent quarrel with Dyson, however, he noticed Tom seemed to treat him "with particular kindness & attention, ... acknowledges that he had been unjust to me; but says, that he cannot wholly justify me[.]" And observed, "May not upon this incident be built a system of forbearance & equality," and though he usually took Dyson's side in the arguments, concluded, "Perhaps Dyson was most in fault.... Extraordinary quality of T.[Tom] Greater essential rudeness in the other."

The next month Godwin found himself writing a letter of rebuke,

---

**Holcroft's anonymous translation of the German play had just been produced at Covent Garden.*

not to the sixteen-year-old Tom, but to Dyson for insulting and striking Tom. The letter shows his matured respect for Tom's qualities:

> Dear Sir. I am inexpressibly grieved at the perusal of your letter to T. C.....
> It was right when he called you a misanthropist. This is the second time you have written a letter to him in which your desire to do good was set at proud defiance; in which your only object was to wreak a spiteful & malignant temper.... You cannot be blind to his talents; you have had many proofs of them. What vices have you to chafe him with that should render him a nuisance on the face of the earth? Why truly that he does not think in all respects as you do. That his opinions you conceive tho' in that you are mistaken are the same as those of Epicurus, Aristippus, Horace, Voltaire & others who have done honour to human nature. What intolerance is this!

He took particular objection to the physical abuse:

> One expression of your letter is too curious to pass unnoticed. You say you struck him from a feeling uncorrected by philosophy, & supported by an opinion that, such modes of reproof were necessary for minds like his.... You have already perhaps done an irreparable injury to the mind, who, like all young people is very apt to judge of philosophy or any set of principles by the conduct of those who profess them.... The doctrine of beating is a very comfortable one, because it ... persuades us that there is no reason for us to be very anxious to subdue the brutality of our nature.
> I trust I need not repeat here the high opinion I have of you or the great love I bear you.... March 21, 1792 WG[17]

In March the Girondins came to power in France; the French monarchy was abolished in September. Meanwhile, as Godwin made preparations for writing *Political Justice*, the *Notes on Tom* ceased. Cooper later recalled to Dunlap that by then Godwin had abandoned his black clerical suit for the dress almost of a dandy, "a blue coat, yellow cassimire waiscoat [*sic*] & breeches, highly blued silk stockings ... hair plaited behind round hat & spectacles."[18]

One day Tom went in and suddenly announced to his guardian that he was ready to make his own way. Engrossed in his study, Godwin was taken by surprise and asked the young man what he intended to do. When he repeated his question, Tom confessed, "'Walk to Paris and join the republican army.'"[19]

Four

"The Die Is Cast"—1792–93

Suddenly faced with the effect of his political activities on his young charge, Godwin briefly put him off, "'We will talk further on the subject to-morrow morning.'"[1] And before the boy's mother got wind of her son's notion to go to France, Godwin came up with the reasonable suggestion that he audition for Holcroft to become a chorus singer. He undoubtedly knew that Thomas Cooper had a voice of good quality. It would eventually become the most significant asset in his stage career, "a fine resonant voice, of good compass, strong in head-tones, musical in cadence, and highly sympathetic[.]"[2]

At the audition, however, Holcroft concluded that without training, Cooper's singing would not do. He also recited a speech of Zaphna [Voltaire, *Mahomet the Imposter*], but it was several days later, when he gave a reading from Shakespeare's *Richard the Third*, that he caught Holcroft's imagination. Once Holcroft agreed that he might have a gift for the stage, Godwin arranged to send him by stagecoach to the theatre in Edinburgh, where Stephen Kemble, younger brother of John Philip Kemble, was the manager. The Kembles' sister, Mrs. Siddons, was also there at the time, temporarily avoiding the stress of the London season while continuing to play the roles that had made her famous.

With money in his pocket and a letter of introduction from Holcroft, the sixteen-year-old Cooper set out to begin a life in the theatre, dressed for the first time as a man, the same modish attire with blued silk stockings that Godwin had adopted, his chestnut hair fashionably tied back and curled.[3] Given his youthful determination, anxiety, and concurrent impetuosity, this first attempt would prove to be brief, a mere summer month away from home, as it turned out. But even here, in the letters he wrote home, the profile of the future star is clearly discernible.

After a long trip, he finally arrived in Edinburgh at nine o'clock at night on Wednesday July 26 "in high health & spirits," as he reported to Godwin, who had moved again with Marshal, to 39 Devonshire Street in London. Beginning the makeshift life of a provincial player, Cooper went on to aver, "but my spirits were damped, when, upon my arrival I could get no bed or lodging either at Edinburgh or Leith, on account of the races which will end on Saturday."[4]

The next morning he went to see Mr. Kemble at eleven and gave him Holcroft's letter. On Friday the company was to open their production of Holcroft's highly successful new comedy, *The Road to Ruin*, which had been presented in London at Covent Garden in February. In his letter Holcroft suggested that Tom be tried out in the part of Young Norval in John Home's tragedy, *Douglas*; the speech beginning "My name is Norval" was a favorite recitation piece for young actors. Kemble agreed to hear Cooper read the role at one o'clock that same day. Failing to keep the appointment, he went ahead and arranged for him to rehearse it with Mrs. Siddons, who was to play Lady Randolph in the play on Monday evening the 31st.

The next day Cooper attended the rehearsal, but Mrs. Siddons did not appear, and afterwards Kemble took him aside to comment. Cooper recounted the conversation to Godwin: "'Sdeath I'm sped I have just rehearsed Douglas with other actors before Mr. Kemble. When I had done he walked aside with me & told me he was sorry to say that he could not trust me with the character. He then made his individual objections. He said that in the two descriptive speeches I had a great deal to [*sic*] much passion.... And that in the scene with Glenalvon the audience would laugh at me." He said he asked Kemble if he did not think that Douglas was very angry, to which "he answered certainly, but that he was angry with good manners, & that he must not vex Mrs. Siddons." Kemble told him that he was really "too young to act characters of such importance" but agreed to see about some other roles, offering to read *Douglas* with him at breakfast the next morning.

The letter Cooper wrote to Godwin shows that he had not accepted this critique, expecting that when Mrs. Siddons heard him read, she would reverse Kemble's opinion: "Perhaps Mrs. Siddons will be there (at breakfast the next day), & I shall probably please her better if she gives me a hearing for I am certain that I rehearsed as well as ever I did to Mr. H. [Holcroft] I have an infallible rule to judge by, the recollection of my own feelings."[5]

Cooper would indeed become an actor skillful in conveying feeling, but in Edinburgh in the beginning Holcroft undoubtedly expected him to audition with Young Norval to show something of his potential and then be content to start off like other newcomers with bit parts. From the first, however, he had no idea of beginning as a humble apprentice adapting himself to the company. Though seemingly foolhardy in the boy, this quality of intention and self-belief, when coupled with more training and experience, would quickly impel him to stardom in America.

Kemble failed to appear at breakfast the next morning, and when Cooper pursued him an hour later at the theatre, Kemble simply told him that he could not play in *Douglas*. He had to accept the disappointment, but with time on his hands, had the opportunity of attending performances to observe Mrs. Siddons. He noted that he enjoyed her performance much more as Lady Randolph than as Jane Shore the week before and looked forward to seeing her as Mrs. Beverly in *The Gamester* next. Despite his frustration, this providential opportunity to see the great actress perform profoundly influenced Cooper at the beginning of his career and helped to shape it. He would espouse the classical "Kemble" style of acting introduced by Mrs. Siddons and John Philip Kemble. As it happened, the style was temperamentally suited to his sense of grandeur, and his naturally graceful physique. As for his own individual quality, "the recollection of my own feelings," this would manifest as a notable ability to portray passions onstage, the romantic element he would bring to the formal classic model.

Meanwhile the novice contemplated Kemble's advice, sharing his thoughts with Godwin in a series of letters home: "Relative to Mr. H.'s [Holcroft's] supposition concerning rant I think it must be false! even from what Kemble himself said, his word was I had to [*sic*] much *passion*, & after ward he said he did not doubt I should make a good actor for I had a great [deal] of *fervency*. by [*sic*] these expressions he could not mean rant the common signification of which is exactly opposite."[6] He was consoling himself with an expectation of playing Lothario in Nicholas Rowe's tragedy *The Fair Penitent* on the company tour Saturday in Newcastle-on-Tyne, because, as he explained to Godwin, "their [the company's] Lothario was very bad & merely a make-shift."[7] His hopes, however, were groundless, since Kemble and Mrs. Siddons *had not even agreed to hear him read Lothario!* But the part of the gay seducer, which requires practiced grace and skill, would prove to be significant for him later on, since the criticism he received for his first performance of it in London was so harsh that it influenced his decision to go to America.

The letter Godwin apparently wrote to Mrs. Siddons for Cooper did not reach her until after he had already been assigned his first part, Mr. Smith in *The Road to Ruin*. He only hoped that when she saw him onstage, she would want to hear him read Lothario. At the same time he admitted that the comic actor who was currently playing the part, LaMath, an acquaintance of Holcroft, was "infinitely superior" to Lee Lewis, who was ranked as first comic actor of the company. Audiences, however, loved Lewis in the part of Goldfinch in *The Road to Ruin*, and he became famous for his portrayal of the lively and foolish young dandy; at Covent Garden, almost completely rebuilt that summer, he would open the fall season in Holcroft's play.

Continuing his letter the next day, Cooper gave Godwin an account of his own first appearance on the stage, as Mr. Smith. It had gone reasonably well: "I did not come off with great applause but I was not hissed which I in some measure expected because it was not known by any body that this was a first appearance." But he said he was "very much mortified to see Mrs. Siddons in one of the boxes. What will she consider a bare justice if she forms her judgement from this performance since, if I did nothing strikingly bad there is nothing sufficiently prominant [*sic*] to make any impression & as she is at present in a very bad state of health the indolence resulting from that may prompt her so to do." However, he told Godwin that that night as they sat in the green room [actors' lounge], the actor who played Old Dornton whispered in his ear "that he percieved [*sic*] in me the seeds of a great actor & I had only to take care of myself & be careful in having my words."[8] Unfortunately, he failed to take that very good advice.

He continued to agitate for the part of Young Norval but had little hope, for as he told Godwin in another letter, Mrs. Siddons was still in bad health and said she was not willing to play roles "that require her greatest exertion." Pointing out that she had already acted Jane Shore, Portia, and Desdemona at Newcastle and still intended to act Mrs. Beverley and Lady Macbeth, he vented his frustration in a harsh critique of Stephen Kemble's acting: "I am as you say at a loss for a subject; the strangeness of which will vanish when you consider that I am deprived of the characters in which I expected to shine; that I am obliged to sit down with a black gown over my shoulders as a dumb senator (which I have twice done) & hear Mr. Kemble hold forth with most impetuous rant, with sudden ill-timed unmeaning risings & fallings of voice, to astonish the vulgar & confounding the wise by not articulating a single syllable; & to hear Mr. Woods repeat his words in one dull, heavy, monotonous sound[.]"

More or less against his will, the young aspirant was learning his craft by observing the other actors, pouring out his criticism in the letter home: "This circumstance is so remarkable in Woods, that having repeated a part of a speech in Lord Hastings with tolerable propriety & having made a pause introducing a totally different feeling & passion, & by his pause & the length of it, rousing every individual to the highest pitch of eagerness & expectation he begins to speak & on the instant, destroys all pleasure by the repetition of the very same sound. I uttered at the very first syllable an involuntary groan; (this was the first time of my seeing him) & a dirty sceneshifter cursing him expressed his dissatisfaction in very characteristically awkward manner—" Despite this, he noted Woods' "remarkably graceful action & easy deportment[.]"

Otherwise he felt justified in complaining, because he saw "a number of dull fools who scarcely even pretend to know their right hands from their lefts, fill up the other characters without my being considered worthy to utter a syllable...." On a better note he told Godwin, "My reception was such as I could wish: the actors are all very civil & the highest are not distant & proud. Mr. Bell, others of some consequence, give me advice in general insignificant enough but tolerably good in it's [sic] kind." He also reassured him, "You need be under [no] apprehension concerning money, for I have had a guinea every monday."[9]

But he was not unaware that Kemble was annoyed with him. A letter written two days later begins, "My courage is as great as you could wish considering that I stand upon a shaking foundation every time Mr. Kemble sees me, I percieve or think I percieve a kind of discontent, arising from want of determination, in his countenance." Asking Godwin for news "of Mr. Paine's & France's proceedings," his mother's health, and whether George Dyson had gone to France, he confided, "I do not keep company with any of the actors except in the green-room."[10] From the beginning he followed his instinct to maintain a life separate from the theatre. Years later in America when he was famous, William Wood remembered that Cooper firmly resisted "all attempts to exhibit him at parties as an artist, or an object of social curiosity."[11] At a time when actors were not generally accepted socially, he would be called "the gentleman actor." Recognizing this, in his Philadelphia studio Gilbert Stuart, famed for his formal portraits of George Washington, also painted Cooper at least twice, dressed in the formal attire of a gentleman.[12]

The conflict with Kemble quickly reached a climax in the payroom the next Monday. When Cooper ventured to ask about travel arrangements for the company tour to Lancaster, Kemble replied, "'Why really Mr. Cooper I think the best thing you can do is to go back to London.'" Already prepared to bargain rather than accept dismissal, Cooper responded: "I told him that I believed if he would give me a hearing in Lothario, I could please him. He said I was not at all fit to play it. Then he began to talk in a hesitating way about my being of no use on account of my being inexperienced in stage matters. I said that if that were true in every instance that plays would be acted as long as and no longer than the actors at present existing should live. In short I argued the case a little with him told him the characters I had learnt in London." He said Kemble ended by admitting that "he had a great respect for Mr. Holcroft" and would "endeavour to bring me forward by little & little."

That evening he was to be "one of Mrs. Siddons's train (dumb as usual) in *The Mourning Bride*. On Wednesday ... the second witch in *Macbeth*[,]" but Kemble now said that if he had thought, he might have offered him the chance to play the feature role of Malcolm instead and suggested he learn it for the next time the play was performed.[13] The irrepressible boy fatefully replied that instead of waiting until the next town, he was ready to play Malcolm there at Newcastle. The outcome was heroic tragedy:

> The die is cast & when, having tottered for some time, I thought myself growing firm at that instant this fate was reversed, & I fell headlong without hopes of recovery.... I told you in my last of the doubtful manner of talking of Mr. Kemble and at last of his saying that he would keep me & endeavour to bring me forward on account of his respect for Mr. Holcroft. Irresolute blockhead! he has again altered his mind. Now he has got the shadow of a reason for his final determination to which though one of the most irresolute I believe he will adhere; but observe though I call it the shadow of a reason I do not mean to say that I was without blame, I am conscious of it in it's [*sic*] full extent.... He desired me to study Malcolm against the next time it was acted. But the next morning I told him that I would undertake it for that time as I had two before me; he consented I went through the part very well & tolerably perfectly till I came within two lines of the end of the play (I speak the last speech), and there I wanted the word the noise behind the scenes, the play being nearly over, prevented my hearing the prompter & in an instant some people in the back of the gallery, as I guessed, began to hiss and immediately every body else began to clap which lasted for a minute & as we were so near the end it was not adviseable to wait the conclusion of the bustle to say the few words that remained—the trumpets sounded & the curtain fell. My blame consisted in want of courage or recollection, in not skipping to the next line the very instant they began to hiss & it was impossible to catch the word. Mr. Kemble made this his handle declared I was totally unfit for the profession & that I had not one single requisite for an actor & in fine said he, "As a friend I advise you to return to London. I cannot keep you."

In that letter, written to Marshal, Cooper also said he had offered to stay for little money and replace Mr. Charteris, Jr., "a foolish fellow about my age," who was leaving, but Kemble had the treasurer pay him five pounds to let him go. He then attempted to join the sharing company

Charteris was forming but was refused. Determined to continue on his own, he asked Marshal for help in finding a four or five-hour-a-day job in London at which he could earn ten shillings, sixpence, enough to live on.[14]

Kemble offered to take care of his trunk until he told him where to send it, but moved on with the company to the next town at the end of the week. He was left alone at Newcastle waiting anxiously for over a week for Marshal or Godwin to answer his letter and tell him what to do. He wrote again August 24 in desperation:

> [A]llowing you to miss the return which I confess I think strange in my present situation yet when a second post arrives & there is no letter my surprize [sic] is doubled. I can only account for this circumstance by the miscarriage of one of our letters if this fate attended mine you can apply to my mother who recieved a letter from me on Wednesday & she can tell you that I am at present alone, that Mr. Kemble has said, "Sir I have no farther occasion for your services." In my letter I said or at least intimated that I should not act without your advice why you should refuse your advice I cannot tell; but though you refuse you should have acquainted me with your refusal since I said I should delay doing anything till I heard from you. I [hope] I have money enough to maintain myself here till an answer *can* come… which will be next Wednesday and if I do not hear from town before or by that time I must take measures without advice suited *to the disparation of my situation.* [I hope you will pardon my laconic or snapping manner of writing. I am in a very laconic humour.] Tho's Cooper[15]

If Godwin received this communication and sent assistance, it never reached him. He spent his last penny riding back to London in a cargo boat of coal.[16]

When he got home, he found Godwin intensely involved in finishing his book to keep up with the escalating events in France; his publisher was already advertising it. In January, on the twenty-first, the King of France was executed; the first of February France declared war on England, and three weeks later England declared war on France. In the midst of these events, on February 14, *An Enquiry Concerning Political Justice* went on sale in London.

In his definitive essay Godwin developed the basic philosophy of anarchism. The ideal state as he saw it would evolve naturally in an atmosphere of individual freedom and true equality, effected by the abolition of laws of property, punitive laws, religious laws, even the marriage contract. One can imagine the interest the publication elicited in Cooper; not only had he espoused Godwin's political principles, but also the book made Godwin famous overnight. After reading the first 250 pages his sister Betty wrote Godwin, "[Y]ou, with an almighty power, burst the fetters with which prejudice shackles the understanding, and draw it from the darkness of its dungeon to feel the fervent heat, and behold the infinite brightness of your soul renovating Pan."[17]

With the completion of his publication, Godwin moved out of the lodging with Marshal, to a small house on Chalton Street where he would live alone, but he and Holcroft continued to foster Cooper, arranging that same February to send the young man, now seventeen, to the theatre in Portsmouth. As a favor to Holcroft, the Portsmouth manager, Collins, had consented to take him on, even though the company was full and all the parts already assigned.

Five

"My Fortune Smiles"

An Irish Benefit—1793

When Grace Mary Cooper heard from Marshal that the Portsmouth manager, Collins, was in London, she was afraid he had come to London to try to forestall her son's joining him. She wrote anxiously to Godwin, "I doubt the disappointment will quite do him up, however strong his mind may be for his years, I fear he is too young to bear such repeated ill success[.]" She went on, "I hope Mr. Collins saw Mr. Holman."[1] She hoped Collins was in London to see a former member of his company, Joseph George Holman, make his debut at the Theatre Royal, Covent Garden.

The very day his mother wrote Godwin, Cooper was already in Portsmouth writing Godwin too, an ecstatic letter: "Well, here I am! 'My fortune smiles & gives me all that I dare ask!'" He reported happily: "I called on Mr. Collins this morning; he recieved me very politely—desired me to call on him at three o'clock & he would go over with me to the theatre. Mrs. C. proposed an amendment that I sh[ould] dine with them & go after dinner—So I did. Mr. C. was very well pleased with my rehearsal—I walked with their son to a lodging which he knew—when I went out of the room Mrs. C. said she should expect me back to tea. to [*sic*] tea back I came having agreed for a remarkably nice room at 9 shil per week, & now I am writing in their apt—with Mrs. C. saying: 'come Tippy bring it.' which is the reason *for my writing so* laconically."

He told Godwin that Collins very much desired the words and music for Mrs. Martyr's air in *The Midnight-Wanderers*, suggesting, "[I]f Mr. Holcroft could procure the music by means of his musical connexions & interest he would very much oblige me, & serve Mr. C." He also asked Godwin, "Inform Mr. Marshal that I play for the first time on Monday the 4th inst. If he have a mind to come down I can procure him an order."[2]

In a reply Godwin apparently asked that he write him personally all the details of his new position; he did not want to have to keep up with the boy through his mother. Cooper wrote back that he had already sent her the information the day before and was being kept very busy, but conceded, "as necessary information cannot in London be conveyed half a mile I will with pleasure endeavour to do it from seventy miles distance." From then on he showed his guardian the respect of giving him precedence, asking him to convey his news to his mother instead. This interchange gives evidence of Godwin's strong intention toward him, even though he was now living on his own, as well as his mother's continuing involvement. Still only seventeen, this kind of support undoubtedly kept him going in a profession fraught with risk and hard circumstance, and he wrote Godwin a detailed answer to his inquiry:

> You desire to be acquainted with some of the gentlemen of the company. Their names are as follows.—Mr. Tyler—Curtis, Stanwix, Gill, Maxfield, Kelly, Woolley, Baker, Davies, Barrett; Mesdames Tyler, Maxfield, Kelly, Davies, Collins, Ball, Lings Rivers…. Mr. Curtis is a kind of a pompous fool; never seems to attempt anything in acting; stands always in one posture, & as erect as if he had a spit through his body. Mr. Gill is— nobody. Mr. Stanwix is a young beginner & he has been but nine months on the stage. I dont [sic] know well what to make of him. his [sic] understanding is above mediocrity but I believe he will never be a good actor. he plays french parts & fops…. Kelly is a jack in all parts; a young man and would have merit in some cast if he did not undertake all. Woolley, Baker, & Davies are low comedy men. & all have an equal & middling share of merit. Perhaps Woolley is the best…. When Mrs. Davies, Mrs. Ling, and Mrs. Rivers are mentioned I have mentioned all the women who are better than non-entities.

Characteristically, Cooper was never able to understand or agree with the stock company system that allowed a man like Mr. Maxfield, the hero in tragedy at Portsmouth, to go on one night as Richard the Third, and the next as a sailor in *Captain Cook* without any lines or action. Still determined to play heroes himself, he would nevertheless stay with the Portsmouth company for over a year, his first real job in the theatre. At the end of his first three weeks, he reported to Godwin that he was playing several secondary parts, including Worthy and Philip in *The Brothers*, and "frequently in Don Juan." He was earning "only" fifteen shillings a week, but that was the same as everyone else, with the exception of Tyler and Barrett.

George Joseph Tyler, a "good-natured rather formal" man of about thirty-eight, was the chief singer for the company and received an enviable salary of one pound, eleven and six per week. In 1796 he would go to America to act singing parts, as well as second leads and feature roles, with the John Street Company in New York, where he had a long, successful career. Giles Barrett, an auxiliary who had come to Portsmouth to replace Holman, Cooper deemed "a very bad actor." Six feet tall and about forty-seven years old, Barrett was a comedian and some-time manager. He had played Don Juan at the Royalty and considered himself a wit. Cooper remarked, "He is a wit but of all the dull who profess that character I never knew a duller.... He was complaining ... 'I am in a darned scrape—I almost think I am a fiddle I am in such a scrape'—at the running his stick backward & forward across his arm by way of illustration."[3]

Four years later both Barrett and Cooper would be in America in rival companies. August 18, 1797, Barrett opened as Don Felix in *The Wonder, A Woman Keeps A Secret* at the John Street Theatre in New York, and five days later at the theatre in Greenwich Street, Thomas Wignell introduced Cooper and Mrs. Merry to the New York audience in *Venice Preserv'd*. The proceeds for Wignell's stars were $1,000, as compared to $374 for Barrett at the John Street, where Dunlap commented, "Barret [*sic*] is not equal to the first place in a Company *now & here*."[4]

While acting with the Portsmouth company Cooper stayed at a public house. Thieves were common, and when the wooden box with his belongings broke on arrival, he wrote home special delivery to have a portmanteau with key sent to him straightaway directed to the theatre. Otherwise he said, "I am very well pleased with my situation except that Portsmouth is a very unsociable place. I'm not acquainted with a single person unconnected with the Theatre. It is impossible to play any of my characters they are already in possession & it is not in Manager's power to make alteration."[5] During Passion Week there were no plays and no pay, and he began to imagine himself abducted and impressed as a sailor: "I expect every day to be pressed, & not appearance or friends can save one. Masters of houses have been taken away. I know a common sailor who some time ago was a player."[6]

In April he began to feel pressure mounting at the theatre when he was given only two days' notice to learn the part of Sandford in *Who Is the Dupe,* and only five for the part of Edmund in Holcroft's *School for Arrogance.* Meanwhile he had learned the part of Lord Dartford, expecting to play it any night, and was understudying another part for Barrett. A day or so later he was told to learn the part of Meanwright in *Such Things Are* for the same night, so he gave the part of Edmund back to Maxfield. In an apparent reply to a query by Godwin, he reported, "My health is as well as can be expected." Continuing their political dialogue, he told Godwin he had observed French privateers being brought into the harbor at Portsmouth and mentioned, "What a glorious speech is Mr.

Fox's [Opposition leader Charles James Fox] in answer to Attorney General relative to the King's."[7]

On June 10 the company began touring, first to Chichester for ten days, four back in Portsmouth, and then on to Winchester for two weeks. In a running reply to Godwin's remonstrances regarding his scant correspondence, on July 13 from Winchester he wrote asking, "how your book sells?—whether you like your way of living...." He also showed a maturing awareness of family responsibility, reporting that he had written his sister, vis à vis her dissatisfaction with her job as a provincial governess, "a pretty sharp answer immediately which I hope will cure her of her disorder whatever it is."

Explaining his financial situation, Cooper told Godwin that on tour they were only being paid by the night and had to bear their own travel expenses, "allowed nothing extra for our continual removings." The bookings were also scarce, only one night in a week at Winchester for which they each received four shillings.—" [Y]ou may conclude we are all chop fallen—It is your maxim that a little wholesome adversity is a very good thing for a young man to encounter—so that ... I trust you will give me credit for a little wisdom—that a few of the dregs of folly are purged away by the purifying physic of—bread & water." Since they were not to be dismissed until they reached Southampton, they were advanced one shilling, but they were facing the prospect of two weeks without work. He assured Godwin he was "in perfect health, as I hope this will find you" and said he might be back in London toward the end of the following week or the week after.[8]

On the nineteenth in another letter, also from Winchester, he said not to expect him after all. The tour had been revived by a special request for a performance from a local lord, "a bespeak from the Marquis of Buckingham[.]" He began with some excitement: "I am just come from the theatre whence we have dismissed two from the gallery & one from the pit." The play-going audiences tended to be rowdy, and performances also suffered from the pace the actors were forced to keep up. He recounted an incident that had occurred at Wincester:

> George Barnwell (George Lillo, *The London Merchant*, 1731) was played—you recollect that the uncle comes on with a book & speaking a soliloquy on death—The uncle has not or did not choose to have leisure to learn the soliloquy but thought if he carried on a book of the play that he might read it he did not reflect that the stage would be darken'd & when he looked in the book he found he could not read he recollected the first words "oh, death—& repeated them three or four times in great agitation calling at the same time for George Barnwell to come & kill

him. but George was laughing so heartily behind the scenes that for some time he could not relieve his uncle & his uncle said no more than—"Oh death"—do-do—till his nephew came & stabbed him & laughed at him—in the agonies of death—

He also corrected Godwin's accusation, "'not a word about your health,'" by diplomatically suggesting that Godwin had failed to read his assurance concerning his health in his previous letter, faulting his own bad handwriting; in fact, Cooper's generous classic script is not difficult to read.[9]

From time to time a well-known performer would attach himself to the company for a few nights. John Quick, the small, "quick," actor of comedy at Covent Garden, had joined them at Chichester and the four days back at Portsmouth—"a very pleasant man in company & very familiar." At Southampton they expected Charles Incledon, a young tenor famous for his trills and falsetto, and perhaps Holman as well.[10]

It was in October that Cooper wrote from Southhampton saying he was having differences with the managers; this time, unlike his confrontations with Stephen Kemble in Edinburgh, he had more justice on his side, if as much pride. Ever since the time of James II, when managers had replaced the King as paymasters for the performers, actors had drawn up their own programs and distributed their own tickets for their benefits. The actors of long standing in a company took their benefits first, so audiences were scarce by the time newcomers like Cooper took theirs. He had just had his first benefit: "Glory be to thee, O God, for the manifold goods which day after day thou bestowest upon me. Would you believe it? I have had a benefit—such a benefit—a kind of Irish one by which I have lost upward of six pounds—at least I remain that much indebted to our managers!—How strange, how despicable are the dispositions of tyrants[.]"

He described the unfair treatment threatened him by Davies, Collins' co-manager: "The morning after my night—this Davies came to me begging me to do something for him in a pantomime which is performed tonight for his benefit—I readily consented—Things have turned out so that I am not of much consequence to him to night—& this morning instead of the smiling, smirking face of yesterday he addressed me with a stiff hibernian frown: 'Mr. Cooper I want some money; I must have money—Goddamit Sir I'll not pay the salaries till you have paid me—Blood Sir why am I to pay money out of my own pocket?'" He explained that the usual method of making up such a loss was by deducting three or four shillings a week from the salary, but that on account of his great deficiency, Davies said he might take his whole week's salary at once, rejoining, "In case he attempts that it is my present intention to leave him immediately—not secretly—no—what I dare do—I dare do openly; & if he pursues other steps I have arrived to such a happy disregard relative to my personal affairs that it will scarcely give me a moments [sic] concern[.]"[11]

Davies had also asked Holcroft, through Cooper, for the rights to *School for Arrogance*, but since Mr. Harris had the exclusive option on the play at Covent Garden, Holcroft had necessarily refused him. Cooper said Davies complained, "'[I]f Mr. Holcroft had really been inclined to serve me he certainly could not have refused so small a favour. Mr. Harris would never know it.'" He added, "I smiled within myself at the confined ideas of selfish men."[12]

He also told Godwin that after his benefit Mr. Tyler, taken up with his own importance, had treated him as a newcomer with careless disregard: "The absent politician too has—attempted—to speak to me. 'Mr. Tyler have you heard any news to-day—Oh Mr. Cooper—about your night (a pause) I have not seen the star today—Sir walk this way if you please.' I was going to follow But he met Mr. Somebody & immediately began settling the business of the nation—He dared imagine that it was for me to wait his pleasure—about half an hour after he repeated his request & I told him I was otherwise engaged—" Sardonically he explained, "[T]he other weak interests are supremely blessed with the happy gifts of fawning & servility—yet I have not so much of the spaniel about me; I cannot take my hat off to the great man's great servant. If I were to lose 50 pounds & 50 benefits I cannot bow to & flatter the man I despise[.]"[13] Soon after he came to America, Tyler told Dunlap that at the beginning in Portsmouth he had thought Cooper "a most unpromising boy and was astonished, when in New-York, to hear that this same good-for-naught stripling was playing Hamlet and Macbeth with success in London."[14]

Making do with what little money he could save and borrow, Cooper remained with the company at Southampton. In another letter a month later, in response to Godwin's suspicion of "an appearance of reserve in my letters," he rejoined that he had not made over much about the failure of his benefit, because he was unmoved by it himself: "If I did not expatiate at large on the subject it was because I had no desire to excite any man's compassion; for I feel no compassion for myself; or in other words I am quite indifferent about it as I have told you before.—I have lived partly upon a little money which I had saved and partly on credit; which has involved me in debt near two pounds. But I shall considerably decrease it by means of about a guinea which I got last night by joining with two others who had failed, and buying a bad stock-night of the managers at an underprice—this with the loan of a guinea which you are so kind as to offer me will pretty well bring me about." His early life had toughened him, so he was able to adopt an attitude of indifference, toward the money, as to the critical notices, which served to engender the lofty mystique which would provide him the fortitude for the demands of his career.

He went on to explain to Godwin that he had not known about the opportunity for a second benefit when he last wrote. The managers had ended settling the benefit loss by allowing him and two others who had failed to hire the house on an *off* night at a reduced price. He said his own benefit was *Such Things Are*, plus the afterpieces, *Hog in the Well* and *The Romp*; the joint benefit, *Every one Has His Fault* and *Modern Antiques*. He planned to stay with the company if they restored him a salary at the next town and paid his one still outstanding bill, for the printing of his benefit tickets, to which he expected they would agree. Otherwise he said he would refuse to play for the manager's benefit the last night and leave early. He closed his letter to Godwin with "a childish wish"—not to tell his friends he was coming to London for the holiday so he could surprise them.[15]

"A Wretched Set of Mummers"—1794

The reunion with his family and friends must have been a happy one, for all during the past year of writing Godwin, his mother and sister, and Marshal, Cooper had continually asked about all of them, including Holcroft and Dyson, and his younger brother Jack. When he left to go back to the company in January, he added Godwin's sister, "Miss Godwin," to his salutations. The trip he had just made from London to Newport, where the company was engaged, showed the strong physical endurance he had developed:

> I left hyde [*sic*] Park corner at five o'clock on the Sunday. I left you at two—& proceeded some twenty or thirty miles when I was overtaken by the Southampton mail. I got a four shilling cast on the outside—& arrived at Southton [*sic*] gloriously wet at ten o'clock on monday night—I set of [*sic*] to Cowes the next morning at seven by the mail packet which was opposed both by wind & tide, & could make no way—& the mail was obliged to vent in an open boat; & as I could row I got into the boat leaving the rest of the passengers on board. I now pulled against wind & tide for upward of twelve miles—without one minute's rest & I dont recollect ever to have undergone so great fatigue before—I arrived at Newport however by three o'clock in the afternoon on tuesday according to my promise—when contrary to my expectation I had nothing to do in the evening's entertainment—

Five—"My Fortune Smiles"—1794

In fact, his only reward for the timely exertion was a reduction in salary from fifteen shillings a week to ten, and after Newport there was no work at all for several days.

When the company reached Chichester, they were able to get a seven-week engagement, but because of the managers' "great impatience" to open the Portsmouth Theatre, after three weeks they divided the company, sending Cooper along with some others back to Portsmouth. Collins also directed him to learn new parts, including the role of George Barnwell in *The London Merchant*. Lillo's play, a repertory staple, is a moral tale about a London apprentice, corrupted by a prostitute, who murders his uncle, but at his execution rises to redemption in cautioning others.

Cooper reported to Godwin that so much traveling and extra work had left him little time for his own study, but he had managed to learn Lord Hastings in *Jane Shore*. He had also begun to study Jaffier in *Venice Preserv'd*, but had decided to put it aside until he had learned the leading role of Pierre. Loving the good life and a good shot at that, he admitted that he had had time enough at Chichester to do some poaching from seven to nine in the mornings and "in utter defiance of the laws of the constitution under which I exist dined twice or thrice on partridges."[16]

Just how long Cooper stayed with the Portsmouth company that year is not known; if he wrote Godwin in the spring and summer, no letters survive. By the time he had left London to return to the company after the Christmas holiday, Godwin was beginning to be distracted by the arrests of prominent reformers; he was also starting a novel to promote the ideas in *Political Justice—Things as They Are, or The Adventures of Caleb Williams*. In May he finished the book with a Preface to delineate his moral purpose, referring to the current conflict over "things as they are" versus reform. That was the same day the British government seized the papers of the radical London Corresponding Society. Pitt's government arrested the popular orator John Thelwall, a shoemaker Hardy, the well-known philologist Horne Tooke, and ten others on the capital charge of high treason. May 26 *Caleb Williams* was published, but out of fear, the printer withheld the Preface. As a thriller of pursuit, the book was an instant success, printed 26 times in Godwin's lifetime.

Meanwhile in France, June marked the beginning of the Great Terror. The Jacobin extremists now in control put thousands to death and incarcerated British reformers who had gone to Paris to witness the birth of liberty, including Tom Paine, who had fought to save the King's life. Godwin, whose role it was to infuse truth into the society through his writing, had not been arrested, although it was said that *Political Justice* escaped prosecution only because in a debate in the Privy Council William

Pitt observed that it was too expensive to be of general influence, that "'a three guinea book could never do much harm among those who had not three shillings to spare.'"[17] But there was a clear difference between writers like Godwin and Holcroft and the radical activist politicians of the Opposition; the Jacobins quoted Godwin for their own purposes. Meanwhile Godwin's disciples, the poets Coleridge and Robert Southey, planned an ideal community in Pennsylvania, "Pantisocracy,"—Joseph Priestley had already emigrated in April.

Godwin was out of London when he saw the London paper for October 7 with the news of Holcroft's detention; also charged with high treason, he had been placed in Newgate Prison with the others. Although Holcroft had a volatile personality, he had repeatedly spoken out for reason and truth and against violence. The only conceivable excuse for his arrest was an incident that had taken place several months before, when he had gone to see a friend, a reformer who had been detained at home under the watch of an officer. The semi-literate king's messenger who was standing guard there at the time misinterpreted Holcroft's assertion of his opposition to violence as a personal criticism, and in an exchange, accused him of association with the radicals. Cooper later recalled to Dunlap that Holcroft was "apt to oppose peoples prejudices in conversation, is talkative and often offends."[18]

In preliminary hearings a grand jury had found *true bills* against twelve of the reformers who had been arrested, including Holcroft, so the death penalty became a possibility. As soon as Godwin wrote and received a reply from Holcroft, he rushed back to town and shut himself away at home over the weekend to write a defense, seeing no one except Marshal and Dyson. He wrote a carefully reasoned argument based on the Constitution, which confined treason to acts against the King's life or actual war against the state; it ran anonymously in the *Morning Chronicle* on October 21.[19]

That same day Cooper wrote Godwin a letter, marked on the outside "To be delivered immediately," in which he told him that he had joined a strolling company at New Theatre, Stockport, Cheshire, and was in desperate need of money. He explained, "We are to play in theatre to be sure; that is, in a place built for that purpose only, but we shall come under the vagrant act[.]" The Licensing Act of 1737 had classed itinerant players as rogues and vagabonds, subject to penalties as such. However, they were generally allowed to practice their profession unrestrained, unless they created undue disturbance, and in 1788 a new act had secured them firmer legal status.

The company had been traveling constantly since closing an engagement at Liverpool two weeks before. He remarked to Godwin:

Whether the god of wisdom presided in my brain at the time I made the resolution of joining these strolling players at Stockport I know not—whether you may think the step wise ... I am equally ignorant. But well I know that it is now a fortnight since we closed at Liverpool and that in the interim I have travelled fifty miles bag & baggage across the country—And that by these means my stock of cash is so reduced that without a supply before tomorrow twelve o'clock I shall [be] obliged to dine with a certain duke with whom I have kept company before today; but (heartily despising every thing and titles among the rest that put me in mind of usurpation & inequality,) whose company I would very willingly renounce for the time to come. Nevertheless I stand prepared to encounter any tricks or mischief fortune may be inclined to put upon me continually repeating the first dozen lines of that ode of Horace beginning, "Justum & tenacem propositi virum—"

Recalling Cooper's accounts of his early struggles in the British provinces, William Wood said, "He often spoke with pride of the approbation bestowed on his performance of some very inferior characters, and the courage which a night's success gave him to labor on and hope."[20] In the letter from Stockport he admitted he had reservations now about the situation in which he found himself, but told Godwin he was too far away and too much out of pocket to consider leaving right away. Moreover, he considered that at least he was at the front of a company: "Here then I am—& here we open tomorrow I donot [sic] play till saturday when I make my appearance in Barnwell—I have no doubt of my success—for what trifling degree of merit I may have will receive additional lustre from the

Mr. Cooper as Barnwell. From an engraving by J. Rogers, after a drawing by Wageman. Courtesy Harvard Theatre Collection, Houghton Library extreme dulness of the set of devils I have got among—... But the sweets of superiority—'Oh tis better to reign in Hell than serve in heaven.'"

Asking how his novel was selling, Cooper told Godwin that he might leave for London in eight or ten weeks "unless I should meet with very great success." Having read about Holcroft's arrest in the newspapers, he wanted to know, "how is Mr. H's family governed in his absence—tell me any occurrence relative to Mr. H's imprisonment if any there is not mentioned in the papers ... let the Holcroft family know I have not forgotten them." He added, "Though indeed if Mr. Holcroft's trial comes & a consequence which I tremble to think on should take place I shall be in Town on the instant." He joked about the party they had attended at Holcroft's the last night he was in London: "mention me ... to Mrs. Revely [Godwin's close friend, Maria Reveley] ... the lady who supped with you the last night I was in Town at Mr. Holcroft's—she is a painter. Tell her I would come all the way to London bare foot to see her perform the office of hangman to Mr. P. [Pitt]—which I recollect she said she should have no objection to." He also asked, "Is George Dyson yet out of his swaddling clothes— that is does he yet live entirely as his own master or is he still at home with papa & mamma[?]" and "How does Jack* go on."[21]

Mrs. Merry as Alzira (Voltaire, *Alzira*, 1836).

Only a week later Cooper wrote Godwin again, on the twenty-eighth, now outraged at the manager and making

*At the time Cooper went to America his brother Jack died, aged eighteen (Mrs. Shelley, Memoirs).

plans to leave. A chance occurrence had tipped the balance. He had been slated to perform George Barnwell, but the play was canceled, and his willingness to take on a secondary role in another play instead, put him under the manager's hand:

> All the devils in Hell seem to conspire against me—when success seemed placed within my reach and I had nothing left to do but to nod my head and become a hero some damned untoward accident prevents it. Barnwell could not be played as I informed you it would—But last night to forward the manager's business I undertook to play Roldan in Columbus at a short notice & give up an appearance part; the consequence of which was that the manager relying upon a continued obligingness in doing his dirty work this morning gave me a list of parts & grinning told me I promised very well—but that I must do all the parts there specified. There were to be sure a great many *good* parts & most of them respectable but he told me that in my turn I must also deliver messages.

Cooper retorted to the manager that "the parts expressed in his list would very well satisfy me indeed; but that as to the delivering messages I would not do it in heaven." He explained to Godwin that if it were a good company, a few messages would have been all right, but—"I hardly think it would be right to stay even if I did nothing else. They are such a wretched set of mummers. Perhaps you will reply—that I can do my business properly tho' they did not I say no they seldom speak a word of the author the business is a jest—& likewise the man who attempts to treat it seriously[.]" He

From a sketch of Thomas Holcroft (left) and William Godwin at the Treason Trials, 1794, drawn by Sir Thomas Lawrence in the courtroom. Private collection.

ended his letter with a flourish: "I shall see you shortly. I will black shoes at the corner of Goodge street for 1 shil per day sooner than be any thing but the leader among a set of wretches I despise—Io Triumphe[.]"[22] Assuredly, he would make no such accommodations to any manager in future.

That letter was written on the same day the Treason Trials began in London, so on December 1 when Holcroft was brought before the court, Cooper was most likely back in London. Clearly innocent, Holcroft was quickly acquitted by dismissal, but when he asked for a half hour to speak to the court, to explain how diametrically opposed he was to violence and the kinds of charges for which he had been imprisoned, he was denied it. This refusal was a significant symbol, for although Holcroft was freed, both he and Godwin would be maligned by association in the wave of anti-Jacobism that followed, affecting Cooper as well.

Six

"A Young Gentleman"

Mr. Holcroft—1795

The next word from Cooper is a letter dated January 20, right after he had left Godwin's. Over the holidays he had had discussions, undoubtedly impassioned ones, with both Godwin and Holcroft regarding his future. Having ruminated over what had been said, he was writing to tell Godwin his decision—to abandon the theatre: "The die I believe is now finally cast—and if it be the result is insignificance—non-entity—death to the hopes my ambition has oftentimes formed and on which my mind has continually brooded with enthusiastic pleasure—The little portion of mind, I (perhaps) have hitherto retained has now yielded; it receives it's [sic] fetters, not indeed without murmuring, but the curses it pours forth, and the tortures it endures are equally unavailing and unproductive of any material resistance."

It was when the young actor had lost his first chance to play a leading role, the ill-fated clerk George Barnwell, that he had quit the Stockport company, and now he was writing to inform Godwin that he had decided to accept a position as a clerk with Mr. Dorset, the family benefactor who had helped support his sister. Dealing in extremes as usual, he said since "love of fame," which Godwin considered "a bad motive for praise-worthy conduct," had been his "only spur to intellectual exertion," he had made the distasteful decision "to become a slave."

He said he was giving up the theatre for good to go into business, "to become totally an everyday man."—Though not without torment: "Your last words to me on Monday night were:—'and then become a mere vegetable'—The damned idea has harrassed me ever since—Whenever it recurs to my recollection I curse the hour that gave me birth—I curse the trifling improvements I have received which only enables me to discover the wretchedness of the sphere in which I am doomed to act without giving me power of emancipating myself from the shackles of ignorance and attaining the heights of true genius—'The vast, the unbounded prospect lies before me—but shadows clouds, and darkness rest upon it...' Oh!—had I the power to dispel those clouds—to enlighten that darkness—"

For leading him into the theatre, tempting him with the golden apple, he blamed Godwin: "I almost doubt whether I ought not to curse you since you it is who have brought to my knowledge the existence of something sublimely beautiful, but which I am doomed never to attain and without which my life must be a series of despair, envy and misery—Why did you not permit me to remain quiet in my primeval ignorance? You have acted by me something in the same manner as religious enthusiasts report the creator to have acted when he placed the tree of knowledge in reach of our first ancestors—they tasted and damnation was the consequence—"

It was Holcroft, however, who had most likely lectured their young protégé with some stringency about his inordinate ambition and commensurate discouragement; Godwin was more guarded and quiet in company. Cooper went on to confide to him, "I feel half inclined to go and quarrel with Mr. Holcroft I do not know and have not enquired why I feel that inclination ... though at the same time I have the utmost veneration & love for him.—But my mind is all chaos—it is weighed down by unsurmountable causation—but still retains the useless quality of deprecating and groaning at its situation."

He admitted that the only motive for his decision was to "search after riches which according to my present determination is the object I must pursue—for among the rest of my vices I take pleasure in those things which riches can procure[.]" But added, "Though I feel at present determined to accomplish that end—I suspect it is out of the nature of things that it should last sufficiently long for the purpose." Withal, he decided he could not totally relinquish his longheld animus, to distinguish himself: "At any rate I am sure I shall not die [unless that event happen suddenly] without perpetrating some deed of atrocity or of virtue by means of which my name will be either extensively execrated or revered."[1]

With a flourish under the *C* of his name, he took a plunge into the business world in London. However, Betty had left Dorset's protection three years before, because, as she had explained to Godwin, he had become possessive of her time and demanding of her obeisance to his benevolence.[2] And Cooper's doubts proved true, for although he would one day make—and lose—a great deal of money, it would not be in a counting house; he soon left Dorset as well.

In a letter to Godwin July 25 from Exeter he protested what must have been an accusatory letter from his guardian; Godwin was undoubtedly worried about what he intended to do, particularly since Cooper had borrowed a little money from him for the summer: "You say that my *pretence* of a ten days ramble appears to be a *cloak* for a visit to Bath—What criminality there is in a visit to Bath that should seem to require a cloak I cannot perceive—but take my word for it whatever desperate villainy I may engage in it shall not be under a *cloak*; and when (as you express it) I sink into vice, it shall not be into it's *sourness*; it shall be into the dashing whirlpool that openly destroys every thing around it—Therefore whenever vice becomes my object notorious shall be the fact—Depend on it I have nothing to do with *cloake!*—"

He explained that he had been at Exeter for a fortnight and had gone on to Exmouth to see Holcroft, who was staying at nearby Broadclyst; his mother had told him Holcroft was seriously ill due to a fall from a ladder. He also revealed his current intentions to Godwin: "I shall remain a fortnight longer for the benefit of sea bathing & the instructions of Mr. Holcroft."[3] He had indeed conferred with Mr. Holcroft, and back to the theatre he was going. While convalescing, Holcroft had offered to coach him, presumably to instruct him in the Shakespearean roles he would play for his debut.

Originally an actor himself, in 1780 Holcroft had published a series of articles on acting in which he emphasized the emotional truth necessary to raise acting from mere imitation to art, using Macbeth as his example:

> An actor who speaks the Dagger soliloquy of Macbeth from observation of other Actors, and not from a strong conception of the feelings of a man lost in thought, bewildered by the tumultuous passions which agitate his mind, and liable to fancy a thousand chimeras from the time of the night, the bloody deed he is about to execute, and the wanderings of an over-heating imagination, will stare, stalk across the stage, grasp at the dagger, and use all the other mechanical motions he has observed; but his eyes will have the glare of vacancy; his very feet will confess the confused state of his ideas; and his whole deportment will contradict his lips: it will be evident he has not those emotions which he says he has; and the indignation of the audience will rise against the impostor, who has the effrontery thus to insult both their feelings and their understanding.... Passion is not communicated from one to the other by the attitude of the speaker or the force of the dialogue; it is thinking aloud, and depends upon the imagination of the speaker, the strength of his conception, and the goodness of his judgment.

He went on to describe the actor's art in the intervals of silence: "[H]is deportment should in dumb shew describe what the next sentence will confirm." Pointing out that "it is in this dumb shew that Actors are in general deficient," he concluded that "fortitude and presence of mind are indispensable for a great Actor; because without them his ideas would be liable to frequent disarrangement, his countenance thrown into confusion, and every feature, limb, and attitude contrary to the tone of the passion."[4]

In view of Holcroft's tutelage, it is not surprising that Macbeth would generally be regarded as Cooper's most distinguished representation, his dagger scene regularly singled out by the critics. Moreover, while he adopted the formal style, for which he embodied the ideal, as a young man rising from early loss and poverty, he was himself a romantic figure, and as such, naturally added more passion to his art. Focused by the training under Holcroft, he would become noted for his emotional truth, always a basic measure in theatrical criticism; he would also be respected for eschewing stage tricks. An uneven actor, however, from time to time he would be guilty of violating Holcroft's precepts.

The fine American light comedian James Edward Murdoch recalled Cooper's acting as "half-way between" the classic Kemble and the famous romantic British actor of that time, George Frederick Cooke.[5] In point of fact, though occasionally accused of rant, as well as an unpleasing sibilant *s*, his ability to express a depth of feeling while maintaining the formal demeanor was one of the hallmarks of his acting for which he was generally lauded throughout his career. The delicacy of his facial features suggested to some that he was ideally suited for comedy and romance; but a later critic in New York, viewing Cooper as "a man of proud spirit and acute sensibility" who had "deep tenderness of feeling," noted, "His countenance was remarkable for its mobility of expression";—a significant asset for an actor—"his dark eyes were beautiful"; and his voice "of uncommon volume" with "tones of peculiar, silvery sweetness[.]"[6] These qualities enabled him to represent nuances of emotion and reaction in either mode. He chose to emphasize the tragic roles but practiced comedy as well to good effect. This flexibility was an important component of his success and influence in the widespread touring he undertook in America.

Kemble, the sober, even solemn, scholar-actor had originally studied for the priesthood and played only in tragedy. The gracefully controlled style he had developed was said to be born of the defect of an asthmatic voice, which he would thus preserve for the occasional burst of passion. When Washington Irving saw him in *Venice Preserv'd* in London in 1805, he wrote to his brother about Kemble's voice, "Some of its tones are touching and pathetic, but when violent exclamation is necessary it is evident from the movements of his head and mouth & chest that he is obliged to use great exertions." In contrasting Cooper with Kemble, Irving added,

"It would be a long time however before C. would be equally *correct* in his performances. Perhaps he would never be so—his style is different and with a little correction—its warmth & richness would perhaps make up for the want of Kembles correctness & precision. Actors are like painters. they [*sic*] seldom combine all these qualities but excel in different styles."[7]

During his time with Holcroft Cooper also took dancing and fencing lessons to learn how to move gracefully on the stage. At the end of the summer, Holcroft had to stay at Broadclyst to continue his recovery, experimenting with conquering the pain through the philosophy of Mind, while Cooper returned to London to collect some back salary Dorset owed him in order to repay Godwin the money he had borrowed.[8]

That summer Godwin had met Mrs. Siddons for the first time. On Cooper's return, when he heard him recite, he recognized the advance he had made in working with Holcroft over the summer, so when Holcroft himself returned, together they made plans for his London debut. The manager of Covent Garden, Thomas Harris, had just produced *The Deserted Daughter*, perhaps Holcroft's best comedy, in May, so they were able to arrange with Harris for Cooper to perform a series of leading roles that October at the Theatre-Royal, Covent Garden.

First Appearance—1795–96

At the time of Cooper's debut, only two "patent" theatres were allowed to operate within a 20-mile radius of London, a restriction imposed by the Licensing Act of 1737, and both were in a state of financial difficulty. A plan by which first, Covent Garden, in 1792, and then, Drury Lane, in 1794, had been rebuilt and approximately doubled in size in order to accommodate the public was backfiring. As the masses began attending the theatre, the serious theatregoers, who had frequented the theatre in the first half of the eighteenth century, stayed away. Since the new theatre-going public could not appreciate even the most obvious fine points of the play itself, music, horse shows, and spectacle had to be added at great expense to attract them. Even so, only the pits and galleries would fill, except on special occasions, such as the yearly visit of Royalty, who cared little for serious dramatic art themselves.

Many critics complained that a lack of actors of genius, except for the rare Mrs. Siddons, John Philip Kemble, Charles Mathews, and very few others, accounted in large part for the fall-off in theatre attendance by people of discrimination. However, a newcomer, particularly one as young as Cooper, could be counted on to arouse special interest. On Monday,

Theatre-Royal, in Covent-Garden,

This prefent MONDAY, Oct. 19, 1795,
Will be prefented the Tragedy of

HAMLET.

Hamlet by a YOUNG GENTLEMAN,
(Being his Firft Appearance.)
Ghoft by Mr TOMS,
Horatio by Mr HARLEY,
Laertes by Mr MIDDLETON,
King by Mr RICHARDSON,
Oftrick by Mr BERNARD,
Polonius by Mr MUNDEN,
Rofencrans by Mr MACREADY,
Guildenftern Mr Claremont, Marcellus Mr Williamfon,
Francifco Mr FARLEY, Bernardo Mr CROSS, Prieft Mr POWEL,
Player King Mr THOMPSON, Lufianus Mr DAVENPORT,
Sailor Mr LEDGER, Gentleman Mr ABBOTT,
Grave-diggers, Meff. QUICK and REES,
Ophelia by Mrs. MOUNTAIN,
Player Queen by Mrs. PLATT,
And the Queen by Mrs. POPE.

In Act V. a DIRGE, fet to Mufic by MR. SHIELD.
The WORDS from SHAKSPEARE.

The VOCAL PARTS by Mrs. Martyr, Mrs. Clendinning, Mifs Stuart, Mrs. Watts, Mrs. Lloyd, Mrs. Blurton, Mifs Walcup, Mrs. Mafters, Mrs. Norton, Mrs. Follett, Mrs. Coftelle, Mifs Ives, Mifs Leferve—and Meff. Haynes, Linton, Street, &c.

To which will be added (Firft time at this Theatre) the Farce of

The GHOST.

Farmer Harrow by Mr KNIGHT,
Trufty by Mr POWEL,
Clinch by Mr FARLEY,
Sir Jeffery by Mr DAVENPORT,
Capt. Conftant by Mr CLAREMONT,
Belinda by Mifs IVES,
And Dolly by Mrs DAVENPORT.

NO MONEY TO BE RETURNED.

On Wednefday, 14th Time, the laft new Comedy of the
DESERTED DAUGHTER,
with the grand Ballet Pantomime of OSCAR AND MALVINA.
On Thurfday Mifs GOUGH will make her Firft Appearance in this Kingdom,
in the Character of Alicia, in the Tragedy of JANE SHORE.
On Friday, 4th time, a New Tragedy called The SECRET TRIBUNAL.
Mrs. SERRES will perform Polly in the BEGGAR's OPERA on Saturday.

2

From the Playbill for Mr. Cooper's London debut.

October 19, 1795, at the age of nineteen, he made his first appearance, as Hamlet. The announcement in the *Times* that day does not give his name, but simply states, "Hamlet by a YOUNG GENTLEMAN being his first appearance on any stage." Established members of the company supported him: Joseph Shepherd Munden, chief comedian of the theatre, as Polonius; John Quick, whom he knew from Chichester, one of the grave-diggers; Mrs. Pope, the Queen. The afterpiece was the farce of *The Ghost*.

It was said that at the time of Cooper's debut, "His person had grown more into masculine bulk and manly shape; his face had become more marked and expressive, and his voice had swelled into a more full deep tenor."[9] He was received with enthusiastic applause, and the critics generally recognized his talent. The reviewer in the independent paper, the *Monthly Mirror*, which ran a series of three articles on the debut, said that the performance, "for a first appearance before a London audience, taking all its disadvantages and terrors into account, was, beyond a doubt, *unusually brilliant*." He went on to describe the debutante:

> Mr. Cooper is, in person, of the middle size, his features are not strongly expressive of any particular character; there is more softness and playfulness, than spirit or energy about them; yet, with artful management, they may suit either tragedy or comedy: naturally inclinable perhaps to the latter.
>
> His voice is, in tone, pleasing; capable of more modulation than he seems to know how to give it; firm and extensive in the upper division; in the lower, musical and articulate. Indeed he can have nothing to lay to the charge of nature for a scanty supply of her gifts: if he does not make use of them properly the fault rests with *himself*.

Without question, from the outset, the fact that he was Holcroft's pupil had a material influence on the assessment of the novice, as the *Mirror* reviewer stated: "Mr. Cooper has suffered as much from the hyperbolical praise of some, as from the indiscriminate censure of others. The true state of the case is this: Mr. Cooper has a friend in Mr. Holcroft: he was represented to be *his* pupil. Party, the foe to every thing generous or just, instantly made its appearance. The prints of *opposition* were unanimous in the most extravagant eulogy, while some of the *contrary* character were in the other extreme."

One side regarded him as "an actor of an astonishing genius: with powers of discrimination that ranked him at once with the first performers of the day. One, indeed, as if gifted with prophetic *inspiration*, went so far as to affirm that, in the course of five years, he would be the best actor that ever trod the English stage." The reviewer commented, "*Ridiculous, impudent* assertion!—This is surely the very *bathos* of puffing: infatuation itself could scarcely conceive any thing more injurious to the young actor." On the other side he reflected, "It were hard, indeed, for an actor to suffer for the *principles* of his *tutor*[,]" and went on to explain, "The name of *Holcroft*, it should seem, was sufficient to blast the fame of *Cooper*; and, as if by a principle of consecutive necessity, a *critique*, as it is called, made its appearance, deficient of all candour and honesty, and every way injurious to the talents of the performer[.]"

By laying out the imbalance in the criticism thus far, the *Mirror* reviewer laid the basis for a fair appraisal, "an intermediate course, as remote from adulation as ill-nature[.]" He deemed that Cooper's faults in the performance stemmed from reliance on art at the expense of true emotion, his first act Hamlet not truly "grieved." This suggests that on the first night, a daunting experience, as he said, even for this most determined young man, Cooper did not achieve the kind of emotional definition in which Holcroft had instructed him: "Mr. Cooper ... was as *dégagée* with *Horatio* as, by and by, more applicably with Rosencrantz and Guildenstern. Nothing was ever spoken with less feeling, with less effect, than the fine defence of *Hamlet* from the charge of his mother, '*seems*, madam, nay IT IS.' He was no better in the *soliloquy* immediately after, he was angry, he was boisterous, but he was not *passionate*. There was an expression of *discontent* that the Almighty had forbidden self-slaughter: there was the same expression of discontent, that the world had become a matter of indifference to him. In short, it was *Hamlet* disappointed, it was Hamlet *chagrined*, it was every thing but Hamlet GRIEVED."

In the scene in Act One where Hamlet first meets the Ghost he did not think "Mr. Cooper's *caution*, on approaching the *platform*, either natural or characteristic.... Of course he would not *peep about*, as if appalled at his own shadow; therefore we think Mr. Cooper has been seduced by a novelty for the *sake* of novelty only." And in the opening address to the Ghost said he was "not sufficiently solemn ... or he never would have pitched his tone so *high* at the commencement of the address[.]" But went on to affirm his success in the speech otherwise.

As the scene progresses, at the point when Hamlet, consumed with his vision of the Ghost, breaks from Horatio and his other friends, he faulted Cooper for too long a pause for effect in turning back to Horatio and his friends while he should more properly have fixated on the ghost. Referring to "a custom with some actors, ... to stop before the delivery of the last quotation, for the accustomed *gallery tribute* ... a *clap-trap*[,]" he warned, "[L]et us caution Mr. Cooper against this subserviency of spirit, lest, in the anxiety after undue applause, like some other accommodating actors of the present day, he should be *caught in his own snare*."[10]

The reviewer granted that in the mad scenes "Mr. Cooper was little inferior to the *stated* Hamlets of Covent Garden ... as far as *conception* goes, except in relating the progress of his melancholy to *Rosencrantz and Guildenstern*[.]" But in the "*To be, or not to be*" soliloquy said he "appeared to be amusing himself more with an idle problem of mathematics, than exercising a reasoning faculty on a question of the last moral concernment. Thus he spoke the *second*, 'to die—to sleep,' as follows: 'to die to sleep;' but Hamlet does not knock off his arguments so rapidly.... Mr. Cooper was, through the whole of this soliloquy, cold, awkward, trifling, and injudicious."[11]

In the scene of Hamlet's advice to the players, he again saw "*more of art* than of *nature*" in Cooper's performance, though he commented favorably on his delivery: "It is not to be denied, that, for a *novice*, he spoke the instructions with much ease and general propriety[.]" This scene would be considered the peak of Cooper's performance of the role by most critics in future; he had himself been a strolling player in Cheshire. And the reviewer went on to praise the originality of his conception of the play scene itself:

> It is but justice to say, that, in the scene where the *murder of Gonzago* is represented, Mr. Cooper was every thing that the situation of the character required. It was here that he formed the only attitude that bore any thing like grace or picturesque appearance; and, at the same time, struck out a bold and original conception, which had a most electrical effect.
>
> "He *poisons* him—in the *garden*—for his *estate*:—you shall see, anon, how the *murderer* gets the love of Gonzago's *wife*."
>
> This mode of *emphasis*, pointing out the exact *parallel* in which the circumstances of Gonzago's murder ran with those of his father's, and *tenting* Claudius at once *to the quick*, we do not remember to have seen adopted by any former Hamlet. The improvement is obvious, and so is the actor's gradual relinquishment of his seat at Ophelia's feet, and advance towards the king as he finds the plot work the desired effect.

"This scene," he said, "may be styled Mr. Cooper's master-piece." And concluded, "Upon the whole, we are inclined to think very favourably of Mr. Cooper's abilities: he possesses understanding and powers, but in his utterance he is disgustingly broad and provincial, in his action embarrassed, and, in the general disposition of his person, inattentive to all the rules of grace and proportion."[12]

According to "Thespis" in the *Oracle and Public Advertiser*, Cooper's "instructions to the PLAYERS were well delivered, and drew down very general applause." And in the play scene he deemed him "superior to his competitors—The forcible iteration of every term connected with *murder*, *poison*, the *garden*—all collateral to the usurper's guilt, evinced sound judgment, and the tone with which he conveyed 'our withers are *unwrung*,' will never cease to delight us." He concurred to some extent that "[t]he famous rumination, 'To be or not to be,' was indifferently given; his reflection was too light; and in one line he mistook the emphasis, as he will see, by looking at the two lines together—It is not 'what *dreams* may come'...." But of the soliloquy upon the going out of the players said, "[A]fter the rant about *Hecuba*, he was so impassioned, natural and impressive, as to leave the critic nothing to wish or dispute."

This critic also praised several of his line readings: "When he notices his joy at *Polonius*'s taking leave, and expresses no greater willingness to part with anything except his *life*, he produced the best effect imaginable." In the closet scene, later considered among his best in the role, "[H]e gave the sarcasms with great *poignancy*, and the eulogium upon his *father* with forcible grandeur." And "The mixture of sorrowful reflection, when he says of *Polonius's* body to the seekers, 'He will stay till you come,' was new, and accurately spoken." At Ophelia's grave "his 'millions of acres,' shewed body of tone, and management of it, wonderful in a young man." He also noticed in the fencing scene he "had sufficient skill in the weapon—he hit *Laertes* neatly—" concluding, "His death was too quiet; but he no doubt was thoroughly exhausted."[13]

The critic for the *Times*, the government paper, while agreeing that Cooper had talent, was not as generous in his remarks, beginning: "To pourtray the character of HAMLET *well* requires so nice a judgement, a discrimination so correct, it is a wonder any 'Novice in the scenes' should select it for a first appearance. The adventurer of last night does not appear to want talents; but they are much beneath what is necessary for the princely Dane." He aimed his sharpest criticism at Cooper's deportment in his delivery of the advice to the players: "In correcting the players, there should be a grace of action, a superior elegance of manner, which he entirely wanted.... [H]is voice [is] tolerable; his tones provincial. He trammelled up some of the sentences with an affected velosity, very unsuitable to the *firma pedestris*;—so that they came not 'trippingly, but *jiggingly* off the tongue.'" He apologized for his own brevity, however, by noting that "[t]he curtain dropt to a very good house, but so late, that it is impossible to tread further through the fields of criticism."[14]

When Cooper performed Hamlet again at the end of the month, the same critic reviewed his second appearance in the role more favorably, saying, "MR. COOPER, on his first appearance, shewed so much conception and feeling in this character, that it would have been injustice not to have attended his second performance of it, and judge of him when his embarrassment was a little worn off." He now gave him full credit for absorbing the criticism of his first performance: "The attention he paid to the hints of candid criticism shew his modesty and good sense; he was much less provincial in his accent, and more even in his tones. There is no doubt but study, experience, and a readiness to adopt the advice of the judicious (which bad actors are too great to submit to), will make him a capital Performer. The requisites seem all to be in his possession."[15]

He was first announced by name in the *Times* on November 2, "HAMLET, by Mr. Cooper, (being his 3rd appearance)." The following day the *Times* reviewer, noting that he played "to a large audience," said, "Mr. Cooper received what he deserved—continual applause." He also praised the production: "The music of the Requiem was given exquisitely well. The whole piece is managed with correctness and elegance as to scenery and decoration."[16]

On November 6 Cooper was cast as "the gallant, gay Lothario," in Rowe's *The Fair Penitent*. The part of the young seducer, reminiscent of the rake, Lovelace, in Samuel Richardson's *Clarissa*, which Godwin had read him as a boy, was the part he had longed to play in Edinburgh. Unfortunately, it requires a kind of smooth deportment which, judging from the *Hamlet* reviews, he had not yet mastered. To make matters worse, the stage director, Lewis, put him in a suit of clothes that was too small. In telling him the story later, William Wood recalled Cooper "often declared ... that from the first moment he appeared, before he had uttered one word, he was assailed by a degree of disapprobation (so cruel a contrast to his former greetings)– as for a time wholly to paralyse exertion, and which he resented in an indignant manner, which completed this unexpected failure. He fled from this scene with a feeling of resentment towards his countrymen which no time had the power to soften." All things considered, the bitterness of that reception did not seem justified to the young actor, who, while he had a degree of critical success, had also been attacked in the papers as a protégé of "'a most ferocious duumvirate of *disorganizing Jacobins.*'"[17]

Cooper made one more appearance at Covent Garden on November 30 as Macbeth. The *Times* critic's assessment of the performance was undeniably harsh, but his suggestion that the young actor get more training was not unreasonable:

> [I]t would give us the highest pleasure, if for his sake, and that of the Stage, we could speak of him "*otherwise than he is*";—his HAMLET promised something; his LOTHARIO was neither gallant, gay, nor even Gentlemanlike; and his MACBETH is a
> "Real mockery!"

He certainly possesses some requisites, and may become a good Player. He should be recommended to study more off, and less on, the stage. He should try experiments in provincial Theatre, there he may practice attitude and enunciation: this will not degrade his talents, for talents he has. Mrs. Siddons had much less promise when she "travelled for instruction"—and returned "The Arabian bird." The metropolis will not patiently climb up the hill of excellence with any Performer, and if he did not see that he had no attraction last night, why then—"there is No Speculation in those eyes."[18]

Although kinder than the *Times*, the reviewer in the *Mirror* shared the opinion that he should serve a longer apprenticeship in the provinces: "Mr. Cooper, in the scenes prior and subsequent to the murder, particularly in the *Dagger Soliloquy*, displayed considerable skill—certainly beyond what, from so young a man, could have been expected. But is he competent to the *first line* of business in our Theatre, taking his present capabilities in their *full extent*? We Think Not.—Would it not be advisable to give him a *progressive* trial of skill, by which he may get rid of *certain habits* that at present preclude him from a general cast of characters, of equal importance with those in which he has hitherto been brought forward? We Think It Would"—going on to censure the management, "Unless the Managers mean to pursue their accustomed system of *elevating* an Actor at first, that by and by they may more sensibly *degrade* him, at a time when such degradation would affect his *feelings*, as well as his reputation."[19]

At the end of these five appearances, Harris offered Cooper a contract to play secondary characters with the company at Covent Garden, but Caesar or nothing, Cooper turned him down. Taking the fifty guineas Harris paid him for the five nights he had acted, he left London before the opening of *Pericles*, in which he was also scheduled to appear. In his *Memoir* of Cooper, Joseph Norton Ireland remarks on a "beautiful engraving of him (then in his twentieth year), in the character of *Pericles*," which appeared in the frontispiece of an edition of the play adapted for his performance at Covent Garden and published in July;[20] but he would never perform the role. Withdrawing from society, he went off to Wales.[21] It was there that he studied the part of the lonely misanthrope in Richard Cumberland's sentimental comedy, *The Wheel of Fortune*, which, providentially, he would perform for his first appearance in America.

No matter what prejudices may have been attached to Cooper as the result of his political associations, he had been well received in London. Then ninety-five years old, the actor Charles Macklin, famed for his portrayal of Shylock, and a distinguished acting coach as well, had gone

Six—"A Young Gentleman"—1795-96

backstage to see him after his debut. Eccentric to the extreme and a hard and severe critic, Macklin had taken Holcroft with him to Ireland in 1770 as an apprentice actor and treated him badly, but he remarked that Cooper's first performance was "the most successful appearance, in one so young, that he had ever witnessed."[22] In 1775 Mrs. Siddons' London debut at age twenty had been a failure; she had not returned to make a successful appearance there until she had played in the provinces seven more years. John Philip Kemble was twenty-six when he made his first London appearance to indifferent success. Considering that in 1795, Kemble, the leading tragedian in London, under contract at Covent Garden, was thirty-eight years old, it is clear that the contract Harris offered the nineteen-year-old Cooper was excellent.

Mr. Cooper as Pericles. From an engraving by W. Skelton, after a drawing by Graham. Pub. G. Cawthorn, July 16, 1796. Harvard Theatre Collection, Houghton Library.

In the spring, 1796, the *Monthly Mirror* "personal notes" mentioned John Quick acting by command for the King at Windsor, Mrs. Siddons for Tate Wilkinson's company in York, Holman traveling West, and said "Mr. Cooper rusticates at Swanzea, where he is to play for Masterman, Hamlet, Penruddock, Mordent [Thomas Holcroft, *The Deserted Daughter*], Macbeth, &c."[23] On the strength of his recent success at Covent Garden, he was able to move about the provincial companies playing leading roles in much the same way he later did in America.

In March Cooper wrote a letter to Godwin from Bath, where he was taking the waters for his health and acting at the Theatre Royal. His tone was cavalier: "I do not know exactly how to address thee—Whether am I to consider thee my grandpapa—or my wise and illustrious cousin—or whether with the familiarity of a companion—I should slap thee on the back and enquire if the smiling pot-girl at the corner has yet yielded her luxuriant charms to thy ardent embraces—I ... have not been able to determine—therefore shall write as chance and my natural inspiration may dictate." With his eye still on London, he asked Godwin to read the actress Mrs. Robinson a favorable notice of his performance of Macbeth that appeared in the *Portsmouth Gazette*; he copied it in his letter:

> "On Thursday evening Mr. Cooper (who performed with such distinguished success in the course of the winter at the Theatre Royal Covent Garden) played the part of Macbeth at our Theatre. This character has ever been considered by the nicest judges of the Drama as one of the most difficult to represent in all Shakespeare, the requisites for its effect being so versatile and numerous—When we observe, that the whole of Mr. C.'s performance bore the evident dignity, the most correct conception and admirable delineation we are confident we pay no more than a just tribute to that merit he so eminently possesses."

Expecting to play Hamlet the next week there in Bath, he ended the letter with intoxication, "May the goddess fame attend thy steps through life—& when thou diest (if that event ever happen) may they transform thee into materials so pure and bright that thy rays may illumine the latest posterity."[24]

On her way back to London Cooper's sister Betty traveled to Bath and Bristol to see her brother perform Penruddock and wrote Godwin a glowing letter:

> "I tremble for Penruddock"
> Tremble, my dear Sir, no longer for the attention the plaudits, the expressions of delight visible in the countenance of two numerous audiences (for the time of year) have evinced most forcibly, that my brother has lost no credit by the performance of this arduous character. I assure you, my fears during the last week were far from trivial; & I went to Bristol in the expectation of hearing expressions of disapprobation for beside, that I imagined he was not perfect in the character, I knew he had to combat prejudice in favor of an old established performer, Mr. Dimond, whose best part it was considered. I summoned heaven & all my heroism, determined unshrinking to receive the blow. These resolutions proved needless. Throughout he produced greater effect than he had ever done before, except in the play scene in Hamlet. The next day at Bath he played still better; he perfectly electrified the audience in his scenes with Henry, particularly, and each time of his reappearance,

Silence was vociferated with impatience, and at the end of almost every scene—the "exclamations" of *Very Well, Bravo, Excellent, Better than Dimond, As well as Kemble, Better than Kemble, The most natural actor* were repeatedly heard. I wish you had been there, you must I am sure have been pleased, critic as you are. I was never more electrified.[25]

In August Holcroft, thinking Cooper still in Wales, sent a letter to him there; it actually caught up with him in early September at Cheltenham. Cooper had written to Marshal when he was sick and in a mood of not uncharacteristic despondence, and Marshal had evidently shared the letter with Holcroft, for Holcroft began by speaking truth to what he perceived to be the young man's error: "'You do not like the word lamentation. You will less like the word that I am going to use. But, before I use it, I will most sincerely assure you I mean it kindly. I do not like rodomantade heroics. They are discordant, grating, and degrading. They are the very reverse of what you imagine them to be. It was not from report, but from your letter itself, ... that I collected my idea of lamentation: and compared to your sufferings, I repeat, Jeremiah never lamented so loudly....'" He was continuing to instruct the young man personally, and Durang later surmised that he and Godwin had succeeded in influencing his character for the best: "We think these lessons were deeply inculcated in Cooper's mind.... He did honor to his great instructors."[26]

Holcroft went on by "'reminding'" him, "'though you did not wish me to apply for a London engagement for you it would have looked quite as friendly had you written to me without this personal motive[,]'" and then told him about the American offer: "'Mr. Wignell, the Manager of the Theatres of Philadelphia and Baltimore in America, has applied to me; offering you four, five, and six guineas a week, forty weeks each year, for three succeeding years: & ensuring benefits to the amount of 150 Gs.'"

He also gave his advice: "'I have reflected on the subject and have consulted your other true & tried friend, Mr. Godwin: and, notwithstanding that this offer is so alluring, it is our decided opinion that, were it ten times as great, it ought to be rejected. As an actor, you would be extinct; and the very season of energy and improvement would be for ever passed. I speak of men as they are now constituted; and after the manner as experience tells me that their habits become fixed: eradicably fixed. Mr. Godwin indeed expresses himself with great force, mixed with some little dread lest money should be a temptation that you could not withstand.'"

"'However,'" he concluded, "'we both know it to be but right that the decision should be entirely your own; and I therefore send you this information. Be kind enough to return me your answer, and without regarding my or any man's opinion, judge for yourself. It is right that Mr. Wignell should not be kept in suspence.'" And added a postscript about an Irish offer: "'A Gentleman has just been with me on the part of Mr. Daly who is to be in town in nine or ten days and wishes to engage you for the winter Season but his I think as prejudicial except that it is nearer home and not so durable an engagement as America Ireland is certainly the school of idleness However all these matters must be left to yourself.'"[27]

Upon receiving this letter, Cooper hardly hesitated before making up his mind to accept Wignell's offer. He replied to his sponsors' advice by pleading the need of a change of air for his health.[28] Ironically, his decision not only assured his fame, but also, in years to come, afforded Holcroft's plays an international reputation. When Cooper met the New York manager, William Dunlap, Dunlap already knew and admired the writings of Godwin, but it was through Cooper that he became familiar with Holcroft's plays and introduced them in America, where they proved to be as popular as they were in England.

That fall, surrounded by his good republican friends, Cooper prepared for his trip to America. In addition to the letter to her brother in Washington, Godwin's future wife Mary Wollstonecraft gave him a letter of introduction to the Irish republican, Archibald Hamilton Rowan, who was in America after escaping imprisonment for treason in Dublin at the same period Holcroft had been tried in London. "Dear friend," she wrote, "The bearer of this, Mr. Cooper, is a very ingenious young man, for whom an intimate friend of mine, Mr. Godwin, has particular affection. By shewing him any attention you would oblige Mr. G. as well as myself; and I am much mistaken if his countenance does not prejudice you in his favour, for it is the sort of one I like to see on young shoulders—"[29]

On September 11 Godwin and Holcroft accompanied Cooper to the coach where he was to meet Wignell and his other recruits. The party would board a Gravesend packet traveling down the Thames River to join their ship for the voyage across the Atlantic. Cooper later recalled to Dunlap the picture of his two friends, both by then with short, unpowdered hair, standing by the coach to tell him good-bye.[30]

SEVEN

The Wheel of Fortune—
1796–98

Cooper was a gambler, if not by nature then by the haphazard nature of his situation. Immured to any idea of saving for his future, as soon as he had money to spend, he indulged in gambling as a sport. In traditional British fashion, he would bet on anything—the speed of a horse, the height of a room, the outcome of an election.[1] Impelled as he was, in 1796 he took a gamble on his future. He was too impatient to stay with a London company and slowly make his way up the ladder, especially since his promoters, Godwin and Holcroft, were misperceived as Jacobins; after the Terror in France they were permanently out of favor in London. Despite their persuasive advice to the contrary, he decided to cross the Atlantic.

Along with Cooper and Mrs. Merry, Thomas Wignell recruited the distinguished character actor, William Warren, who, with William Wood, would eventually succeed him in the management of the Chestnut Street Theatre. In all he hired some fourteen actors, including the well-known comedian, John Bernard, from the Covent Garden Theatre; a pair of distinguished dancers from that theatre, Mr. and Mrs. Oscar Byrne; and a couple of senior actors, Mr. and Mrs. L'Estrange, with their daughter.

William Warren wrote a *Journal*[2] in which he recorded their voyage to America aboard the *Sansom*. In it he refers to Cooper as "T.A. Cooper," so it appears that by that time, if not before, Cooper had added the middle initial *A* to his name. He probably did so in order to distinguish himself from the English chemist and journalist, also named *Thomas Cooper*, who had followed his mentor, the radical scientist Joseph Priestley, to Pennsylvania two years earlier. As the story has been handed down, Cooper's friends in America later encouraged him to expand the *A* to *Abthorpe*.[3]

On Tuesday, October 18, 1796, after almost a month at sea, the ship dropped anchor at Sandy Hook, off the New Jersey coast. Warren listed

Cooper as one of five, including the captain and Wignell, who were the first to disembark, boarding the U.S. revenue cutter that would pilot the ship to harbor in the East River. Since there was a yellow fever epidemic in Philadelphia, the group had to stop over in New York, the commercial center that would prove to be the keystone of Cooper's career. The evening after their arrival, Wignell took them to meet playwright-manager William Dunlap at the old John Street Theatre, where the resident American Company was performing Richard Cumberland's sentimental romance, *First Love*.

The thirty-year-old Dunlap, son of a successful merchant in Perth Amboy, New Jersey, had begun his interest in the theatre while he was studying painting under Benjamin West in London. Once he returned to New York, unable to make a living as a painter, he had joined the management of Lewis Hallam and John Hodgkinson at the John Street. He had signed on with them primarily because they offered him control of the play selection and the opportunity to produce his own plays, but he had failed to calculate the financial burden that would accrue.

Hallam and Hodgkinson, who were in continual conflict, needed Dunlap's money, but Dunlap had no appreciable theatrical experience. Nor did he have the strength of personality necessary to stand up to the egos of the other two, who also had wives who were actresses in the company. Hallam had been the chief actor prior to the arrival of Hodgkinson, who was some twenty years younger. After his arrival Hodgkinson, who had learned his trade touring the British midlands with the Bristol stock company, gradually took over most of Hallam's parts. The inevitable ill feeling between them reached a climax when the aging Mrs. Hallam took to appearing onstage drunk. Eventually Hodgkinson refused to act with her at all; thereafter the two actor-managers broke off communication with one another, except through Dunlap.

Wignell left Cooper in the green room while he went to find Dunlap. He first gave Dunlap a message from Holcroft, apologizing for a lapse in the correspondence the two had been carrying on, and then said, "'I have with me a young man, educated from infancy with Mr. Godwin, of the name of Cooper.'" The young actor could not have entered the scene at a better time. Dunlap went immediately to the green room and sat down with Cooper, asking him about his life with Godwin. Cooper explained, "'I have lived with him from infancy; I am his son, not in the course of nature, but much more than a common father is he to me; he has cherished and instructed me.'" Dunlap recalled the moment later and noted, "Such was the first interview between Mr. Cooper and one who for years was connected with him in theatrical affairs and by reciprocal acts of friendship."[4]

Seven—The Wheel of Fortune—1796-98

From a painting of the Old Holliday Street Theatre, Baltimore, July 4, 1839, by William Thompson Russell Smith, oil on canvas. Courtesy Eugene Applebaum.

After a week in New York Wignell took Cooper, Mrs. Merry, and the others to Philadelphia to join the rest of the Philadelphia Company. They made their way by stagecoach over rough roads to the Delaware River, where they boarded a packet ship, arriving in Philadelphia on Sunday afternoon, October 23. In the history he later wrote for the *Philadelphia Sunday Dispatch*, Charles Durang described Cooper as "an airy, a dashing and handsome youth[,]" remarking particularly on his young age when he first came to America.[5] Dr. John Irving, who later saw him "put under the standard to decide a bet," said he was slightly less than five feet, nine inches in height, but his slender figure made him appear tall, as he is often described. With dark blue eyes, chestnut hair, and rosy English cheeks, he needed little or no makeup onstage, except in character parts.[6]

After a short stay in Philadelphia, everyone except Mrs. Merry, who remained in the city to rest and settle into her new home, proceeded to Baltimore, where the Philadelphia Company habitually opened and closed its season with a month of performances. In 1794 Wignell had built a neoclassical brick theatre there, first known as the "New Theatre," and later, the "Holliday Street." The Baltimore audience rushed to get tickets whenever the players were coming to town.

Cooper made his American debut at the New Theatre in Baltimore on November 11, 1796, as Penruddock in *The Wheel of Fortune*, the title wonderfully apt for the young actor himself, both in character and situation; William Warren, who played the father, Mr. Tempest, recorded the date.[7] The play opens to the bitter melancholy of Penruddock, who has been withdrawn from the world for twenty years in a lonely woods cottage because of the loss of his bethrothed Arabella to his best friend Woodville. By chance Woodville's vice of gambling causes him to lose his fortune to Penruddock. The embittered man immediately sets out for London to seek his revenge, but finds himself so touched by Woodville's son that he relents and gives the young man the inheritance: "Henry is young, and, like the promise of a forward spring, flatters our hopes of harvest; it were hard to let him wither in the bud—he too is thoughtless, rash, impetuous, but he's a soldier and a lover; with them I sympathize—besides, his mother's in his face [Act IV]." The success of the play, which had opened on February 28, 1795, at Drury Lane Theatre in London, arose from the depth of the pathos aroused by the transformation from misanthropy to benevolence in the central figure of Penruddock, played to excellent effect by John Philip Kemble. Cooper acted it to equal favor in America.

In his *Recollections* Wood noted that Cooper, and later Mrs. Merry, "were received with an enthusiasm which abated little during the many years they repeated their visits. In private, too, they experienced the elegant hospitalities which the Maryland people know so well how to dispense."⁸ As late as 1828 Cooper would be a reliable draw in Baltimore, which saw a large increase in Shakespearean productions once he joined the company.⁹

In early December the company returned home to Philadelphia, which at the time was the largest and most cosmopolitan city in America. After the American Revolution, immigrants from Ireland and France had flooded into the port, and an influx of people from rural areas coming to seek opportunity had swelled the population to 42,000 by 1790, when the city became the temporary U.S. Capital. The neat and fairly priced public markets were said by visitors to be the best in the country, and the streets were paved and some even lit at night.

By the time the New Theatre on Chestnut Street had opened, on February 17, 1794, the demand for entertainment had begun to outweigh a resolution, passed by the First Continental Congress in 1778, banning theatrical activity as a source of "idleness and dissipation." Philadelphia had repealed its ban in 1789, and other cities soon followed suit. Built diagonally across from the seat of the legislature, Congress Hall, the Chestnut Street Theatre had a façade of arches and columns in the classical style of the Royal Theatre at Bath in England. The interior was painted gray and ornamented in gold, and over the stage was a motto referring to the lifting of the bans, "The Eagle Suffers Little Birds to Sing." The stage was raked [sloping down from back to front], projecting several feet past the first section of boxes, and the pit was also raked, something new in America, effecting an element of intimacy. With a capacity of 1155, though much smaller than London's Drury Lane, it nevertheless acquired the nickname "Old Drury."

In the early years of the republic, the audience section of the theatre, illuminated like the stage with oil lights and candles, remained lit during the performance. Part of going to the theatre was the chance for social intercourse, for beauty and fashion to see and be seen. In addition to the gentry, however, now all classes of society began attending, with resulting conflicts, lively interaction, and reaction. At the Chestnut Street Theatre and the Boston theatre, the underlying class struggle manifested itself in heated political debates between the Federalists and the Democratic-Republicans.¹⁰ People also expected long evenings of entertainment when they went to the theatre, so in addition to the play, performances included a variety of arts—farce, song, ballet, opera, even juggling and circus. Withal audiences could become loud and unruly, particularly up in the gallery where prostitutes were admitted. Actor Francis Wemyss, who served as manager of the Chestnut Street later on, disliked the grand chandelier suspended from the dome in that theatre, partly because as he said, "it exposes to view, that very portion which should be kept as much as possible in the shade[.]"[11]

When the New Theatre was under construction, Mrs. Bingham, a queen of Philadelphia society, had come to Wignell and asked him to sell her a private box in the European manner. Upholding the democratic ideal, Wignell had refused her, so she and her set rarely attended.[12] President George Washington, however, attended frequently; he had been raised acting in amateur theatricals, plays such as Joseph Addison's *Cato* about the Roman hero. A great admirer of Wignell's comic acting, Washington had attended his performances in New York City when that was the U.S. capital, including his benefit at the John Street Theatre in November 1789. The following year Wignell had left New York to take theatre to Philadelphia when the capital and Washington moved there.

When the President attended a performance in Philadelphia, often for a charitable benefit, he occupied the east stage-box, which was suitably fitted out with red drapes and the U.S. coat of arms. The newspapers even took to announcing the prospect of his visits, and on these occasions a soldier was posted at each stage door, a military guard also in attendance. Wignell, dressed formally in black, his hair powdered in the current fashion, greeted the revered leader carrying two wax candles in silver candlesticks to lead him to his seat; and as Washington entered his box, the orchestra struck up the President's March ("Hail Columbia"). The pit and gallery, having packed the house to see their hero as well as the play, generally shouted demands for "Washington's March" ("The March of the Revolution") as well.[13]

On December 9, 1796, Cooper made his Philadelphia debut at the Chestnut Street Theatre in the character of Macbeth, which would prove over the course of his career to be his most distinguished Shakespearean representation. The charming John Moreton, one of Wignell's original company, played Macduff; Warren, Banquo; L'Estrange, Duncan; and Wignell, the first Witch. Mrs. Oldmixon, who was a favorite singer in light opera and comedy, played in the afterpiece, the farce of *The Prize*.

The audience, as well as the *Gazette*'s theatre critic, greeted young Cooper warmly:

> The performance of this play, last evening, contrary to expectation, drew a full house. Many of the characters in the play were weakly cast, and the piece was, of course, not given with that strength we have been accustomed to see in it. Some amends were, however, made, by the splendor of the new dresses and decorations, and the fine performance of COOPER.

Seven—The Wheel of Fortune—1796-98

Commencing his Theatrical career in America, as he had done in England, with the character of Macbeth, the ultimate effect will probably be very different. If Mr. Cooper's Macbeth has been thought worthy of censure in England, we shall, with all due deference to the London Leviathans in Critique, take the liberty of forming an opinion wholly opposite. Whether this is to be attributed to a deficiency of judgement in the writer of these remarks or to the performer's advances in improvement in the interval, I know not: the general applause of a numerous audience, is at once a striking reinforcement of the latter opinion, and forms a decided testimony to his merit.

Mr. Cooper had, however, attained the highest respectability, previous to his departure from England....

The reviewer went on to compare him to the actor who would be his chief rival in Philadelphia: "Mr. Cooper's voice is clear and sonorous; and though he did not perhaps come up to Fennell in energy of tone and countenance, he certainly possesses in an eminent degree, all the stamina of a first rate actor. The principle speeches were given with a nice discrimination and accuracy of judgement, above all at his death."[14]

At the time James Fennell, a polished English gentleman ten years older than Cooper, was the reigning favorite in the Philadelphia theatre, despite his unpredictable behavior and frequent absences. Six feet, two inches in height, with gray eyes, blond eyebrows and lashes, light brown hair, and fair, rosy complexion, Fennell represented the perfection of an aristocratic nobleman. Educated at Eton and Cambridge and intended for the law, he had first acted at Edinburgh in 1787, the part of Shakespeare's Othello, which was always considered his best role. Flamboyant and intelligent, he was received by the best society in Philadelphia, although acting was still not considered a socially acceptable profession. His weakness was a tendency to overextend himself in shakey financial ventures, which eventually led him into a disastrous salt speculation. Sadly this genial man ended up in debtors' prison and died in obscurity in 1816.

Durang recalled the inevitable rivalry between the two actors that ensued from the time of Cooper's arrival: "I well remember a great division of public opinion in regard to the relative merits of Fennell and Cooper. The literati, generally, approved the former. But Cooper gradually rose above him, till he soon outshone all competitors on our boards.— I am free to say, that I never could see that excellence in Fennell which was at one time claimed for him as an actor.... I must write with due *reserve*. Fennell's *Glenalvon* (John Home, *Douglas*) was said by excellent judges to have been a very natural and powerful performance."[15]

Cooper, who had left England rather than play secondary roles, was expecting immediate advancement in America. On December 14 he played Hotspur in Shakespeare's *Henry IV*. Then, due to the illness of the company's popular leading man, John Moreton, on the 19th he had his first opportunity to play Hamlet in America. In his portrayal he introduced the American audience to the romantic style of historical dress for Hamlet, which Joseph George Holman had first introduced at Covent Garden October 9, 1793.[16] Moving away from the anachronism of modern dress generally in use, he replaced the neckcloth and wig of a contemporary gentleman with a black bugle shape dress, trunkhose, and white ruff collar in the style of a Van Dyck portrait, which became the standard costume for the Danish prince thereafter. Durang applauded "[t]he picturesque beauty of the dress[.]"[17] Not surprisingly, portrait painters of the day, notably Thomas Sully and Rembrandt Peale, chose to paint Cooper in the role of Hamlet.

Shakespeare was the best known and most often performed playwright in America, but offering the necessary variety, on January 30 Wignell produced an extravaganza, *Columbus (or) A World Discovered* [Thomas Morton] with Cooper as Columbus. In this a reviewer in the *Gazette* congratulated the young actor for "a very chaste piece of acting" remarking, "[H]e has been censured for overacting; but we observe that his performance is considerably improved in this particular, and we doubt not, but in a short time, he will be considered as an actor of the first reputation, at least his performances fairly promise it."[18]

With this success, for his benefit April 3 Cooper chose another spectacle, Nathaniel Lee's *Alexander the Great*, and as a newcomer, to ensure a good house he employed a managerial coup. He hired an elephant for sixty dollars to be in Alexander's triumphal procession and let the word go out. In *Mirror of Taste* Stephen Cullen Carpenter told the story that has become part of the star's legend: "Mr. Cooper therefore poured in a whole broadside of printed notices, which were put into every hand, and a huge playbill, which glared at the corner of every street in letters of elephantine size, informing the public that the distinguished performer already mentioned, had kindly consented to act a principal part in the entertainment of the evening. No sooner was this announced than the whole city was in one hubbub of curiosity—one twitter of delight; and Mr. Cooper had so many *friends* who were all at once intent upon giving him their dollar at his benefit[.]"[19] The elephant, "duly caparisoned for war, made his first appearance in a Philadelphia theatre, in the procession upon the entry of Alexander into Babylon."[20] By Cooper's original contract, his benefits were insured to the amount of 150 guineas, but more than money, "fame ... is my deity," as he wrote Godwin.[21]

In May William Dunlap came to Philadelphia and attended a

Seven—The Wheel of Fortune—1796–98

rehearsal at the theatre. This was the second time he had met Cooper, but the first time he had a chance to see him on stage, and as it happened, the young actor was playing an unsuitable part, the Serious Father in Thomas Morton's comedy, *The Way to Get Married*. "Yet[,]" Dunlap commented, "in this he exceeded expectation."[22] At the end of the season Mr. and Mrs. Whitlock, who was Mrs. Siddons' sister, left the Chestnut Street Theatre for John Joseph Solee's Company in Charleston. Their departure opened places for Cooper, Mrs. Merry, and the other new arrivals, who "although brought out as stock actors, ... yielded a brilliancy in their spheres and elicited qualities so attractive that, from the early period of their engagements until the arrival of Cooke and other stars of later European celebrity, they were not equalled or in any way eclipsed."[23]

From a portrait of Thomas Abthorpe Cooper as Hamlet attributed to Rembrandt Peale, ca. 1805–10, oil on canvas, 24 × 20 inches, accession number 1960.1, negative number 40943. Collection The New-York Historical Society.

Wignell took his new actors to New York in August, 1797, and set up a temporary theatre on Greenwich Street to complete the company's season. The Charleston Theatre Company also arrived in New York to play at the John Street Theatre, while Hodgkinson took the American Company to the Haymarket Theatre in Boston for a tour. For the first time, New York had theatre available every night of the week. Cooper made his first appearance there on August 23 in the role of Pierre, to overwhelming success.

A couple of weeks later, however, Fennell also appeared, booked by Wignell and Reinagle, to give his favorite portrayal of Zanga in Dr. Young's melodrama *The Revenge*. A critique in the *Gazette*, signed by "Philo Drama," gave Cooper's rival full credit: "The excellence of Mr.

Fennell on Friday in Zanga was witnessed by the reiterated involuntary applause of a discerning and admiring house." The critic went on to speak of Cooper as "a child of promise" and added, "Those who have seen Mr. Cooper in Pierre, do not despair of seeing him great where he has scope for greatness."[24]

Undaunted, Cooper continued to play leading roles much of the time, including Columbus, Shylock, and Hamlet. His Hamlet was so successful that he repeated it for his New York benefit. When Fennell played his most famous role, Othello, on November 11, Cooper flatly refused to play Iago; Warren had to take the part. Dunlap wrote Hodgkinson, "'Wignell, deceived by the name Fennell gained (by) in Zanga has treated Cooper *en Cavalier*, and will find himself injured by it.'" Cooper warned Wignell that he might depart for the Charleston Theatre, but Wignell temporarily subdued him by threatening to have him arrested if he broke his contract.[25]

Wignell's Company clearly won the summer competition with the Charleston Theatre in New York, and due to a siege of yellow fever in Philadelphia, Wignell extended the engagement to three months. Despite this success, however, he suffered considerable financial losses from the venture, and returning to Philadelphia, where earlier in the season he had tried raising ticket prices ($1.25 for a box seat, and $1 for the pit), diminished sales forced him to cancel the increase.[26] Meantime, although Cooper's contract provided for a "rising salary" of 4, 5, and 6 guineas a week, 40 weeks a year, for 3 succeeding years,[27] as a result of his financial struggles, Wignell got in the habit of paying him in notes which he was unable to honor when they came due.

On New Year's Day, 1798, Cooper took advantage of a temporary lameness to return to New York, and when he arrived there, had no desire to go back to Philadelphia. He wrote to Wignell the first week of January demanding payment of a note issued to him by the Philadelphia manager; when he had tried to redeem it, he had been threatened with legal prosecution for endorsing it. Supported by a number of New Yorkers he had come to know during the past summer and fall "who preferred him to all tragedians they had hitherto seen,"[28] he also asked Wignell's permission to act an engagement with the American Company at the John Street Theatre under Dunlap's management. Wignell refused his request, but Cooper went ahead and performed there anyway. On January 5, 1798, he played Pierre, followed by a performance of Penruddock the next day.

These appearances were a blessing for Dunlap, for in general thin audiences were causing him extreme financial difficulty; many theater-goers feared for their safety in the old John Street building and were waiting

Seven—The Wheel of Fortune—1796–98

for the opening of the new theatre he was building on Park Row, facing City Hall Park. The American Company had been founded by the contemporaries and immediate fellow-actors of David Garrick at Goodman's Fields Theatre in London. Though without the genius of Garrick, the actors who made up the company had imbibed his manner, readings, and general stage business. When the U.S. government's headquarters moved from New York to Philadelphia in 1790, and Wignell left New York to found the Philadelphia Company, he had made the first break in the American Company's monopoly. Durang points out that this was the defining moment in modern American stage history, "the final dissolution of that sharing scheme of principal actors, first projected at London in 1752—a kind of a republic in advance, to be first tried in the new world, by the *'mimic world*[.]'"[29]

Wignell himself had been instrumental in the competition and democratization of the theatre that eventuated in Cooper's secession for personal starring. Once Cooper broke with Wignell, he began to develop a career as an independent star. He was the first actor to do so significantly, to the increased profit of all concerned. And with the opening of a new century, the expanding settlement of territories in the vast new nation would give limitless opportunity and impulse to the Americanization of what had been the conservative British theatrical scene in the Colonies.

In a letter dated April 1, 1800, from Philadelphia Cooper wrote Godwin giving him a detailed financial account of his first three years in America. He was responding to a letter Godwin had apparently written to him taking him to task for his "extremely limited remittances" to his mother back in England, perhaps to himself as well. He began by giving Godwin's criticism his full respect and gratitude in the manner Godwin had required of him: "I am extremely happy to have the opportunity, which I had not the courage to seek, forced upon me of acknowledging my errors. Perfectly aware how negligently and unworthily I had treated my best, I may almost say my only friend, my astonishment at seeing a letter directed in his well known hand was only to be equaled by the tumultuous variety of sensations, which immediately took possession of my mind; but these all subsided in delight, before I had finished the first paragraph. I never before so truly felt the fulness and dignity of your goodness. I will make no promise, but I hope to improve." He went on to say, however, "While candid in acknowledgement I must not submit to mistaken censure." He explained that he had repaid 29 pounds Wignell had loaned him in London and 40 pounds for his ship's passage. Also, his second year benefit fell "short—50" and he had 40 pounds' worth of

From a painting of the interior of the Park Theatre, NYC, 1822, by John Searle, watercolor on paper, 38 × 23 inches, accession number 1875.3, negative number 229. Collection The New-York Historical Society.

Seven — The Wheel of Fortune — 1796–98

Wignell's notes "at present which he being insolvent I shall never get the money for." He might also have added that Mrs. Merry was earning a star's wages while performing with him, and the declining Fennell receiving more money for six or eight scattered nights than he, Cooper, was being paid for three months of steady acting.

Wignell finally agreed to make good on the bad notes he had paid Cooper if he would meet him back in Philadelphia. Instead, the next day, when Cooper returned to Philadelphia to collect, intent on recovering his "juvenile tragedian,"[30] Wignell had him arrested. However, Cooper put up bail and returned to New York on January 23, 1798. That evening at Dunlap's, he and the New York manager talked about Godwin, his "friend and father." He described Godwin to Dunlap as "a small man delicately formed, about 40 years of age," and Holcroft, "a man of about the same height but muscular and aged about 54." He told Dunlap that "Mr. Godwin has no fortune but from his writings: that he is at present much afflicted by the death of Mrs. Godwin (Miss Wolstoncraft) [*sic*] whose death being in consequence of childbirth, was painful in the extreme and that she showed a distressing reluctance to quit the world." He arranged to play in three of Holcroft's plays for the American Company—the Count in *The School for Arrogance,* Young Dornton *in The Road to Ruin,* and Cheveril in *The Deserted Daughter.* He also asked that Hodgkinson give up the part of Romeo to him, marking the beginning of his challenge to New York's established star.[31]

Eight

The New House

The Park Debut—1798

Cooper was much in evidence on January 29, 1798, when Dunlap and Hodgkinson, in desperation, opened the new Park Theatre before it was finished. The prelude farce, *All in a Bustle* or *The New House*, described the backstage commotion opening night, alluding to Cooper's dog Chance as running off with one of the actresses' wigs. Cooper, however, did not take part in the evening's production of Shakespeare's *As You Like It*, hoping to come to a satisfactory agreement with Thomas Wignell before acting on the Park stage. Instead, during the near-riot as people crushed into the new house, he took the place of one of the box door-keepers to help restore order.[1]

On February 20 Wignell announced in the Philadelphia papers and on handbills that his theatre would close for a few days "'in consequence of unavoidable circumstances having intervened beyond their [the managers'] control[.]'" The announcement explained as the causes for the difficulty "'the unfortunate indisposition of Mr. Moreton, the injurious defection of Mr. Cooper, and the unprecedented, peremptory refusal of Mr. Fennell's to perform the character twice announced for him.'" It also stated that Cooper's violation of contract was "'the subject of a suit now depending in the Supreme Court[.]'"[2]

In his April 1 letter to Godwin Cooper recounted the resolution of the lawsuit: "[O]n my arrival here [in Philadelphia] to my utter astonishment the jury were in the act of considering their verdict!! and that verdict was five hundred Sterling pounds damages at par against me, merely because my lawyer had not given me notice that I might appear & defend my own cause; which having been all along my intention I had not told him a number of circumstances which I should have brought forward in extenuation and justification." He also noted the loss of salary during "my quarrel & separation from Wignell" before the new engagement was procured.

Eight—The New House—1798

On February 22 Cooper made another trip to Philadelphia, this time to pay the forfeit for the breach of contract. On Saturday the 24th, in the presence of two witnesses, Thomas Taylor of Philadelphia and Gilbert McEvers of New York, he formally presented Wignell and Reinagle with 500 pounds sterling, which had been collected for him by his New York friends. The Philadelphia managers, who could ill afford to lose Cooper's services, refused to accept the money, and a day or so later, sent for Cooper again, insisting that he return from New York. Cooper remained firm, but sent $1,200 by Wignell's lawyer, Mr. Dallas. Wignell refused it, pressing for the whole sum instead, in exchange for Cooper's freedom. However, now Cooper refused, returning to New York with the money.[3]

Cooper made his first appearance at the Park Theatre on February 28 as Hamlet, with Mrs. Hodgkinson as Ophelia and Mrs. Melmoth, the Queen. A notice in the newspaper announcement of the performance gives an idea of the value Dunlap attached to his contract with the theatre:

> TO THE PUBLIC
>
> *Mr. COOPER, by certain unfortunate circumstances, being prevented from the future exercise of his profession for nearly the term of two years, unless he pays the penalty of his article with Mess'rs Wignell and Reinagle—the managers of this Theater propose to appropriate the profits of this, his first night's performance, towards the discharge of the same.*[4]

The receipts amounted to $895, one of the few full houses since the Park's opening night.[5]

In effect Cooper's 1798 contract with Dunlap marked the beginning of his career as a star. His opening night as Hamlet was an unqualified triumph, and from then on he performed leading roles almost exclusively. A reviewer in the *Commercial Advertiser* March 2 noted, "The play was specially designed to introduce to the patronage of the citizens of New-York, a gentleman, who, tho much distinguished as a performer in the company that visited us last summer, has recently become united to ours." He first praised the actor's personal qualities:

> Beauty of person, and features naturally adapted to the expression of very various passion, ... seem so necessary to success in many parts, that no combination of genius and judgement of which we have any knowlege [*sic*], has been sufficient to secure to an actor a decided popularity without them. We look for something uncommonly attractive or imposing, in a hero. How much soever we may have rationally persuaded ourselves that greatness of character is not appropriate to this or that size, we always experience something like disappointment in finding nothing

remarkable in his appearance of whom we have heard much and often. Few performers will permit the spectator to depart with so little disappointment of this kind, as Mr. Cooper—His person, countenance, voice, gesture and manners, were admirably calculated to impress on the audience the liveliest realization of the personage he represented.

The performance itself he pronounced "transcendantly excellent."—

[W]ithout making any invidious comparison ... it may be proper to say that never did this country witness a more masterly exhibition than that which astonished a delighted auditory on this occasion.... To have gone through with so difficult a part as that of *Hamlet*, respectably, is no mean praise: what then is that of having surpassed every expectation! As instances of wonderful felicity of execution, the *advice to the players*, the *scene with the queen*, and above all the *play scene*, may be cited.—They who were incapable of feeling the excellencies of those scenes, must relinquish their pretensions both to judgment and sensibility."[6]

Dunlap thought the play scene "the finest thing I ever saw." And after seeing Cooper in the part again in March added, "I saw most of it and think it the best acting I ever saw. Cooper says old Macklin attended each of his representations of Hamlet in London; asked to be introduced to him and paid him high compliments."[7]

At the time Cooper was launching his career in New York, it is ironic to note that the elegant John Moreton came to the end of his stage career in Philadelphia. Still a young man himself, Moreton died after taking chill lying on the stage floor during a performance on a bitterly cold night. A particularly personable actor who had been an early protégé of Wignell, Moreton was most gifted in comedy but also gave sensitive performances in tragic roles. William Wood said of him, "Hamlet and Romeo, with him, might have wanted force and intentness, but in grace and tenderness, it is doubtful whether either have been surpassed or even reached by his successors."[8]

On March 2 Cooper made his second appearance at the Park as King John in Shakespeare's seldom-acted play of that name. The reviewer March 5 described the production as unusually extravagant: "A more splendid exhibition of scenery was never witnessed in this city, and probably never in this country; the dresses of the performers were dazzling and well-imagined; and the whole conduct of the stage in the highest degree creditable." He went on to praise the performance: "Mr. Cooper and Mr. Hodgkinson, as *King John* and *Faulconbridge*, kept pace with each other; while the gaiety and spirit of the one gave additional force to the majestic energy of the other, and the gloomy grandeur and fitful passion of the first, was relieved and heightened by the unyielding courage of the last.... And nothing could surpass Mr. Cooper's performance in the two principal scenes with *Hubert;* the first for the dexterous management of dark, but agitated passions; the second for the wonderful bursts of remorseful indignation." Concluding, "On the whole, our citizens must be insensible to all that is elegant and enchanting as a spectacle, and all that is excellent and admirable as tragedy, if they neglect this piece."[9] Unfortunately, however, the lavish production expenses at the Park, added to the regular running costs of the theatre, continually exceeded the income. The only relief was Cooper's performance of Romeo on March 9, which brought out the ladies and $735.[10]

André—1799

Cooper continued to enjoy a congenial relationship with Dunlap. As Dunlap noted in his *Diary,* he and Cooper were companionable, chatting about their mutual friend Godwin and consulting about plays, as well as matters of management. At the end of March, 1799, Dunlap produced one of his own plays, *André,* a blank-verse tragedy portraying the execution of the British spy Major John André, captured during the American Revolution while attempting to bribe the American general, Benedict Arnold. The growing public spirit of nationalism made recent American history a favorite subject for popular plays, the playhouses themselves platforms where members of the audience aired their contrary political views sometimes to the point of riots.

Dunlap had worked on *André* for nine years, and it is a more serious study than most of the kind of patriotic pieces being written at the time. Arnold was still alive in England, André dead less than twenty years. Focused on the moral dilemma, the play emphasizes the sentiment for amnesty, due to the fine character and appealing youth of André, as opposed to the infamy of Arnold; a Federalist himself, Dunlap projects a conciliatory attitude toward Britain. But as in fact, General Washington makes the hard decision to execute André in order to maintain strict justice and dominion in the young Republic, and the play affirms this eighteenth-century viewpoint and decision.

The production of *André* was the only time in George Washington's lifetime that the General himself was presented as a character in a play. Lewis Hallam played Washington and Hodgkinson André, while Cooper was assigned the part of Bland, the American officer who defends André. Aside from the secondary nature of the role, Cooper did not want to play Bland, because in pleading for André's life, Bland was directed to tear the

American colors from his cap and throw them to the ground. Since Cooper was British, he and some of his friends feared that the public would identify the anti–American action with the actor himself. One day when Cooper and Dunlap were out together, Cooper riding on his mare and Dunlap walking alongside, Dunlap spoke of the fact that the actor Chalmers had refused the part of McDonald in the play because he did not have enough time to study it. Cooper took the opportunity to suggest that Hodgkinson might play McDonald so he himself could play André. Dunlap replied that he "should not dare ask Hodgkinson to exchange."[11]

Six feet, ten inches tall, with a round face, broad nose, and gray eyes of unequal size, Hodgkinson had been a potboy in his father's pub in Manchester until he ran away to Bristol to join the theatre. Dunlap recalled that the uneducated Hodgkinson had once mistaken "anon" for the name of an author in the listings for a poetic reading.[12] But as an actor Hodgkinson had achieved an exceptionally brilliant career with the American Company; he appeared to be intuitive about character and had an excellent memory, a source of some unfortunate comparisons for Cooper.

Not overly in awe of anyone, Cooper began to agitate for the part of André. Dunlap's *Diary* indicates that just three days before the first performance of the tragedy, he still hoped to change parts with Hodgkinson: "Read André in ye Green room. Some words pass'd between H & C again this morning. Rehearse André." Finally, that afternoon Dunlap called a halt to the quarrel: "Afternoon Cooper sent me a letter wishing André put off: I call'd on & told him I would rather see it imperfectly represented than put it off, for I knew of nothing else to enable me to pay Salaries on Saturday. I sat with him some time. I told him he was wrong in respect to Hodgkinson this morning: he laugh'd & assented." And the next day, Cooper "in his rattling way made up with Hodgkinson[.]"[13]

A large number of veterans of the American Revolution were in the first-night audience, so Cooper's fears proved to be well grounded. Dunlap explained: "The play was received with warm applause, until Mr. Cooper, in the character of a young American officer, who had been treated as a brother by André when a prisoner with the British, in his zeal and gratitude, having pleaded for the life of the spy in vain, tears the American cockade from his casque and throws it from him. This was not, perhaps could not be, understood by a mixed assembly; they thought the country and its defenders insulted, and a hiss ensued—it was soon quieted, and the play ended with applause." He also described the weakness of Cooper's performance in general, however, which he said was "*trying to the author as well as actor and audience.*"—

Our friend Cooper was at this time rather in the habit of neglecting such *parts* as were not *first*, or exactly to his mind. Young Bland was not the hero of the piece, and very little of the author's blank verse came *un-amended* from the mouth of the tragedian. In what was intended as the most pathetic scene of the play, between Cooper and Hodgkinson, the first, as Bland, after repeating, "Oh, André—oh, André,"...approached the unfortunate André, who in vain waited for *his* cue, and, falling in a burst of sorrow on his neck, cried, loud enough to be heard at the side-scene, "Oh, André!—damn the prompter!—Oh, André! What's next, Hodgkinson?" and sunk in unutterable sorrow on the breast of his overwhelmed friend, upon whose more practised stage cleverness he relied for support in the trying scene[.]

That performance brought in "a temporary relief" of $817.[14] The second night Dunlap wrote in an alteration having Bland replace the cockade in his helmet, and he was gratified that "the whole performance, on the second night, met the warm approbation of the audience."[15] The third night was the last, however. The next year, in 1800, Thomas Jefferson's election to the Presidency put an end to Federalism and the lingering monarchialism of Washington and Adams, and in 1803 Dunlap rewrote *André* as a musical piece, *The Glory of Columbia—her Yeomanry*. In line with Jefferson's vaunted return to *true republicanism,* the "Revolution" of the new century, Dunlap's play now emphasized the British André's guilt, glorifying the common American soldier, and won popular success when it opened on the Fourth of July.

New Successes—1799

Back in his preferred repertoire, Cooper played well for Dunlap. He acted Macbeth for the first time in New York on February 1, 1799; until that performance Hodgkinson had always played the part. In the next day's edition of the *Commercial Advertiser,* the reviewer reported: "Last evening a numerous audience attended the representation of Macbeth, and we believe, left the house with but one sentiment, *that they had never seen the play truly exhibited before.* Mr. Coopers [*sic*] Macbeth is only equalled by his Hamlet."[16] On April 26 to perform Othello, a new role in his repertoire,[17] he painted his face, in contrast to the blackface Fennell had been using, "more nearly the color of a mulatto."[18]

The sudden appearance thereafter of the Philadelphia star, who made his Park Theatre debut on May 1 as Jaffier to Cooper's Pierre, produced a favorable comparison: "Few things can excel the performance of the excellent Fennel [*sic*]. The power of expression by countenance and gesture he possesses in an eminent degree; and in the part of Jaffier he found full scope for his exertions.... The fire and force of our favorite Cooper, broke forth in an eminent degree, he was well fitted in his character, and he did it full justice. His powers are so acknowledged that they need not commendation; it is sufficient to say, that in the presence of Fennel we saw no diminution of his excellence, and his powers received lustre from the comparison."[19] Before Fennell left, they played together in Frederick Schiller's tragedy, *Don Carlos*, with Cooper as Don Carlos to Fennell's King Philip. Then Cooper proceeded to finish the season in a variety of offerings: Shylock, Columbus, and Frederick in *Lovers' Vows* [Kotzebue].[20]

That summer, in July, perhaps to avoid the mounting debts at the Park, Hodgkinson left New York to manage the Haymarket Theatre in Boston. Hoping to profit, he arranged for Cooper's first Boston appearance on July 27 as Hamlet with Mrs. Hodgkinson as Ophelia. Unfortunately for all concerned, however, a yellow fever scare shut down the engagement.

A little over a month later, on September 6, 1799, Cooper made his first permanent personal commitment to the United States. Allying himself with the city that had promoted his fame, he married Joanna Johnstone, daughter of an old New York family of property.[21] Joanna, who was seven years older than Cooper, was the widow of a sea captain, Upton, and she brought three small children with her to the marriage. This rather surprising match for the young Cooper may have arisen from his need for the closeness of family amid the turbulence of his ambitions. Perhaps it also echoed—or answered—his mother's unresolved widowhood.

Meanwhile the fever caused Dunlap to delay the Park Theatre season until early December. To the list of financial losses Cooper sent Godwin he added, "the yellow fever came and robed [*sic*] me 5 months employment." When Dunlap finally opened, to try to please the public and ensure financial success, he offered a series of plays he had translated and adapted by the German dramatist, August von Kotzebue, melodramas that were currently sweeping Europe. He had told only Cooper the secret of their foreign origin, since the American audience might have boycotted them had they known. Shakespeare would continue to be the most widely performed playwright in America, the British inheritance underlying the strong oral tradition and longing for romance in early nineteenth-century America. However, the enjoyment of melodrama grew out of this inclination, and as the new century proceeded, in the quest for financial survival, the theatre would necessarily reflect cultural trends away from the aristocratic toward the new nation's evolving egalitarian character. The new century also marked the beginning of the modern industrial nation, and the public required constant novelty.

The first of these highly publicized offerings was *The Stranger*, which Dunlap had introduced the past season. He said that he "got possession of a wretched publication in which the plot and part of the dialogue of Kotzebue's play were given" and wrote his own from it. Cooper played the title role, a melancholy figure not unlike Penruddock, but in this case a bereft husband whose wife has deserted him and their children for another man. Dunlap rejoiced that "Mr. Cooper was well studied in the principal character, and produced great effect[.]"[22] The critic for the *Commercial Advertiser* also expressed delight with the execution of the play, saying, "The scenes between the Stranger and Francis his faithful attendant, were managed by Mr. Cooper and Martin in a masterly manner; .... When the Stranger reminds Francis of the little white cottage on the borders of the wood, and the honest servant in reply mentions the children whom he had seen playing by its door—the writer of this is a Father—and the words, the action and the look of Mr. Cooper, with the corresponding and appropriate demeanor of Mr. Martin, went home to his heart.... When the Stranger is touched by the unaffected proofs of Francis's attachment, and compares it with the falling off of his wife, the burst of passion, as conceived by the poet and executed by the performer, has few—very few equals."[23]

The Stranger started a trend, and Dunlap followed it with two heroic dramas set in South America, *Pizarro* and *The Virgin of the Sun*, as well as *Lovers Vows*, all by Kotzebue, whose scenes of affecting sentiment, in both the domestic and the spectacular, struck a popular note with Americans. Evidently the New York manager, who had entered the theatre with the intention of lifting public taste to serve the democratic ideal, had resigned himself to reality. Dunlap noted that these plays "were stigmatized by the actors as *Dutch stuff*, and by other epithets equally characteristic." He went on to reflect: "When a theatre is supported by a power, whether in a government or an association, which will not look for profit from it, but rather, if any deficiency of money from the receipts occurs, is ready to make it good, as in France ... then such a theatre will be truly a school of morality, of patriotism, and every virtue; the glory of the fine arts, and the delight of the wise and the good: such a theatre would be what the theatre of Weimar was when Göthe was its manager[.]"[24]

Nine

"Fame Is My Deity"

New York City—1799–1800

At the beginning of the 1799–1800 season, after suffering financially in Boston, John Hodgkinson returned to the Park Theatre in New York with his wife, who was also under contract to Dunlap. With the reappearance of the New York veteran, Cooper's efforts at the theatre decidedly declined. Now married and still under the financial and emotional stress of the lawsuit, which Wignell had continued, instead of becoming more exact in his roles, he became less so. He had quickly tired of the flimsy German plays. His forte was Shakespeare—he had a wider Shakespearean repertoire than any of his contemporaries—but when he played Macbeth on November 27, his "German Shakespeare" colored his Shakespeare. As "Crito" noted in the *Commercial Advertiser*, "Cooper in the principal character exhibited occasionally marks of real genius, his conception was sometimes very just, his tones fine and attitude striking; but after all justice compels us to say, Macbeth is certainly not his Chefd'oeuvre. He assumes the character and appearance of a murderer too early; he should remember that to *introduce* Macbeth as a villain is to destroy the moral of the piece."[1]

As the season progressed, criticisms of Cooper pointed to an increasing carelessness in his study and acting of parts. While Crito acknowledged him to be "unrivalled in Hamlet on the American stage," he qualified his praise: "but he must also permit us to say that it requires much study before he can be allowed to have arrived at perfection; he ought to avoid all approach to rant, remembering that it is 'the sin that most easily besets him' in common with other players of no uncommon merit." He also took the opportunity to criticize a line-reading: "He has a method of endeavoring to ally sense to sound indiscriminately: in pronouncing the line 'Or that the everlasting had not fixed his *cannon* gainst self slaughter!' he stops with all the strength of his voice and with an improper inflexion on the word '*cannon*,' but that word has no antithesis either expressed or implied, and is therefore unemphatical, and so in many other instances which we cannot now remember sufficiently to particularize, but we submit the observation to his own good sense to profit by in future."

Crito went on to laud him for his performance of the scene when Hamlet enters his mother's bedchamber: "[N]othing is equal to his attitude and his eye when the ghost appears to him in the chamber scene with his mother; we do not think it going too far to say it cannot be excelled and it serves to show to what a superior degree of excellence Mr. Cooper may with attention attain." However, evidently he had let his eyes wander during the scene at Ophelia's grave, and the critic pointedly censured his reckless inattention: "[A]t the time when the body was letting down into the grave, and Laertes ranting over it, we were shocked to see him carelessly surveying the boxes and recognizing his acquaintance, we will not say gazing at particular ladies. It was an indecency which we hope never again to witness."[2] As Cooper's mentor, playwright Thomas Holcroft, had himself pointed out, "The eyes ... are more expressive than any other feature: to suffer them therefore to be wandering, inattentive, without meaning, and void of passion or sentiment, are unpardonable faults, and faults that he would find inferior actors continually guilty of."[3]

The following week Cooper recovered by giving an outstanding performance of Romeo, as Crito attested: "Mr. Cooper in Romeo, gained universal applause, and acquired additional credit. Whatever may have been said of his Hamlet or his Pierre, we pronounce without hazard of contradiction from any person of correct taste, that his Romeo, taken throughout, is the most finished piece of acting he ever exhibited." The critic faulted him for expressing undue agony in delivering the line "*Tybalt slain,*" since in slaying Tybalt, Romeo "but revenged the death of his dearest friend, by taking that of the author of it." And like other critics from time to time, he alluded to a technical problem, his tendency to play too far upstage: "The interesting reflections the author makes, when Romeo embraces the cold, and as he supposes inanimate form of Juliet, could not be heard by the audience, from his being too distant; if he could contrive to remedy this, it would be an improvement." But he went on to extol the performance: "In the scene where he is informed of Juliet's death, and in that of his entrance into the Church yard, Mr. C. surpasses all we have ever seen; cold hearted must he be, who does not here feel the blood curdle in his veins."[4]

The theatre season was interrupted by the death of George Washington on December 14. The hero President expired from a throat infection just prior to the opening of the new century, and the removal of the federal government from Philadelphia to the new capital city he had created upstream from his beloved Mt. Vernon. The Park Theatre closed for a week—"'In consequence of the afflicting intelligence of the death of General Washington,'"[5]—and reopened on December 30 with *The Robbery*.

To begin the performance the curtain opened on a stage draped all in black, with the words, "MOURN, WASHINGTON IS DEAD" displayed in bold letters. Then America's young star, Cooper, appeared to recite a monody written for the occasion by the American novelist, Charles Brockden Brown. However, Brown had written extra lines at the final hour, and Cooper was poorly prepared. In the New Year's Day edition of the *Commercial Advertiser*, Crito described the debacle:

> [H]e began to speak in the very tones of Mrs. Melmoth, artificial and declamatory, ... He edged a little nearer the prompter, caught his cue and went on—stopt [*sic*] again—moved on a word—stopt again—the ladies cast down their eyes ... the Pit groaned aloud, and a small hiss began to issue from the gallery—when some good honest fellow got up and clapped his hands, which encouraged our *favorite Cooper* to start once more, and to go quite thro the piece, consisting in all, perhaps of 60 or 70 lines, much to our own as well as his relief. To add that he pronounced it very ill, after the above, is, we presume, unnecessary, as no man can ever speak with propriety and effect, whose whole attention is constantly occupied in the sole business of recollection.

And remonstrated: "If Mr. Cooper's sensibility is hurt at our remarks, his conscience must at least acquiesce in their justice, for how will he excuse it to us, that after having had the Monody in his possession ten days, he has had the unparalleled assurance to present himself on the stage in such a state of utter deficiency, as to call up the sympathetic emotions of shame in a whole auditory? If what we have now said, is not sufficient to reclaim him, perhaps he may learn, when it is too late, that he is not so firmly rooted in the *blind* affections of the public as he has hitherto persuaded himself to believe."

All he could say of Cooper's performance in the play that evening, a new adaptation by Dunlap, was that he "*got thro with* the part of Orlando."—"We do not say that he played ill from beginning to end, for he was so totally deficient in point of recollection, that he could not fairly be said to play at all; he not only mistook the name of his beloved mistress, ... but he was even obliged to look up to Jefferson [the well-known comedian, Joseph Jefferson] to know when to set [*sic*] down." He went on to admonish Cooper by praising Hodgkinson for "the admirable accuracy of *his* study[.]"[6] On January 8 Brown's monody was again recited—this time by Hodgkinson.

Despite his growing competition with Hodgkinson, Cooper's irregularity continued. During the second week of January he forgot his lines in *Hamlet*. Crito noted, "Mr. Cooper was extremely and shamefully defective in his study[,]" going on to comment, "for him to fail, so very grossly as he did in the fine soliloquy, in which he revolves the awful consequences of suicide, is such an outrage on all taste and feeling, as ought to have been instantly followed by a banishment for the evening." However, he applauded his much-touted scene with the players, saying there he "was better and more chaste than we have ever seen him before; he has now hit the true manner, and we do not wish him to alter it." And in the chamber scene said, "he was as he ever has been, excellent[.]" But he ended by noticing that again Cooper took the coffin scene to scan the boxes: "We were obliged once before to notice a want of decorum in his looks and behaviour, when the coffin was letting down into the grave, and *he now repeated it*."[7]

At the end of that week Cooper had to go back to Philadelphia again to answer Wignell's suit against him. Meanwhile, his debts were mounting, as he explained in his letter to Godwin: "[J]ourneys I was obliged to make ... my absence from the service of my then employers & my law expences [*sic*] have amounted at least to—80[.]" Also, his salary with Dunlap was one guinea per week less than it had been with the Philadelphia Company, which amounted to a loss of 22 pounds in five months, nor were his New York benefits insured as they were in Philadelphia. Yet, as he protested to Godwin's complaint, he had still sent thirty pounds sterling home to his sister Betty for his mother.

Although the loss of income was a major concern, it was probably what Cooper thought to be Dunlap's ill treatment that caused him to break with the New York manager in the spring. In his letter he told Godwin that he had obtained a one-day leave of absence from the New York Theatre because he was being "excessively ill-used" by a man in Philadelphia, one of Wignell's lawyers. Going to Philadelphia, he did not find the man that day, but when he did, with characteristic flourish, challenged him to a duel. The duel apparently fizzled, but the unexpected delay made him late getting back to his New York engagement, so Dunlap had to change the play.

On his arrival back in New York he said he wrote "a note with an ample apology & offering to pay 3 week's [*sic*] salaries for my defalcation & to pay also for every name that had been struck from the box book during my absence on account of his being under the necessity of changing the play." Meanwhile, however, he heard it repeated that Dunlap, "enraged at the disappointment did little less than proclaim me liar on the stage before fifteen hundred people." Commenting, "Evils seldom come alone[,]" he said he remonstrated with Dunlap, who gave him no satisfaction, so he told him, "I should have nothing more to [do] with him."

He went on to protest to Godwin: "He was my debtor and for the two night's [*sic*] absence fined me near six hundred dollars—" Concluding, "Living is very high in this country & every article of consumption proportionably exhorbitant. Strike a balance it stands thus which is all I have had to subsist upon for three years & a half with the expensive life of a player." Anticipating Godwin's criticism, "Perhaps you may say ... 'But why all this? Why these inprudencies and losses! [*sic*]'"—he countered, "I can only say that if there has been any error in propriety to cause them, I am ignorant of it, and on my conscience I will declare that were every thing to do again, my conduct would be precisely the same."[8]

Later in his *History* Dunlap explained that more than this dispute, the production of the melodramas was the source of Cooper's disaffection: "That Mr. Cooper had become discontented with his situation in New-York, before the unfortunate failure in keeping his appointment and its consequences, no one can doubt. Hodgkinson's eternal appearance before the public, and eminent success in the German plays of the present season, threw the tragedian into the shade. The necessity for producing these attractive novelties rendered *Hamlet* and *Macbeth*, and all the glories of the drama, for the time a dead letter." He recognized, "In proportion as his consequence decreased, the carelessness for performing his duty increased, and every new character Mr. Cooper *went on for* (to use the stage phrase), was almost invariably marred by an ignorance even of the words of the author. It was perhaps well for his future fame and excellence that circumstances removed him from the stage of New-York at a time so inauspicious to his improvement as an actor."[9]

It was at this point that Cooper settled the lawsuit with Wignell by agreeing to return to Philadelphia for the following season in time for the Washington opening. In actuality, the conflict with the two managers was impelling him to develop the role of the independent star. With the entrepreneurial spirit of the new country, he would eventually set up regular weekly touring between the two cities, raising the value of his services. Therefore, as he told Godwin, he remained buoyant, "Surrounded with difficulties (though, *dieu merci*, not yet with prison walls) oppressed with poverty, & burning with resentment against individuals, still enjoying health, my animal spirits undiminished, *mente mihi consciâ recti*, I remain firm and even happy amid the shock." In fact he had proven to have the talent, persona, ambition, and energy to engage the public's interest and admiration. The happiness of dearly bought freedom he was finding worth the price he was forced to pay, for after little more than two years in America, he was achieving the stardom he had always aimed for.

With this success in view, to Godwin's query regarding negotiations with Harris at Covent Garden for his return to London, Cooper replied that "Harris's offers" were "too indefinate [*sic*] to have any effect upon my conduct."—

> I am three & a half years older than when last I saw you. I have traveled much, have seen great variety of men from the highest to the lowest class of society, *in great variety of situations* & under the dominion of great variety of passions. I believe honour & justice to be *rara aves* and am convinced that interest is almost the universal *primum mobile*. In ninety five [*sic*] if Harris's interest had said "aye" in my favour no contingency would have induced him to say "no." Whenever I arrive in England (should that time ever come,) if my exertions are likely to be conducive to his emolument he will avail himself of them. But I am not in a situation to trust to chance. Therefore that time is probably far distant.

He explained, "Though a situation in London is the height of my ambition; no money should induce me to remain there, unless that ambition were gratified in all it's [*sic*] points." And clarified his position: "I would not accept Mr. Holman's place in the theatre. I would not play the *Mr. Darnly*s and the routine of walking gentlemen in modern comedy, in which he has been ever brought forward. Such business damps feeling, deprives a man of the most useful excitement to exertion, the consciousness of the dignity of his profession." From the provincial theatre, he had indeed come very far, and he had no interest in the light parts as a career, for he considered himself primarily a tragedian. In 1793 Joseph George Holman had left the Portsmouth Theatre right before Cooper arrived there to make his London debut. For a time he had had success playing, for the most part, young lovers; but apparently by 1800 his position at Covent Garden had become tenuous.

Invoking Milton's Satan, Cooper vowed he would never go back to Covent Garden unless he were offered the first position in that theatre: "Aut Caesar aut nihil. If Mr. Harris will bind himself to give me every character that Kemble plays and to offer me *none* which Kemble would refuse I shall be at his service. Otherwise, though I grant that 'Pestilential is the atmosphere of this wild, immeasureably spread'—Yet 'I would rather reign in hell than serve in heaven.'"

He held out the possibility of a trip to London, "I am present under engagements to go to the West indies [*sic*] for a short time in June next: if I receive a favourable answer from a merchant who has promised to procure for me the theatre at Martinique. Should my plans there prove successful, I may perhaps be in England in November—" going on, however, to reveal his growing commitment to America:

> But shall most certainly return to this side of the globe unless I can procure the situation already described—my emoluments here may be very considerable—& my fame which is my deity is at it's [*sic*] ne plus ultra. The theatres in this country are very nearly in every respect equal to those in London, & the stage department at N. York much superior to any I ever saw.... Should my schemes succeed, and I visit dear England! once again, I may engage with Mr. H. [Harris] but till I have positive direct and *inevitable* offers & those such as I would accept; I will never expose myself, by quitting America *prematurely*, to listen to terms the fulfilment of which would be wounding to my feelings & destructive of my happiness.

He concluded gracefully: "Trust me I have a most burning desire to prostrate myself upon British ground and kiss the first stone that shall meet my lips; to see again those dear friends whom I have left behind; to renew those sentiments of cordial feeling, which really constitute the happiness of this otherwise miserable existence; to recall past times, to hear & to relate adventures, and with transport to survey a gilded future through hope's prismatic glass."[10]

Philadelphia—1800-01

In the new contract he signed with Wignell Cooper consented to play, among other roles, Alexander in the heroic spectacle *Alexander the Great*. His original contract had guaranteed that he would not have to play the part again, for it was inimical to the stature of his intent, the literary standards Godwin had set for him, to say nothing of the degree of exertion it required. However, this new agreement with Wignell restored their amicable relationship.

As a boy Charles Durang went to see a performance of *Alexander*, which was introduced by a pantomime, *The Siege of Oxydrace*, an extraordinarily elaborate offering with real horses and a contingent of 80 U.S. Marines in costume. Recalling, "The scaling of the walls ... was exciting[,]" he said they formed a "tortoise" with their "Grecian shields," on which Cooper, as Alexander, with his men, "fighting at every step," climbed to throw rope ladders over the battlements "and precipitated themselves, apparently, into the city." Then, "On the bridge, at the back of the stage, *Alexander* was seen battling with overwhelming numbers in hand-to-hand contention[.]" Durang reflected, "Cooper scaled the walls—fought as described, although he was not, nor never was, a melo-dramatic actor."[11]

In the *Port Folio,* a new weekly begun in Philadelphia in January, "Oliver Oldschool," (elegant man-about-town Joseph Dennie) praised the mounting of *The Siege* and noted that in playing the role of Alexander, Cooper "bestowed upon it, its appropriate colouring of youth, animation, and impetuosity." Those qualities, close to Cooper's own, may have come naturally enough to him, but the critic went further to compliment his discretion: "In a part, so highly drawn, that it often seems to 'stretch the modesty of nature,' he never degenerated into insipidity, nor soared into extravagance."[12]

Having determinedly decided to remain independent, Cooper replied to another letter Godwin wrote him the end of December with regard to the position at Covent Garden, reaffirming in strong terms that he would never have let Harris use him to supplant Holman. Thanks to his distinguished guardian, he had been brought up in such an atmosphere as to espouse fervent and undeviating principles of honesty and fair play:

> I can now imagine Harris's inducement to think and talk of me, an obscure being in another world. He was at war with justice, and preparing to play the tyrant; and every instrument to effect his purposes or screen him from the bad consequences of his ill-conduct was to be grasped at with avidity and without distinction. Strange indeed if among great variety of implements he should find none adapted to his purpose. He had no particular election—He ran no risque [*sic*]—He made no promises of the least importance—What sportsman would not shoot among the bushes concealing a deer?—If the object be hit, the remuneration is glorious—if missed, who values a charge of powder & shot.—But I should have been the worst instrument he could have selected from the world, to effect any such iniquitous purposes. If I had been in London at the time, and Mr. Harris had wished to engage me on my own terms as a necessary preliminary to the discharge of Mr. Holman (or Mr. Any body) I would have rejected the offer and insulted the proposer. If there be any vice which I detest worse than every other it is tyranny. In every form which it can assume, and to *whatever end* it be exerted it shall have my active opposition, my unequivocal and unconditional execration.

His experiences both in London and America had intensified his resolve: "Perhaps I feel more strongly upon this subject because by the operation of petty tyranny and apparently insignificant I have had my happiness diminished (frequently, pro tempore destroyed); my pecuniary resources miserably curtailed, so as to frustrate the purposes which it was my intention and my duty to cultivate, and upon which the well being of those dear to me depended; and my character and life almost at stake. But as yet I have withstood it's [*sic*] attack, and begin to rise superior to it's effects. Yet tyranny & tyrants shall never find quarter with me mentally or personally. My motto is—*Lex Talionii*."[13]

That said, he did not, however, decline to judge himself as well: "That hardness of character of which you have often complained, is, I fear, more firmly than ever rivetted to my existence. The fortiter in re I possess abundantly, but the suaviter in modo will never assist my progress with it's winning influence. But to a man of your discernment it is superfluous to confess these traits of my mind. My letters are the mirror in which you can clearly discern it's most prominent features."[14] To withstand the heavy winds of chance that had undone his family's property and position, as well as the early challenges in his career, Cooper had developed a kind of mental armor. Early on he had extended this habitual public posture to the theatrical reviewers in Philadelphia, who sat in the pit near the orchestra "with the eyes of lynxes."[15] He turned a cold eye to the critical notices, good or bad, at once preserving both his ego and his energy, while developing the hauteur of a star's persona.

Wood later explained that the public demeanor belied the true nature of the man: "A mistaken notion prevailed, that Cooper was a man of harsh, unkind nature; but nothing could be further from the truth. Undeserved persecutions in his youthful days, no doubt greatly soured his temper, and gave an austere reserve to his manner, which sometimes amounted to roughness. Cooper is not the only instance we remember, where early neglect and unfair opposition tended to render a disposition naturally kind, cold and repulsive.... The few persons who shared his friendship, can bear noble testimony to his frank generosity, truthfulness, and unostentatious benevolence, sometimes bestowed with a reserve which was greatly misunderstood."[16]

Oldschool continued to laud his performances: Matthew Gregory Lewis' melodrama *The Castle Spectre*—"In the part of Osmond, he is perfect, and his genius has full scope to display itself. And, perhaps, no audience has ever witnessed a grander or more impressive delineation of that finely conceived character."[17] Macbeth—"[W]e do not remember, at any other representation of the ambition, violence, and cruelty of the Scottish regicide, to have witnessed a more perfect representation of these bad passions, *raised to bad eminence*. The actor's conception of the poet's sentiment was invariably just, his attitudes were dignified and graceful, his elocution forcible, fluent, and harmonious. In the dagger scene, and in the [scene] with the much injured Macduff, the profound silence, and gazing eyes of a respectable if not a numerous audience, attested the accomplishments of the actor."

In the same review he said of Cooper's performance in Kotzebue's heroic drama, *Pizarro*: "In the most interesting scenes and situations, he exerted all his powers, and deserved all our praise." He then qualified the remark, however, by pointing out that while the Elvira of Mrs. Merry was "maintained with the utmost energy and dignity" throughout, "[i]n a few instances, we detected his [Cooper's] attention wandering, and the occasional whisper of the prompter admonished us, not of the actor's want of genius and memory, but of his being above, or below the drudgery of application." He went on to exhort the "favourite performer" hoping he would "not wince at this slight stimulus to his energy" and ended by asserting his admiration, "We reverence genius; and the few minor faults and foibles are nearly lost in the radiance of mental glory."[18]

Cooper clearly put his strongest intent into moments of heroic climax. These heights were offset, particularly in his younger days, by memory lapses in less crucial scenes, a common fault in early players. Prior to the illumination of the scene with gaslighting (after 1814 in America), productions generally centered on climactic scenes, as did contemporary criticism. Moreover, the stringent demands on a star, the constant traveling and the enormous number of parts expected of him, as well as the burden of the production's success, took their toll on his time and energy.

Oldschool reviewed Cooper's *Hamlet* in February, preferring John Moreton's enactment of the play scene, generally considered the peak of Cooper's performance of the role by the London and New York critics.[19] Again in March he pointedly criticized the star's deficiency, this time in Irish playwright Arthur Murphy's tragedy *The Grecian Daughter* [1772], describing it as "mortifying, to behold Mr. Warren, following the tyrant [Cooper as Dionysius] round the stage, to supply him with words, appropriate to those forcible gestures and expressions of countenance, of which he is so complete a master."[20] Perhaps his admonitions had an effect, however, for in April he was able to laud his outstanding performance in Shakespeare's popular comedy, *Much Ado About Nothing*: "The glory of the evening was Mr. Cooper's Benedick. To our satisfaction, the memory of a favourite actor was disciplined and tenacious, and his look and tones were responsive to nature."[21]

Ten

Rising Returns—1801–03

William Dunlap regretted Cooper's departure, which both weakened the American Company and added to Hodgkinson's power, a continuing source of irritation. He noted in his *Diary*, "[I]f any stranger was to read this might he not say are you thus constant attendant on Hodgkinson & does he never come to you? the truth is, I wish to keep my house free from visits which partake of the Theatre and particularly Hodgkinson's[.]"[1] Soon he sought a new agreement with Cooper. As Charles Durang put it, "the managerial author threw the cold water of his repentance on the fire of Cooper's anger, and honor and interest wisely shook hands."[2]

Dunlap not only secured Cooper's agreement to return, but he also persuaded Mrs. Merry, despite her increasing ill health, to keep a starring engagement she had previously agreed to fulfill with Cooper in New York that summer. Dunlap told her that he had borrowed money on the strength of her commitment to him, so against her doctor's advice, Mrs. Merry undertook the hardship of touring for a limited engagement, at a star's salary of $100 per week and a "clear" benefit [all proceeds]. Cooper supported her for $30 a week, and Dunlap promised him an increase to $50 for the winter season.[3]

On July 1, 1801, the stars opened with *Venice Preserv'd*, following with *Romeo and Juliet* two days later. Though weakened physically, the brilliant Mrs. Merry undoubtedly acquitted herself with excellence. However, in recalling the engagement, Dunlap said that Cooper's "unexpected excellence" in the light comic part of Lothario in Nicholas Rowe's *The Fair Penitent* was "more vivid in our remembrance than any other portion of this very perfect exhibition."[4] He knew that Cooper had suffered unduly harsh criticism for his performance of the role in London in his debut engagement after his connection with the radicals had become known.

While they were still in New York, Hodgkinson was scheduled for a benefit on Monday July 13, but considered it a weak night, so to have more time for the building of elaborate machinery for his pantomime, he asked Cooper to take his benefit that night instead and give up Wednesday the fifteenth in exchange. Cooper assented, provided Mrs. Merry, with the manager's approval, would play with him, to which she agreed. Due to the extreme summer heat, however, she left for home the next day. When Hodgkinson learned she had gone before playing for him, though she had already declined him, he was so enraged that he wrote a letter berating her professionalism to the *Commercial Advertiser*. He then proceeded to engage in a vitriolic exchange about the matter with William Coleman, slated to become the editor of the new *Evening Post*, who, as "Amicus," strongly defended Mrs. Merry.[5]

Cooper had accepted Mrs. Merry's stipulations, that half of his benefit proceeds would go to the manager, and he would play for her benefit in Philadelphia. After completing the New York tour, she would remain resident at the Philadelphia Theatre, passing on the destiny of prime national stardom to the young co-star whom she herself had discovered. Cooper had the stamina required. In taking up regular touring between cities, he even entertained wagers on proposed feats of travel. At one point he made a bet that he could walk from Philadelphia to Baltimore in twenty-four hours. On this occasion Durang said he had himself followed by a man on horseback "to see that he fairly walked, and he put the man to bed on the road as he was knocked up in following him." The innkeeper at Bush, Maryland, twenty-five miles out of Baltimore, said that Cooper passed by his place going six miles an hour; and he arrived at the theatre in time for the morning rehearsal.[6] He also managed to wine and dine with social companions in every city he frequented, never taking himself or the theatre too seriously.

Another bout of yellow fever delayed his first season back in New York until November. He opened on the sixteenth [1801] as Frederick in *Lovers' Vows*. Throughout the fall he alternated with Hodgkinson in the popular melodramas, and another critic, "Thespis," appeared on the scene in the *Evening Post*, begun that month by the Federalist Party. When Cooper was assigned the slight role of Edward Smith in *The Force of Calumny*, Thespis remonstrated, "This actor never attempts by extraordinary effort to give consequence to any secondary character. Either he cannot or will not do it."[7] In fact, early on with the low-grade strolling company in Cheshire, he had been robbed of a chance to play his first lead by agreeing to play a lesser role the same week. Experiences such as this had immured him to the folly of sentimental acts in making his way in the profession, and he had no intention of forfeiting his rise to stardom by similar accommodations now. However, he played the feature role of Macduff to Hodgkinson's Macbeth on November 30 with true spirit, and when they repeated this performance on Christmas Eve, Thespis reported, "*Macduff* acquired wonderful interest from COOPER'S manner of personating it on this occasion."[8]

On December 2, when Cooper acted Hamlet, Hodgkinson refused to support him, and when he played Othello on the fifteenth, the beleaguered Dunlap had to present Hallam instead of Hodgkinson as Iago, for which Thespis roundly criticized him.[9] Dunlap was still unable to persuade either Hodgkinson or Fennell to appear in Shakespeare's *Richard the Third* when Cooper played King Richard on the twenty-first. However, every good part in the afterpieces had already been assigned, so Hodgkinson suffered the humiliation of having to play a character in the farce. In evaluating the season, Dunlap said that "Mr. Cooper's performances now assumed a higher tone, and he became the acknowledged hero of tragedy."[10]

The next October in another new paper, the *Morning Chronicle*, started that month for the Democratic-Republicans by Peter Irving, Washington Irving's brother, "L" compared the two actors' interpretations of the character of Macbeth: "COOPER'S *Macbeth* has more guilty cowardice than HODGKINSON'S—When he enters *Duncan*'s chamber, it is with a sudden and hasty exertion. HODGKINSON steals in with slow and cautious steps. COOPER has more horror and apprehension at sight of *Banquo*'s ghost. When he exclaims, 'Hence horrible shadow—unreal mockery! Hence.' it is rather a burst of terror and desperation than a command. In short, through the whole of the character COOPER unnerves his *Macbeth* more than HODGKINSON." Allowing both actors their interpretations, he made no choice between them.[11] In effect, Cooper used more passion than Hodgkinson, veering emotionally toward the romantic expression which suited the current public taste.

At this point Cooper still had his eye on London. He was solidifying his tragic roles with a renewed intention of returning, not to Covent Garden, but to the rival theatre at Drury Lane. Meanwhile, however, that fall his American life further asserted itself. On October 25, 1802, the Coopers had their first child, a son, Thomas Hercules Price Cooper, born in New York and baptized at Trinity Church.[12]

The year before, an Englishman, David Montagu Erskine, had mentioned Cooper to Mr. Richardson, a proprietor of Drury Lane, as "a Young Man who has lately had much fame on the Stage in Philadelphia[,]" saying, "He has a fine person, and great powers; but is dissipated."[13] Erskine, son of the Lord Chancellor of Great Britain, was married to the daughter of a Revolutionary leader in Philadelphia, John Cadwallader, and had spent the past four years in America. As the result of his recommendation, Cooper received an offer to fill the place at Drury Lane to be left vacant by John Philip Kemble's imminent retirement from that theatre to tour the continent.

Kemble had grown weary of trying to run Drury Lane in partnership with Richard Brinsley Sheridan; Sheridan was a member of the fashionable Whig circle surrounding the Duchess of Devonshire and spent most of his time in Parliament. So the British star was negotiating with Thomas Harris, the manager of Covent Garden and a businessman, to go over to the rival theatre. Consequently, an agent for Sheridan, "Mr. Taylor," offered Cooper 9 and 10 pounds per week for three years certain at Drury Lane. In a letter addressed directly to the manager, Cooper restated the agreement on his own terms, the same he had written to Godwin two years before, that he would be given "the whole of Mr. J. Kembles [*sic*] business[,]" and at a salary of "10- 11- and 12 £ per week for three years *certain*" providing Sheridan could secure his release from Dunlap.[14] Evidently some agreement was reached, because Cooper made plans to leave for England.

Taking what advantage he could from the loss of his star, Dunlap promoted Cooper's performance in *Hamlet* on December 22 as his last appearance in that play in America. The *Chronicle* critic pronounced it "excellent" and noted "some scenes in which he was particularly sublime." When Hamlet questions Horatio and Marcellus about the Ghost, he said Cooper spoke the words, "'Oh! Then saw you not his face?' in an accent and manner, that gave it the most pointed meaning. A flash of suspicion seemed to dart across his mind, of the reality of the vision, and the probability of his friends having been the dupes of imposition." And remarked that in his first interview with the Ghost, "the mingled emotions of awe, horror and revenge were so admirably depicted as to excite a thrill of 'reverential dread.'"

Speaking of the first act soliloquy, "Oh, that this too too solid flesh would melt," he said, "In the first part of that passage in which he describes the melancholy that preyed upon his spirits, he was mild and pathetic"; then in Act II, 2, "when he came to speak of man—'How noble in reason! How infinite in faculties!'" went on to say, "His countenance gradually lighted up with a powerful conviction of the sublimity of the subject; and 'In action how like an angel! In apprehension how like a God!' were delivered with a degree of energy and enthusiasm that evinced a most perfect conception of the feelings of the author."[15]

On the twenty-fourth Cooper acted Richard III to Fennell's Richmond, and then went to Philadelphia to make final appearances as

Hamlet, Richard, Pierre, and Macbeth, each of which brought in on the average of $1,200, half to the Philadelphia manager, and half to be shared equally by Dunlap and Cooper.[16]

Back in New York he gave his "last appearance in America," as Macbeth, on January 5, 1803. The house was crowded that evening, and stating "a wish of preserving the manner in which one of the most arduous characters of Shakespeare was represented, by a performer who appeared equal to the task; and who has taken his leave of the American stage[,]" the *Chronicle* critic devoted three days to a critique of his performance in the part.

Describing the first act soliloquy, "If 'twere *done*, when 'tis done," as "a painting that displays the nicest shades of discrimination and which can only be correctly executed by the pencil of a master[,]" he said of Cooper's rendering, " This difficult task of exhibiting the *blending* of passion; of shewing the shuddering emotions with which Macbeth *really* regards the atrocious nature of the contemplated murder; yet, at the same time, of marking the guilty, selfish considerations which call these arguments against the commission of the deed into review, was performed in an admirable manner by Mr. Cooper."—

> Mr. C. was particularly successful in conveying the strong sense of the base and dishonourable nature of a deed which violated the asylum of his habitation: an act so pointedly infractious of that hospitality which was ever held *sacred* by the Scotch chieftain....
>
> His countenance, manner and modulation of voice, in this passage, strongly evinced the struggles of contending emotions, and exhibited the strong conviction of his duties, with the sensations of disgrace and abhorrence, with which he regarded a deed so utterly in violation of all those principles by which his former life had been directed.

He went on to describe his delineation of Macbeth's gradual capitulation to the derisive urging of Lady Macbeth:

> In the commencement of this interview, he says, "we will proceed no further in this business. He has honored me of late," &c. In the progress, we have an opportunity of witnessing the talents of the actor; he has principally to *listen* to her discourse, and to express by *countenance* the varying grades of feeling with which he hears her, till he changes from terror and abhorrence, to a firm and decided resolution of executing the deed.
>
> In this scene Mr. Cooper merited our decided approbation. While she first reproaches him with want of courage, he listens with impatience and aversion. Endeavoring to veil his fears under the specious covering of *principle*, he exclaims,

> "Prythee peace;
> I dare do all that may become a man;
> Who dares do more, is none."

His lady continues to ridicule his timidity, and boasts her superior firmness. He attends to her with evident marks of irresolution; her taunts touch him; he cannot bear the insinuations of cowardice; but his apprehensions still predominate: he fearfully articulates, "If we should fail"— Here Lady Macbeth immediately shews the readiness and security with which the deed can be perpetrated....

During this recital we observe the countenance of COOPER'S Macbeth gradually expand; the doubts and fears with which it was beclouded, vanished; his *apprehensions,* which were the only restraints that kept him back, are all dispelled; he bursts forth into admiration of the spirit of his wife; he enters into her measures; points out additional expedients of security; and announces his determined resolution to commit the act:

> "I am settled, and bend up
> Each corporal agent to this terrible feat."

The reviewer also described the "celebrated dagger scene" which he said "merited the applause he received from the audience."—"Here we have Macbeth on the eve of accomplishing the murder, alone, at the solemn hour of night, and seized with all the terrors of a guilty conscience. His looks, his actions, his stealthy steps, all strongly evince the horrors of his soul, till his affrighted fancy conjures the ideal dagger to his view. Awe and dread seize on his faculties, till, by a powerful effort, he discards the illusion and proceeds to perpetrate the deed." And commented, "This scene was performed in a masterly manner by Mr. COOPER. The inquiring wonder with which he at first contemplates the imaginary weapon; the fixed and fearful gaze with which he regards its slowly moving progress through the air; and the shuddering horror that accompanies his exclamation on perceiving 'upon the blade and dudgeon gouts of blood' were minutely discriminated and strongly expressed."

After the murder he noted Cooper's transition from "marks of guilty trepidation" to "a melancholy expression of self-censure, on contemplating his bloody hands"; and "remorse and grief as he proceeds in relating the occurrences of the chamber." And said, "This recital appears not so much addressed to Lady Macbeth, as the utterance of what passes in his thoughts and is accompanied with a wildness indicative of partial derangement.... His emotions are frantic and agonizing. The last words 'Macbeth shall sleep no more' are not decidedly given as the utterance of the voice, but rather appear the forcible expression of his own feelings."—

> His lady in vain essays to rouse him from this state of desponding horror. His soul is wrapped up in dreadful contemplation of his crime; and her attempts to prevail upon him to return to the chamber, and smear the daggers of the grooms are regarded with abhorrence. She seizes the daggers from his listless hands while he stands passive and apparently unconscious, till he is awakened from this situation by a knocking at the castle gate. Here he is again thrown into the most violent agitation and dismay. He views his bloody hands with mingled dread and remorse, as the accusing evidences of his guilt: he appears unable to leave the hall, though apprehensive of discovery; and remains in a state of helpless and motionless confusion, till forced to his chamber by Lady Macbeth.[17]

By chance, the packet ship on which Cooper was scheduled to leave the day after that performance was delayed, so he acted Richard III again on January 7. He ended by taking leave of America on January 8 in the signature role of Hamlet. Having arranged to leave his wife and baby in "one of our first boarding-houses, at an expense better suited to his hopes than his fortunes[,]"[18] on January 10, 1803, he sailed for England.

PART II

*The American Star,
1803–1849*

Eleven

An American Indeed

Drury Lane—1803

Returning to England with fame from America, on March 7 Cooper made his opening appearance at Drury Lane in the character of Hamlet. Godwin and his second wife Mary Jane were in the audience, and Cooper dined with them on March 9.[1] A *Times* review on the 8th compared the performance to his 1795 debut in the role:

> The tragedy of *Hamlet* was brought forward yesterday evening at this Theatre, for the purpose of introducing Mr. COOPER, from the American stage, in that character. This Gentleman appeared in the same part about six years since, on the boards of Covent-Garden, and evinced judgment and powers which were rewarded with general encouragement. From that period to the present time he has cultivated his talents with more than common success, both on the Philadelphia and New York stage, and raised himself to the rank of a distinguished favourite, not only in the tragic, but in the comic department of the Drama. Those who recollect his former essays in this country, and who witnessed his *début* of last night, will readily acknowledge that his improvements have been great.

The reviewer described his physical delivery: "Mr. COOPER'S person is well formed, his deportment is easy, and his action is marked with that just variety arising from the object to which his attention is directed. His voice is remarkably powerful, and his articulation so very distinct, that not a syllable is lost to the audience. The upper, middle, and lower tones of his voice, are proportionately impressive." Then pointed out: "His best scenes were the first with his Father's Ghost, in which, instead of distorting his limbs, and torturing his body for a striking attitude, he very judiciously was struck with such horror, awe, and reverence, as to remain motionless;—the grand scene with *Ophelia*, and the closet scene. In the latter, he introduced a novelty, which was attended with a happy effect. He did not follow his Father's Spirit to the very portal, as other *Hamlets* have done, but overcome with the momentous question in his thoughts, and the solemnity of the occasion, he fell prostrate and insensible."

He directed his negative remarks toward the confines of the classical style: "His pauses are, however, too long, and his dialogue is, sometimes, too laboured. If he were to divest himself of the solemnity, which marks almost every scene, he would be more affecting." Concluding, "The great merit of Mr. COOPER'S performance" was "manly personification, with a correct delivery of the text[,]" noticing, "He was received by a numerous and fashionable audience with warm and general plaudits."[2]

On March 12 Cooper gave a second performance of Hamlet, and on the 17th played Macbeth. Again, according to the *Times*: "He evinced in every scene a perfect acquaintance with his Author, and displayed powers of voice and correctness of action, which, very different from those manifested in his delineation of *Hamlet*, proved the versatility of his genius." The reviewer noticed, "The house was nearly filled, and Mr. COOPER'S performance was received with reiterated plaudits." He also commented on the production: "The Play has been got up with a taste and splendour that do great credit to the Management."[3]

When Cooper performed Richard the Third on the twenty-first, the *Times* critic remarked, "He certainly has studied the part with great care, and his delivery of the text was in general marked with discrimination and just feeling." He noticed, "His most forceful passages were those which required energy and passion[,]" but thought that "in the soliloquies and the parts in which art and insinuation constitute the most prominent features, 'the cunning of the scene' might have been much improved by a greater degree of temperance and self-possession."[4]

The critic for the *Monthly Mirror* referred to Cooper's "very fine person, a voice of astonishing capacity, and a sound judgement." He summarized: "In each of the characters [Hamlet, Macbeth, and Richard] he displayed great ability, and exhibited some originality of manner. The 'dagger scene' of Macbeth, and the scene subsequent to the murder, were performed in a most masterly style." Like the *Times*, this critic also complained of "tediousness in his pauses," while asserting Cooper to be "a valuable actor," saying "his faults are easily to be corrected; and, if he intend to remain in England, he will, no doubt, become a favourite with the public."[5]

Meanwhile Kemble had returned to London in March, having effected the move to Covent Garden by buying into the management with his sister Sarah Siddons and brother Charles. Consequently, Sheridan offered to renew Cooper's contract with Drury Lane for the next season. However, that, plus a scheduled benefit for June 10, was the only pay offered him for the performances he had already given; the management had apparently spent their money on the production of the engagement for which they had garnered the compliment in the *Times* review. These were not the terms for which Cooper had bargained, and he was justifiably outraged. He thought the benefit hardly worth taking, because by June 10 a large part of the theatre-going public would have deserted London for the country.

Holcroft too had returned to England, in the fall of 1802, only a few months before Cooper. In 1799, after Cooper had left for America, smarting from his bitter experience in the Treason Trials, he had left England to join one of his daughters and her husband at Hamburg, Germany. While he was abroad he wrote letters back to a friend in England which he said were "intended for the public," explaining that he planned to remain in exile "till more peaceable time should again render that country to me what it once was; admirable for its general industry, manners, and morality; and undisturbed by the suspicions and persecutions, with which other countries were, and too often still continue to be, afflicted."[6] One of his plays, *Deaf and Dumb*, was performed to great success at Drury Lane in 1801 while he was still abroad, and again for 24 performances in 1803, but there is no record of his being paid.[7]

On the revival of their friendship now that they were both back in London, Holcroft asked Cooper, presumably in a position of some authority at Drury Lane, if he could arrange for him to meet the famous tragedian George Frederick Cooke, who was at Covent Garden enjoying co-equal rivalry with John Kemble. Cooke had begun a patent house career in London belatedly, coming to Covent Garden in 1800 when he was already forty-four years old. At the time, the manager, Harris, had been looking to replace Holman; Godwin had written Cooper in America concerning Harris' possible interest in hiring him, but Cooper had not cooperated. When Harris hired Cooke, Cooper had commented to Godwin: "Mr. Cooke I have seen. You describe him just as I think he is. I know his abilities and his character; he cannot last long. His present popularity is not wonderful. Is he not the great pop-gun with which Harris has shot poor Holman? and cannot the manager of a theatre make almost whatever pleases him, please the public?" Adding, "But after all I do not mean to say but that Cooke is a much better actor than Holman."[8]

An instinctively brilliant actor in the natural tradition of Garrick and Macklin, Cooke had originally acted in the full range of tragedy and comedy but had gradually narrowed to a limited repertoire. He had an awkward body and notably short arms and generally played the villain. Shylock and Richard III were his most famous parts, but audiences also loved him in the comic role of Sir Pertinax MacSycophant in Charles Macklin's *The Man of the World* (1781). He was a sensitive man with a propensity for the good life, and for alcohol, which may have delayed him in the provinces. However, the pervasive influence of the Kemble family on the London theatre at that time may also have put him off, as it certainly had Cooper.

Taking the opportunity to repay in small measure Holcroft's former kindness to him, Cooper asked Mr. Dwyer, the principle comic actor at Drury Lane, to introduce him to Cooke. For the basic story of this meeting and the subsequent involvement with Cooke, we rely on Dunlap, although his writings have inaccuracies. According to Dunlap, who said he learned the story first-hand from Cooper, in May Dwyer and Cooke accepted Cooper's invitation to have dinner at the Wrekin, a pub between the two theatres in Broad Court. Dwyer had a performance that evening and had to leave early, but Cooke stayed with Cooper, and the two struck up the beginning of what would prove to be a long association. During the course of their time together Cooper spoke of how poorly he was being remunerated at Drury Lane, the only pay for his engagement the benefit in mid–June. Learning of this, Cooke urged him to go ahead with it, but offered to ask Mr. Harris at Covent Garden to let him go for the one night, June 10, to appear in the benefit with him at the rival theatre. At first Cooper declined, but at the older actor's repeated insistence, he agreed to talk the possibility over with his friends. Later, when he told Godwin and Holcroft about the famous actor's offer, they advised him to accept—and in this case he took their advice.

To conclude the business, as well as bring all his friends together, Cooper arranged a supper for May 19. By some chance Holcroft could not attend that evening, but by then both Godwin and Cooke had also asked him to introduce them to one another, so the party proceeded, with Cooper, Godwin, James Marshal, and Cooke. Commenting that "a worse assorted pair seldom met," Dunlap recounted the story: "Cooke was, however, unusually amusing, and Godwin was interested and pleased by him during the early part of the evening; but in proportion as the rosy god inspired his votary, he became less interesting to the philosophic skeptic." In short, Godwin fell asleep. "Cooper by this time indulging himself in our country custom, 'a custom more honour'd in the breach than the observance,' was smoking a segar, Marshal taking his hot brandy and water, Godwin sleeping, and Cooke drinking wine and talking incessantly to the philosopher."

When Cooke realized Godwin was asleep, he began to rail against his philosophy: "'Asleep!—fast asleep! How perfectly quiet he rests—and yet he is a democrat! ... What a noble head—and yet pregnant with such monstrous errors! Errors, that if received would destroy the bonds between subject and sovereign, between parent and child, husband and wife, give a loose and free sway to selfishness and sensuality, involve the world in anarchy and steep it in blood.—such philosophers—O how I detest them! I could wish government to exert its force for their extermination, by death—by torture—' then looking at Godwin's face, 'but not him—not this—O, no no!—his conscience is good or he could not sleep thus or look thus!'"

Despite the unravelling of their bonhomie, Cooke agreed to play Iago to Cooper's Othello for the benefit. Once the plans were settled, Godwin and Marshal went home, but Cooke kept Cooper talking and drinking until six o'clock the next morning when he finally let a coach take him home. The well-known story of how the arrangement for the benefit was made has no doubt suffered some elaborate caricature, invited by Cooke's fame together with his love of the bottle. The plan was that on the same morning at ten o'clock, Cooper would call for Cooke in a post chaise. So done, together they rode the fifteen miles to Harris' country home at Uxbridge to obtain his consent for the performance. On their arrival, Cooper, to preserve the proprieties, said he would ride around the Common in the post chaise while Cooke went in to bargain with the manager. After an hour had gone by and no Cooke, Cooper finally went up to the house to see what had happened to his friend. When he asked the servant to tell Mr. Cooke he was outside, Cooke had Cooper ushered into the library, where he found Cooke drinking wine alone and Harris occupied with other business. Cooper had to leave and continue his wait.

As it turned out, Harris was unavailable most of the day, so it was six o'clock before Cooke finally made it back to the post chaise, mission accomplished. Dunlap said that what had happened in Cooper's absence he got "from Cooke's own account, and other sources." Cooke said after drinking to Harris' health and amidst much conviviality he had made the request to play with Cooper. Despite his initial objection, Harris had finally agreed, completely taken off guard when he realized Cooke was scheduled to perform that night back in London.

To Cooper fell the responsibility of getting Cooke to town in time for the evening's performance, but at every pub they passed, Cooke insisted on stopping for a libation. Cooper finally managed to get him to Holcroft's, but to his despair, instead of tea, Holcroft offered him wine, wherewith Cooke and Holcroft at this, their first meeting, began to extol one another's talents, forgetting Cooper in the bargain. With Miss Holcroft's help Cooper at length succeeded in prying the two apart and getting Cooke to the theatre, but his inebriated condition was so apparent, the audience hissed him off the stage.[9]

The foregoing adventure pointed to what would be Cooper's much more extensive involvement with Cooke later on, as the form and thrust of his transitional career between England and America unfolded. Fortunately, for the June 10 benefit at Drury Lane, Cooke was in good form when he performed Iago to his Othello. However, the performance was cut short in the middle when Mrs. Pope, the Desdemona, was taken violently ill; she died a few days later.

The Provinces—1803–04

After the benefit Cooper left London to act at Liverpool. At the theatre there during the summer, as the custom was, he had the chance to alternate with the prominent actors of the day: Cooke, Kemble, and the popular newcomer, Charles Young. At one point, in the space of only a few days, the Liverpool audience saw Richard the Third acted by Cooper, Cooke, and Kemble. William Wood said the distinguished historian, William Roscoe, biographer of Lorenzo de Medici, who lived in Liverpool and "occasionally favored the public and the players with critical remarks on the most deserving performances," thought the trio worthy of his comment: "In reviewing each actor carefully, he awarded fairly to each his superiority in several scenes. Kemble, he conceived was inapproachable in dignity, duplicity, and finish. Cooke he lauded for rough spirit and untiring energy. To Cooper he gave the palm for his exhibition of despair and guilty ravings. The whole of his fifth act Roscoe pronounced superior to his rivals."

Roscoe concluded his remarks on Cooper's performance by saying, "'Mr. Cooper, the young Richard, gave some admirable acting in several scenes besides; and we hope he will be satisfied, if, for the present, we feel compelled to rank him Richard the *third*.'" Cooper told Wood that "he considered this criticism the highest compliment he had ever received."[10] Wood, who happened to be in England at the time as an agent for the Chestnut Street Theatre, said he was surprised when he ran into Cooper, "having reason to suppose him on his voyage home, as he considered America."[11] Cooper's future plans, however, were indefinite.

In the summer Joanna Cooper and the baby had crossed the ocean to join him at Liverpool. He was still acting there and at Manchester in the fall season. He was introduced to the Manchester audience in December in the role of Richard III. At that performance he found himself facing another challenge from Cooke, but of a different kind: Cooke's adoring public dared anyone except Cooke to play Richard, the great actor's definitive role. From the moment Cooper appeared onstage, cries went up, "'Cooke! Cooke!' 'No Yankee actors!' 'Off with him!'" Totally immured to the clamor, Cooper acted in full voice for the whole of the first three acts. By the fourth, there was a hush, and it ended with "a long-continued applause, lasting nearly to the commencement of the fifth, which began and ended in a tumult of applause." Delighted at the chance for personal heroics, he had turned the threats into a triumph, which he frequently recalled as "one of the brightest scenes of his life."[12]

The critic for the *Townsman* reported, "On Friday was performed the tragedy of 'King Richard the Third,' for the purpose of introducing Mr. Cooper (the American Roscius) to the Manchester audience...."[13] A notice in the *Mercury* attested to his strong achievement: "We have recently experienced a truly rich feast, in witnessing the chaste and excellent dramatic powers of Mr. Cooper, whose delineation of the character of *Richard the Third* proves that he possesses a perfect conception of the meaning of our immortal Bard; nor do we hesitate to pronounce him one of the ablest representatives of the hunch-backed tyrant at present off the metropolitan Stage."[14]

In his performance of *Hamlet*, the *Townsman* critic liked Cooper's conception of the closet scene: "It is not to be supposed that he had time allowed him to make up his mind to what he was about to say, or provide himself with pictures, to take from his pocket, as most Hamlets do. Instead of this, Mr. Cooper wore at his own breast, the portrait of his father the whole night, as did the queen that of his uncle; these were what he here made use of, which had a much better effect, than the other method could possibly have...." And the grave scene: "I highly approve his appearance, in the last act, at the grave of Ophelia, *in a Cloak*. Most performers of this part, I have seen, have come forwards in the same dress they wore in the former part of the play, which is very wrong: for it cannot be imagined, that the Prince would remain any time unknown, without some sort of disguise ... he did not *leap* into the grave but *crawled* into it...."[15]

He also pronounced Leon in *Rule a Wife and Have a Wife* "the best character he has played here."[16] Cooper's successful performance of this role, which involves the metamorphosis of an awkward youth to a polished gentleman, effectively answered the devastating failure he had suffered in London in 1795 when he had played the gallant Lothario in an ill-fitting suit of clothes. Fuelled by that experience, he most likely enjoyed playing Leon, and it became his most celebrated comic role, giving him much success and audiences much pleasure over the years.

Despite these successes, however, now that he was on the provincial circuit and still being poorly remunerated, in a not uncharacteristic manner Cooper started treating the texts of even his most familiar characters with casual indifference. The *Townsman* noted that in his performance of Pierre in *Venice Preserv'd*, "he transposed and altered the text in a manner, that was really deplorable."[17] And when he acted Macbeth in Manchester again in February said, "[I]n some parts of the play [he] displayed considerable merit, in others he fell considerably short of what is to be expected from a *celebrated* performer of Macbeth. He, as usual made very free with his author, ... often made free with contractions, as on the former nights of his performance here," but added, "they were not *quite* so frequent as usual.... He is certainly an actor of some merit[.]"[18]

On the twenty-second Cooper took a benefit in *Macbeth*, and the next day the critic expressed "infinite gratification to state, that Mr. Cooper's benefit was well attended, last night, especially as the *whole of his emolument depended upon it*, for performing *twelve* nights here."[19] The occasion brought in £ 95, and it was noted that "with the exception of Cooper ... the stars were in ... bad case with the rank & file, ... Stephen Kemble [Cooper's erstwhile employer] had to be content on his night with £ 73.13 & Charles Mayne Young with a trifle under £ 61."[20]

Back at his home base in Liverpool Cooper played Richard, Penruddock and Rolla "to crowded houses," and received lavish praise for his performance of Horatio in *The Fair Penitent*.[21] With the completion of these engagements he returned to London to arrange another dinner for his friends, particularly Holcroft, who had been absent at the first dinner, though he had been the instigator of the involvement with Cooke.

Holcroft was particularly interested to see more of Cooke since they had been mutually agreeable on the short visit at his home. However, exposure over the length of a dinner party proved less congenial with the assortment of personalities who made up the company: Cooper, Cooke, Holcroft, Godwin, Marshal, and several others. According to Dunlap, after dinner a reference to the recent death of Lord Camelford turned the conversation to duelling. In characteristic fashion Holcroft delivered a tirade against the practice, contradicting Cooper, Marshal, and everyone else who dared put in a word. Cooke, aroused by several glasses of wine, "with a bitter sarcastic look, and his sharpest tone of voice, after a short pause, which gave double force to his thrust, cried: 'Upon my honour, Mr. Holcroft, you shall have a patent for being paramount—' finishing however with a smile, which might in some measure soften the severity of the reproof."

Abstemious in the extreme, Holcroft reacted with an half hour of silence, while Godwin, in his accustomed manner, smoothed the intercourse. When Holcroft finally spoke again, he apologized to Cooke, but his smothered hostility eventually vented itself on Cooper, the youngest member of the party, who regularly carried a pair of pistols on his sojourns in America. The day after the dinner party, Cooper, no longer a fledgling and restive of his situation in England, wrote him a letter to protest his insults of the previous night.[22] As it fell out, this letter unwittingly ended his friendship with Holcroft, for whom he undoubtedly had a true affection. He did not see him again before he left for America, and the year before he returned to England again, in 1810, Holcroft died.

While Cooper was still engaged in England in 1804, in Philadelphia a "Sketch of the Life of Mr. Cooper" appeared in a March issue of the *Port Folio*. The author, who referred to himself as "among the earliest in this country, to attempt the delineation of a living character, and the subject one of the most eminent of those, whose walks of life, have not been political, that have presented themselves to the biographer," began by alluding to the lack of support for the arts in America:

> In America, where business is every one's occupation, but few remarkable characters have appeared, and scarcely a biographer has been found to distinguish those few, before the world. However congenial the mystery of money-making may be with a cheerful evenness of temper, it is certainly inimical to genius; and where the opulent lounger would foster, the man of trade frowns on the efforts of imagination. Our luxuries are exotick, our entertainments imported, our publick [*sic*] spectacles more or less excellent as they approach the European models, of which they are the distant imitations. The barrenness of our literary domain is not therefore to be wondered at; nor where the soil, though so rank has been hitherto so uncultivated, should it surprise, that when a native plant has sprung up, its virtues have not been recorded, or when a foreign one transplanted, has thriven, though its qualities may have been used and enjoyed, they have not been sufficiently made known, or justly appreciated.

Peter Irving ran a reprint of the article in the *New York Morning Chronicle* on March 6 "with additions," a second part, which then appeared reprinted in *Port Folio* on the thirty-first. At the end of the second piece Irving made a bid for Cooper's return: "It is rumoured, that he has concluded an engagement with the manager of Drury Lane; but, many persons entertain hopes that he may yet be restored to the American stage."[23]

That fall, on September 22, Irving wrote William Dunlap saying he had received a letter from Cooper, who seemed to be planning to visit America but then return to England. Cooper asked Irving to give Dunlap his apology for not having written since his departure for England and then proposed several possibilities, including one that he sail to New York about February 10 for a twelve-night engagement at the Park over a period of four weeks. Intending to pay his own expenses to and from America, he suggested that the terms of his contract be to divide the clear profit with the manager and take a clear benefit the thirteenth night.

On November 2 Dunlap finally received a letter from Cooper himself in which he explained that "he had often wished to leave England, but that his mother and other friends were extremely averse to his again coming to America." He had now persuaded them to allow him "leave of absence for a short period." Keen to depart, he wrote that he was taking a ship for America immediately. He told Dunlap, "'I shall endeavor to get a new play or two for you, but I cannot promise anything. As to actors, I have not seen one in England that should arrive in America with the sanction of my recommendation, except only a comedian called Emery.'"

Cooper's letter could not have come too soon for Dunlap. In the fall of 1803 after his wife's death, Hodgkinson had left the Park to act in Charleston, and as Dunlap explained in his reply to Cooper, "'I have opened my theatre without a man in tragedy superior to Martin; Fennell being engaged in Connecticut making salt.'"[24] As for Cooper, despite what his English family, or he himself, may have thought, or at least hoped, he belonged to the new country and would not return to England again for another seven years. With the proper exertion he could have had a distinguished career as a tragedian in England. As it

From an engraving of Thomas Abthorpe Cooper by C. H. Meyer, London, after a drawing by J. Wood, NYC. Harvard Theatre Collection, Houghton Library.

had happened, however, his career embodied the transition from the old to the new. He had left England when he was still a boy and had matured and won his fame in America. Also, in the years since the homesick letters he had written Godwin in 1800, he had married an American. At twenty-eight years of age he already held the position of the leading actor of the American stage, which his trip abroad only served to solidify. At the very time he returned to England in 1803, U.S. President Thomas Jefferson was negotiating the purchase of Louisiana from Napoleon. Cooper would be the first star to tour the new territory.

Twelve

The United States' Star

New York and Philadephia—1804–05

Cooper returned to America with Joanna and young Thomas in November 1804, accompanied by Mr. George Wilmot, whom he had found backstage at Drury Lane and brought out as a kind of personal valet.[1] The Saturday before his opening in New York, which was set for Monday the 19th, the *Morning Chronicle* advertised "his first appearance after an absence of near two years,"[2] and on the opening day noted, "The reception of Mr. Cooper, on the boards of the New York stage, promises to be equal to the high rank he has obtained in the dramatic scale. At an early hour on Friday, all the lower boxes were engaged, and from the burst of satisfaction which succeeded his announcement, on the close of the Comedy that evening, there is every reason to believe that few remain now to be taken."[3]

The day after the performance the *Evening Post* reported: "Last evening Mr. Cooper, the celebrated tragedian, made his first appearance in Macbeth after an absence of two years. The theatre was crowded at an early hour and on his stepping forward, greeted him with loud and long repeated applauses." The reviewer went on to say, "[H]is improvement has been beyond all expectation. It may now with strict truth be said that as a tragedian Cooper stands in this country entirely alone."[4] As the engagement proceeded, the reviewer for the *Morning Chronicle* congratulated the manager: "Every night on which that gentleman has performed the house has exhibited a scene but seldom witnessed since his departure for Europe. The theatre appears once more to have become the resort of taste and fashion[.]"[5] He pointed out that Cooper had "a more minute and thorough acquaintance with the passions, shades, and situations of the characters, as also a more masterly and energetic execution[,]" and his European exposure had "improved his acting, by rendering him more thoroughly conversant with stage situation, and by giving to his attitudes and gestures a more picturesque and graceful arrangement."[6]

The performance of *Richard the Third* November 30 "produced an unusually thronged and an extremely genteel attendance—the boxes exhibiting a brilliant and profuse display of beauty and of fashion." Commenting that he had seen Cooper perform the role "in styles very distinct and varient[,]" the *Chronicle* reviewer explained, "It is doubtful whether malignity of temper should be made a prominent feature influencing him in the commission of his crimes—or, whether he should be represented with a more daring and unfeeling grandeur of villainy, stimulated by inordinate ambition, ... removing without compunction every obstacle that impedes his progress to the throne." Not presuming to choose, he continued, "Mr. Cooper has formerly given us great pleasure in adopting the latter mode ... the outline he then struck was we think, more bold, grand and impressive, than that he has at present adopted."

He proceeded, however, by asserting that Cooper had now "called out new and appropriate beauties, by a more mature and attentive study[.]" He said, "The Richard of Mr. Cooper exhibits an accurate discrimination in the different stages of the character. While Gloster he is all cunning and dissimulation: ... It is only in his soloquies that the conscious sense of his own superiority breaks forth. But when his plans have proved successful, he assumes with the crown a bolder and more imperious manner." Continuing, "Mr. Cooper's Richard is also distinguished for a vein of dry humor pervading the character[,]" he pointed to the soliloquy on Lady Anne's entrance with King Henry's funeral procession, and the "*courting scene,* ... one of his most successful." Here, he said, "The art of his flattery, the affectation of candor and innocence, the ardent tenderness of his love, and the hypocritical fervor of his penitence, were all strongly and distinctly marked."

And in the tent scene—"His start from the couch—the exclamations '*Give me a horse,*' ... with the trepidation that might be supposed attendant on a critical and dangerous incident—'*bind up my wounds*' with the voice of painful anguish—'*have mercy heaven*' with the despairing and terrified tone of one who conceived himself past all hope" ... [were] fully equalled by the grandeur with which he resumed his self-possession, on rousing his waking powers, from the influence exerted over them by supernatural agency during his moments of sleep." The critic faulted him, however, for "an occcasional extreme of violence, which was not called for by the circumstances of the drama[.]"[7]

David Ogden was in the audience that night and wrote William Meredith in Philadelphia, "Cooper is now playing here, to very crowded houses—he is certainly much improved by his visit to Europe. I saw him last night in Richard the Third—and he was a very villain—he displayed a strength of judgment and genius throughout the whole of his performance of that difficult character which delighted and astonished the audience."⁸ According to the *Chronicle* reviewer, his Shylock also "commanded much applause ... there was so complete an alteration in his deportment, walk, gestures, &c. that he could not have been recognized by his most intimate acquaintance.... The rapidity of his transitions from rage at the elopement of his daughter, and torture at the recital of her extravagance, to savage exultation at the misfortunes of Antonio, were excellently expressed by the glances of his eye, and sudden variations of voice and countenance."⁹

And the final offering, Penruddock, the reviewer considered "among the best of his performances"—

> The chasteness with which he exhibits and preserves the character of the morose and gloomy misanthrope, in the early scenes of the comedy, deserved no less praise than the wild and impassioned energy with which he gives vent to the furious emotions long confined within Penruddocks [*sic*] bosom, and which break forth like a tempest in his interview with Young Woodville, ... the impressive earnestness with which he details his story, the fire of his passion, the varying modulations of his voice, now broken with agonized recollections, ... again swelling with indignant rage, when he exclaims, "*the defamer of my character*," may truly be pronounced above all praise. Its effect appeared utterly to confound the youthful performer who personated Henry, while it perfectly electrified the audience. Nor should our applause be withheld from the skill with which he preserved the softening shades of the character in the concluding scenes, when the violent passions of the misanthrope become exchanged for more generous and more humanized feelings.

He noted, however, "Some of the actors were embarrassed by an imperfect commitment of their parts, and others were unavoidably feeble from having taken them in hand at too short a notice."¹⁰

This first engagement at the Park Theatre after Cooper's return ran fourteen nights and brought in over $10,000. The pioneer Southern manager, Noah Miller Ludlow, spoke of it as "about the first instance on record of regular 'starring' in the United States[.]"¹¹

The first of January Cooper left New York for an engagement in Philadelphia to act with the former Mrs. Merry, now Mrs. Wignell. The Philadelphia manager had married the widowed actress in 1803 but had himself died just seven weeks after. Again a widow, she had taken up the management of the Chestnut Street Theatre herself, with the assistance of William Warren and William Wood.

A reviewer signing "D" reported, "The house was filled with fashion and beauty" to see the pair onstage together again, the sublimely gifted actress with the star she herself had discovered. "Sophocles" said of Cooper, "[H]e was received with the most cordial approbation and joy, and honored during his whole performance with a listening and attentive silence, much more significant of honest heartfelt applause than the usual tumultuous expressions of popular admiration[.]"

He went on to observe: "I did not perceive that striking difference in his acting which we had been taught to expect from a residence in England, ... I have always thought, indeed, that the manly grace of his person, the expressive ease of his action, the immense extent and nice modulation of his voice, and his apparently intuitive conception of the author's meaning, entitle him a great actor—to all these eminent qualities it is said he has added, what perhaps wipes away the only blot in his escutcheon, a proper observance of the duties of his profession, and an endeavour to be perfectly acquainted with his parts—his accuracy yesternight justifies the reported improvement[.]" "D" concurred, saying, "[T]he most prominent fruits of his Atlantic excursion consist of what may be called the drapery or decorations of acting, for he possessed the *soul* and *body* of it before." He reported that his Hamlet was given "a profound and almost breathless attention[,]" his scenes with Ophelia and the Queen, "constant 'streams of burning fire.' He was never too languid—never too ardent." And Mrs. Wignell's Ophelia held "the master-key to the heart."[12] The receipts were even more generous than in New York.

Meanwhile, Dunlap said that after Cooper left, the New York theatre had "sunk irretrievably." Cooper's triumphant return and all-too-soon departure for Philadelphia had only served to point up the ebbing fortunes of the Park. On the strength of the receipts for the star's engagement the creditors had begun to press harder. Dunlap commented, "After a struggle of years against the effects of the yellow fever, and all those curses belonging to the interior of an establishment, badly organized when he found it, the manager's health yielded to disappointment and incessant exertion, and his struggles became proportionably fainter." Even when Cooper reappeared, the attraction of the star could not save the theatre. On February 22, completely destitute, Dunlap had to close. He had joined the Park management in order to ensure the production of his plays but had lost everything in the venture. Taking a philosophic attitude, he retired with his family to his mother's home in Perth Amboy, New Jersey.[13]

Boston—1805–06

Hearing about Cooper's renewed success, Snelling Powell, the manager of the Federal Street Theatre in Boston, wrote to him about a possible engagement, to which Cooper agreed. But by the time the star arrived there in March, the stock company actors were beginning their spring benefits, and their contracts prohibited the manager from bringing any outside performer to the theatre during that part of the season. However, the Boston public, apprised of the opportunity to see the famous actor, began to agitate for his appearance.

A day or so after his arrival, unable to secure an engagement, Cooper went to the theatre for the evening performance; seated in the dress circle, he was seen and recognized. The play went off without incident, but after the curtain fell and Mr. Dickinson came onstage to announce the next night's benefit, Cooper's supporters, who had scattered themselves throughout the house, began to shout, "'Cooper or no play! Cooper or no play!'" The cry became general: "'Cooper or no play!'" In despair, but anxious to keep the situation in hand, Dickinson finally pointed at one of the most prominent agitators and, in a straightforward manner, said, "'Very well, Mr. ____, no play then.'" The next day, news went out that the house that evening was to be "packed by Cooper's friends," who intended to make sure there was "'no play.'" In consequence, Powell closed the theatre and refunded the ticket receipts for the performance.

William Clapp, who told the story in his *History of the Boston Stage* [originally published in the *Boston Evening Gazette*], surmised that Cooper was "somewhat chagrined, probably, at the serious aspect of affairs, and the unjustifiable attempt to force the management to an engagement, which certainly would prove unprofitable to the actors[.]" So he asked for a meeting, and Powell, accompanied by Dickinson, went to dine with him at Julian's. There, "over a chop, perhaps a glass of port, which, 'full of bounty, prompts the open hand,'" they came to terms. By nature Cooper was inclined to generosity, and it was acknowledged that he was "very liberal" in his agreement. Conferring with Powell and Dickinson, he looked over the benefit list and said, "'There, I will play gratuitously for this one and that one, for they are sure of a full house without me[.]'" In arranging for the rest of the benefits, he asked how much the actors would ordinarily receive. Dickinson estimated each could expect to make a hundred dollars, so Cooper said that in adding to their nights, he would share with them what profits came in, but only after each of them had first received a hundred dollars.[14]

After the settlement, on March 11, 1805, Cooper opened in Boston as Hamlet. A member of the audience that night wrote an account in a letter to "a gentleman in the country" which was published in the *Independent Chronicle*:

I HASTEN to give you some account of Mr. COOPER'S *entre* on the Boston stage. The celebrity which this gentleman had acquired, excited much public expectation, and the difficulty which took place among the players previously to his appearance, raised an encreased anxiety.

Immediately on its being known that he was to perform, every ticket was engaged; and the house, at a very early hour, crowded in every part. Something wonderful was anticipated. A display of powers hitherto unseen and hardly imagined. Such a concourse of anxious and enquiring spectators, were, perhaps, never assembled in the Boston theatre.

The curtain rose; a solemn stillness reigned; Mr. Cooper appeared; the theatre rang with reiterated plaudits.

Mr. Cooper is perhaps the most elegant person you have ever seen upon the stage. Of an height, form and age well fitted for the character he assumed; a flexibility of feature ready to give utterance and energy to every characteristic of passion; 'an eye like Mars, to threaten or command;' a voice clear, sonorous and full, extending its delightful melody from 'the lowest note to the top of the compass,' without labored exertion or unnatural force; a mind comprehending with facility the range and extent of the character, and giving every little shade of nice distinction with perspicuity and precision.[15]

The fourteen-year-old John Howard Payne, soon to be the editor of his own theatrical commentary, also attended the performance. He recalled the evening a number of years later in a letter to his sister Eloise:

Cooper was the first actor of note I ever saw. It was in Boston, on the 11th of March, 1805, eleven years ago, when I was a mere boy.... His reception was very ardent. My young mind was enraptured; he enchanted me, though at the time I could not tell why. His deportment to me is always full of natural dignity; his action and whole manner is chaste, vigorous, and characteristic, and his enunciation always fine. I shall never forget his finished style of bowing to the audience. It acted like a mysterious magic over all, and at once made the audience his personal friends.

Payne explained to her, "Cooper is of the Kemble school; not that he is a copy of Kemble, as Booth is of Kean, but is of the heroic style, and becomes such a part as *Othello* better than that of *Iago*." Comparing Cooper to Kemble he went on, "He resorts, too, to less tricks of the stage than Kemble, who enlarges his legs and arms by pads, and consults pictures and artists, to produce personal effects ... he is more natural, while Kemble is more artistic. In natural grace, Cooper is far beyond any actor I have ever seen, and he is, too, the best *Hamlet* on the stage, he is even more scholarly than Kemble, and, if not so startling as Kean, or so grand as Kemble in the part, he is certainly far less rude than the former, and more natural than the latter."[16]

Cooper, accompanied by Mr. Wilmot, had also taken twenty-four-year-old "Billy" Twaits along with him to Boston. Twaits was a low comedian from the Philadelphia theatre whom Wood had engaged in England in 1803. Short and stocky with a long pale face, large mouth, hooked nose and stiff carrot-red hair, he had a powerful, though asthmatic, voice, and had been popular as a burletta singer in England. Returning to New York with Cooper, along the way Twaits enjoyed making the most of the humorous contrast between himself and his fine friend. He led the keeper of an inn where they stopped for breakfast to believe the grand Cooper, traveling in noticeable style with his servant and fine luggage, was a tumbler and rope-dancer onstage. In due course Cooper retaliated with a practical joke himself. Twaits' wife was one of the lovely Westray sisters, and one night while she was performing onstage, he overheard a drunkard insult her and bragged to Cooper that he had confronted the man and soundly rebuked him. From this Cooper devised an elaborate concoction, building Twaits into peaks of anxiety over several episodes by sending him notes from a supposed challenger, and even accompanying him to specified assignations, where the spectral figure repeatedly failed to appear.[17]

At the end of June Cooper made his first trip to Providence. Acting Othello there for his benefit, as usual he painted his face light brown and, following a custom Garrick had adopted, dressed in a Moorish costume. He was, however, said to follow Garrick's great rival, Spranger Barry, in Act IV when Othello succumbs to the belief of Desdemona's betrayal: With the words, "Oh Desdemona!—away!—away!—away!'—Instead of blustering them out, ... he looked a few seconds in Desdemona's face, as if to read her feelings and disprove his suspicions; then, turning away, as the adverse conviction gathered in his heart, spoke them falteringly, and gushed into tears."[18] John Bernard remarked of Cooper, "[H]is Othello, I think, was equal to Barry's itself."[19]

Some of the critics, used to seeing the role played in a British officer's uniform, stringently objected to Cooper's costume innovation,[20] but his performance captivated them. In the final scene of the play, when Othello, "[t]he first paroxysms of rage and remorse having subsided," asks, "'Will you, I pray, demand that demi-devil,/ Why he hath thus ensnared my soul and body?'"—with his accustomed passion "Cooper, as if forgetful of the previous dignity of his character, uttered this sentence with the querulous accent of piercing agony: his knees bending under him and knocking against each other, as if borne down by the accumulated pressure of misery and guilt. Every attentive spectator was then made to feel how much the elevated hero was lost in the heart-broken culprit."[21] He won the Providence audience, and in the years to come "was always welcomed by large audiences, and was the pet, the idol of the town."[22]

In the wake of his success in Boston, Cooper returned to open the next season, 1805–06, in that city, winning acclaim as Coriolanus in Shakespeare's rarely performed tragedy of that name. The influential Boston critic, Joseph T. Buckingham, lauded him in his new monthly, *The Polyanthos*, the first issue of which featured a full-page engraving of the star [by S. Harris] and a sketch of his life.[23] As Glenalvon in the tragedy *Douglas*, he was "'a sun among stars[.]'"[24] In comedy, his Leon in *Rule a Wife and Have a Wife* [John Fletcher] was "a highly finished performance.... He admirably personated the awkward gait and coarse manners of a clown; and was no less successful in representing the polished gentleman."[25]

From an engraving of Thomas Abthorpe Cooper by S. Harris, reproduced by John Howard Payne for the frontispiece of the first issue of the *Thespian Mirror*, December 28, 1805, and by Joseph T. Buckingham for the first issue of the *Polyanthos*, January, 1806. Harvard Theatre Collection, Houghton Library.

For a stunning change of pace to finish the season, at his benefit Cooper offered a new part, Sir John Falstaff, the corpulent knight of Shakespeare's *Henry IV*. In this, Buckingham declared, "Mr. C. was perfect master of the language, and gave it such force and energy in delivery, that not a word was lost.... The voice, the gesture and the gait of *Cooper* were completely swallowed up in the doublet and hose of *Falstaff*." Concluding, "[T]he time is probably not far distant, when Mr. Cooper's *Falstaff* may be reckoned a master-piece of comick excellence."[26]

The house was said to be "crowded to an overflow" for the benefit, and Cooper had invited the Indian Chiefs who were presently in the city.

After the performance when they met him, and "their interpreter explained to them that he was the person whose singularly gross appearance in Falstaff, had excited their attention, they expressed their incredulity in the strongest terms," as John Howard Payne noted in his new "periodical publication," the *Thespian Mirror*, commenting, "[I]t is not singular that they should refuse to credit this surprising metamorphosis."[27] That fall Payne, whose father had sent him to live in New York, had also featured the Harris engraving of Cooper on the frontispiece of his first issue in December, followed by a biography in January.[28]

Reviewing Cooper's performances in March, Payne said of his Hamlet, "[W]hen the shade is summoned to his 'prison house,' and has vanished from his distracted son –'Remember thee? Ay thou poor ghost, while memory holds a seat In this distracted globe....' [w]as uttered with a *pathos* which found its way to every heart."[29] And in late May concluded,

> He [Cooper] is peculiarly the favorite of nature, and almost invariably follows her dictates. His faults have so often been canvassed, that little or nothing is left for the critic, but to complain in the hackneyed strain of his rant; of his want of application; and of the inequality of his acting. Far be it from us to contradict either of these charges; we cannot disprove them. "Every man to his taste," says the proverb; and every man who has seen Cooper, (we should say *admired*, for we should be inclined to censure the taste of any one who has seen, without admiring him) is peculiarly disposed to rest his applause on some *one* of his characters. For ourselves, though we aspire not to the honour of manhood, our taste is greatly in favour of his *Othello*, and next to that his *Hamlet*. But a new star in the constellation of his excellencies, has made its appearance ... *Beverly* (Edward Moore's tragedy *The Gamester*): and in splendour and magnificence, it bids fair to rival and to eclipse the rest.[30]

In January Cooper had written the proprietors of the Federal Street Theatre in Boston requesting a three-year lease on the theatre, but the management was still in Powell's hands at that time. Meanwhile in New York, John Jacob Astor and John K. Beekman had bought the Park Theatre from the 113 original proprietors for the low sum of $50,000.[31] That spring they invited Cooper to become the lessee and manager. He readily accepted on the stipulation that they underwrite a complete renovation of the theatre building, to which they agreed.

To complete the plans for his management, before going on tour for the spring and summer, Cooper made a trip out to Perth Amboy to offer Dunlap a contract to return to the Park, as general superintendent of the theatre and manager during his absences. As Dunlap told it, "He ... made me such an offer as to yearly emolument, to commence that day, as I could not reject, and proposed getting into a carriage in waiting and proceeding to Philadelphia immediately. It did not take long to change dress, dine or lunch, and I was no longer a painter, but all my mind absorbed in theatrical affairs."[32]

The South—1806–07

At the close of the season, Cooper left New York for his first extended tour of the South. "King Tommy," as he was sometimes called,[33] welcomed the adventure: "[S]o did Cooper go to the South in his tandem sulky, ... he had a brace of beautiful duelling pistols, in holsters, on either side of his vehicle; a gun or rifle, in its leathern case, also hung alongside, and over the entire seat and sulky body was thrown a splendid roquelare cloak, trimmed with gold lace.... Thus equipped, in this unique but splendid equipage, followed by his trim English servant George [Mr. Wilmot], mounted on horseback, would he wend his way to South Carolina and Georgia, through boggs, morasses and pine forests."[34]

On Easter Even, April 5, 1806, the famous star thrilled the audience in Richmond with his debut in that city as Hamlet:

> It is difficult to describe the vivid expectations of the audience, who attended the Richmond Theatre last Saturday night to see, criticise and admire the celebrated Cooper. The notice was short; but the house was uncommonly crowded. Every heart throbb'd for the rising of the curtain and every eye gazed with anxiety for the scene that was to present them with the Prince of Denmark,...
>
> The scene at length was shifted, and Hamlet appears at the footstool of the throne. Everything about him was prepossessing. A mourning dress, rich and starred with brilliants; a figure of more than middling stature, firm without being athletic, and dignified, without affectation; a face, whose every feature seemed capable of expressing every emotion: such was the interesting object that stood forth before the audience. But it was not Cooper the player & the stranger, who appeared before you, with an eye expressive of curiosity & the high blush of anxiety upon his cheek. It was Hamlet of Denmark, and at the very first glimpse, you saw the folded arm, the knitted brow, the indignant and discontented eye, which announced, that there was "something rotten in the state of Denmark."[35]

The next week Cooper headed for the theatrical capital of the South, Charleston, where on the 14th he also opened in *Hamlet*. The advance publicity for this first visit built up tremendous expectation in the Charleston audience, which was a knowledgeable one. Stephen Cullen

Carpenter, editor of the *Charleston Courier*, explained that the expectations were beyond the scope of anyone, "reports of so very exaggerated a kind that we doubt whether there ever existed an actor whose performance could rise to a level with them." Describing Cooper's Hamlet as "a showy piece," but uneven, he highlighted "the beauties" of it, in particular the closet scene with his Mother, the scene with Ophelia, both "of the highest order of excellence," and the play scene: "No man ever spoke words better, or gave them more admirable correspondent action than Mr. Cooper that passage: 'He poisons him in the garden for his estate....'" He ended by pronouncing Cooper "a very great and indeed extraordinary performer."[36]

John Beaufain Irving, who lived in Charleston and later became Cooper's friend and companion on his tours there, said of his closet scene in *Hamlet*: "There was a happy mixture of warm indignation, tempered with tenderness; though cruel, he was so only to be kind, and as if he was trying to bear in mind the injunction of his father ... to leave her to Heaven...."

But it was on the second night when Cooper played Macbeth that he fully captivated the Charleston audience, and Macbeth was the one role he repeated during the engagement. In the *Courier* Carpenter pronounced the performance "a wonderful display of dramatic talents." Irving recalled that when Cooper as Macbeth, having just proposed a toast to Banquo in a most restrained fashion, reacted to the second appearance of Banquo's ghost, the audience applauded. Irving also said that in the fifth act, "He shone ... with a lustre unparalleled."—

> [H]is look—his voice and action, in the sentence to the affrighted messenger—
>
> > "Go, prick thy face, and over-red thy fear,
> > Thou, lily-liver'd boy. What soldiers, patch?
> > Death of thy soul! Those linen cheeks of thine
> > Are counsellors to fear. What soldiers, whey-face?"
>
> were ... masterly illustrations of Shakespeare. As he uttered the last line I liked *his turning a little* to the troops drawn up in the rear, as if he apprehended the alarm shown by "the linen cheeks" of the boy might *counsel fear* to the soldiery. And then his exclamation to the next messenger, who reported that, as he watched upon the hill, he looked towards Birnam, and anon "he thought the wood began to move" ... exhibited a climax of passion, and thence a fall to hopelessness. It was the result of judgment and nature. The effect was electrical.[37]

In addition to the *Courier*, Stephen Carpenter was the editor of a national literary magazine published in Charleston, *Monthly Review and Literary Miscellany of the United States*. In that journal he remarked that Cooper's dagger scene in *Macbeth* "was a piece of unparalleled beauty"; and observed that Mrs. Whitlock as Lady Macbeth "appeared to have caught fresh fire from the splendid blaze of his performance of the Thane." He said that although he had seen six famous Macbeths and Mrs. Siddons as Lady Macbeth, he had never seen the fifth scene of Act One performed better than by Cooper and Mrs. Whitlock.[38]

Carpenter described Cooper's person as "of the best size—(tall enough for picturing dignity,) but of a finely symetrised shape, and proportion." He went on to observe, "His face too is very handsome—but being from its symmetry rather deficient in means of vehement expression, he sometimes injures it by an over-strained effort to produce stage effect correspondent to the character he personates." His voice he described as "strong, harmonious, and capable of producing astonishing effects by the lower tones; or by the higher, in the characters where the furious passions are to be expressed."

Noting, "In the impassioned parts he rouses every latent spark of feeling in the audience[,]" he went on to blame the style for diminishing his effect in the "cold, didactic and declamatory" parts, "particularly soliloquies[.]" He explained, "It appears to us, that when he follows his own nature, he seldom fails to be great—where he does fail, he fails, we think, from overstudiously following an erroneous model. As soon as passion breaks him loose from the fetters of studied action and enunciation— when he ceases to measure his words, and to poise his action *secundum artem*, he blazes out into beauties which nature never bestowed the powers of disclosing, without giving along with them many more, if they were let to have their full scope."

He also pointed to what he considered Cooper's "neglect in the management of walk and deportment[,]" which he perceived might "arise from an over-done disdain of what is vulgarly called tragedy strut[,]" encouraging him to take "the middle path ... a certain manner raised a little above the simply dignified deportment of real life, yet not touching upon the extravagant affected stalk of the stage, which we think Mr. Cooper is as well qualified as any man to attain, and which he should study to adopt." And added, "Mr. Cooper also injures his deportment by bending on his knees, and at times by even turning in his toes." Concluding, however: "With all those deductions from his external appearance, which being matters of either neglect or adoption, he can readily mend, Mr. Cooper's person, taken altogether, is the finest we have seen on the American stage[.]"[39]

Cooper had planned to stay in Charleston for twelve nights, but his engagement proved to be so successful with the Charleston audience that he extended it to over a month. The following season he would return for an even longer engagement, trying out the role of King Lear for the first time in his career on May 13 in Charleston. At that time the manager, Alexandre Placide, applied to the City Council for permission to present him in *Othello* as well, but because the play concerns a black hero, the request was denied.

From then on J. B. Irving said Cooper acted in Charleston "with undiminished success, *the putting up of his name* being seen to gladden the hearts of the *habitués* of the theatre, and to act with magnetic influence upon those in the community who can be drawn out only on extraordinary occasions."[40] And on January 30, 1809, the City Council allowed him to appear in the first production of *Othello* in that city.[41] Also, once he began appearing in Charleston, Charleston became a major point on the touring circuit for all the famous tragedians of the day.[42]

It was said that of all the places in America that he came to know, Charleston was the place where Cooper felt most at home. He made many friends in the luxuriant port city and returned to act there regularly until the late 1830s. His eldest daughter Mary Grace accompanied him on tour later on and married a Charlestonian, Frederic Raoul, son of an exiled French Royalist. Over the years the Raouls had entertained Cooper, in addition to many other visiting celebrities, on her plantation in Columbia.

On that first tour Cooper left Charleston May 16, 1806, continuing to gather admirers and friends as he made his way back north. He played Beverly in *The Gamester* in Norfolk on May 29.[43] Returning to Richmond in August, he played Othello there, and the reviewer for the *Richmond Enquirer* described his skill in listening, which Holcroft had emphasized in his acting theory: "It is in this under play of his character: it is at those points of the drama, where every member but the tongue speaks the emotions of the man, that he more than ever towers above his competitors. When Cooper speaks, it is impossible not to devour every sound which he utters: when Cooper listens, his eye, his lip, his forehead, his fingers are almost adequate to supply the cessation of his voice." Then noted, "When he describes his first discovery of Desdemona's love, each feature of his face seemed again to glisten with the recollected joy. But there was a sweetness, a softness in his tone as if it feared to fling the history of his love abroad into the world, a melting cadence as if inspired anew by the memory of his early love, ... which baffle description."[44]

While he was in Richmond Cooper sought out a young English portrait painter, Thomas Sully, and sat to him. Sully was finding it difficult to establish a reputation, so Cooper suggested he move to New York and invited him to paint portraits in the lobby of the Park Theatre, guaranteeing him $1,000 worth of business to start. Sully took the suggestion, moved to New York with his wife in November, and painted numerous theatrical figures "for Cooper." Cooper allowed Sully to draw advances on the money from his treasurer and also arranged for him to meet the noted painters in New York. This generous and clever patronage proved to be a turning point in the artist's recognition, providing a valuable theatrical record for American heritage as well.[45]

Meanwhile, before he left Virginia that summer Cooper made some joint appearances with his old friend the comedian John Bernard, including a "lecturing excursion" in Virginia and Maryland. Charles Durang attended the lecture at the Pantheon in Baltimore describing it as "a discussion on the drama, its uses and abuses." He said, "Several young gentlemen figured in it. Cooper, we recollect, spoke from notes."[46] Dr. John W. Francis, a well-known New Yorker who later presented his reminiscences to the New-York Historical Society, recalled that "Cooper was an incessant reader of Schlegel, who, he said, was the only worthy commentator on Shakspeare [sic]."[47]

Pioneer theatre and life on the road could be rough, as Bernard later recalled in his *Retrospections of America*. Bernard told how one night when he and Cooper were both onstage in the assembly-room of a tavern in Frederickstown, Virginia, while Cooper was performing his famous recitation of Dryden's poem, "Alexander's Feast," a large brickbat came flying through the window narrowly missing Cooper's head and hitting him, Bernard, in the shins. The audience was thrown into confusion, but upon drinking a glass of water, Cooper continued his recitation. Afterward he went outside with a cudgel he got at the bar to find the man who had hurled the missile. Amid a group of backwoodsmen, a great burly braggart stepped forward to claim his prowess, but Cooper surprised him by overcoming him with blows. Then he calmly returned to the stage to deliver Shakespeare's "Soliloquy on Death." Bernard said he greatly admired Cooper's self-possession, "the cool calculation of danger, and its proud defiance." In the years to come, Southern audiences packed the houses whenever "King Cooper" came to town.[48]

The same quality in the man which manifested itself in physical courage and strict punctuality was turned to firm control in the management of the Park Theatre. In turn, this new position gave Cooper specific involvement with the new country's social and cultural establishment. He could now exert his personal influence on standards of administration, repertoire, and performance. Opening his first season October 6, 1806, he set aside his predilection for first place to let his rival, James Fennell, play Richard the Third to his own Richmond, "[t]o make the attraction irresistible[.]"[49] In November he took time out to coach a young actor, Mr. Morse, for his debut. Morse appeared successfully as Pierre in *Venice Preserv'd* to the Jaffier of Cooper and stayed to act in the company; later, for a period, he was the leading actor in the Boston Company.[50] Cooper himself exchanged engagements with the former Anne Merry, now Mrs. William Warren, in Philadelphia, as well as Bernard in Boston. Mrs. Warren, whom Sully painted for Cooper, was the financial success of the season; receipts during her stay at the Park in February averaged $750 per night and almost $1,000 at her benefit.[51] Sadly, this engagement proved to be her farewell. At the end of the following season, on June 28, 1808, she died in childbirth, an incomparable loss to the early American theatre.

Thirteen

Yankee Ingenuity

Itinerant Star—1807–10

At the end of his first season as manager, Cooper fired the Park's resident scene designer, Ciceri, whose elaborate painting had been hailed when Dunlap first opened the theatre. Dunlap had given the gifted Ciceri free rein, and he expected the same from Cooper, but Cooper wisely refused him; the extravagance of his designs had been one of the factors in Dunlap's financial failure. Cooper replaced him with John Joseph Holland, an architect and scene designer from the Chestnut Street Theatre, who had been trained under the celebrated Marinelli in London.

Making this change with plans for the next season, Cooper went back on tour in March. When he got to Richmond he met up with Washington Irving, who was there to attend the trial of Aaron Burr on a charge of treason. In the persona of "William Wizard," Irving described going to the theatre with his friend, the cockney *Snivers*, voicing the general approval: "Snivers ... really thinks Cooper one of our best actors.... I like frowning in tragedy, and if a man but keeps his forehead in proper wrinkle, talks big, and takes long strides on the stage, I always set him down as a great tragedian, and so does my friend Snivers.... On Cooper's giving one of his gun-powder explosions of passion, I exclaimed, 'fine, very fine!'"[1]

The Richmond audience asked Cooper to act the part of Beverly in *The Gamester*, and when he found himself without the proper costume, Irving lent him a pair of breeches appropriate to the character. A few days later in Baltimore, still in possession of Irving's breeches, Cooper found a heart-shaped locket of hair in the pocket and returned it to Irving with an amusing letter and verse:

> "Receive these inquiries, dear friend, in good part,
> And since you have locked the fair hair in your heart,
> Ne'er trust, of the girl who your fancy bewitches,
> Such an emblem of love in another man's breeches."[2]

In New York, during the summer, Cooper oversaw a complete renovation of the Park Theatre with the assistance of his new designer, Mr. Holland. They finished the job below budget, coming in $5,000 under the $15,000 appropriated by the owners.[3] All the original interior material was torn out, and the walls refitted with four tiers of boxes, giving a total audience capacity of 2700. Durang said that the renovation "presented the most splendid decorations which had yet been seen in America."[4] The ceiling was painted like a dome with light purple panels and gold mouldings, and the panels on the front of the boxes were blue, decorated with white and gold and festooned with crimson drapes. Ten crystal chandeliers lit the lower boxes, and a large oval mirror at the end of four stage boxes reflected the audience giving "[a] beautiful effect" according to Dunlap.[5] Washington Irving produced a speech in verse, which Cooper spoke at the opening of the season in the newly decorated house September 9.[6]

With one season successfully behind him and the redecoration complete, Cooper more and more felt free to leave Dunlap in charge of the theatre while he made starring tours. It was about this time that he began a habit of regular touring on alternate nights of the week, riding relays of horses between New York, Monday and Wednesday, and Philadelphia, Friday and Saturday. Coming across him in the streets of Philadelphia astride "a splendid white charger, dressed in the fashion of the English riding habit, viz: blue coat, red waistcoat, buckskin breeches and fair-top boots," Durang regretted not having "an artist's skill" to capture the picture.[7] Sometimes "driving a gig at breakneck speed,"—as Reese Davis James says in his account, "his reputation as a dead shot discouraged bandits," adding, "He could have routed them without recourse to weapons."[8] Before her death Mrs. Merry repurchased a pair of horses she had sold him to save them from the hard usage, which Durang explained was not "the result of cruel disposition," but "merely the consequence of impulsive youthful freaks." He recalled seeing Cooper in the depth of winter, "December or January, when it was snowing and blowing from the northeast with terrible violence. Thus, without being hardly able to see half the length of a square, would he start for New York, and be there the next morning at rehearsal."[9]

He became a familiar figure legendary for his physical prowess and punctuality, "never failing to 'come to time,' which was considered through the heavy sand roads of New Jersey a Herculean performance[,]" as Henry Dickinson Stone recalled him in his *Reminiscences*. He said, "Cooper was, probably, taking him all in all, the most remarkable actor in the two hemispheres ... playing his most arduous *roles* many consecutive nights," explaining this endurance as the result of his being "scrupulously temperate" and "exceedingly frugal in his diet."[10] Unlike Fennell, Cooke, Kean, or the Booths, he never drank to excess and was renowned for his dependability. In regular commuting between New York and Philadelphia, he failed only twice to keep his engagements, because of weather, and in one case risked his life to get to Philadelphia by paying a pilot boat to attempt to cross the North River for Jersey City when it was icebound.[11]

Cooper's family was not as strong as he was. Joanna bore him two more children, but both died in infancy; only young Thomas survived. Then Joanna herself became ill with pulmonary consumption and died on January 9, 1808.[12] She was buried in the churchyard of Trinity Church; the marker still stands.

We have only a brief personal glimpse of Joanna in the summer before the 1806–7 season, when she was assisting her husband by serving as companion to the pretty and petite British actress Julia Jones. Cooper was trying to spirit Mrs. Jones off to play with him in the south, getting her away from Robert Treat Paine, who was trying to rehire her for the Boston manager, Snelling Powell. Dunlap said that although Joanna was polite to her, she was dissatisfied to accompany her, since she had it that Mrs. Jones was the mistress of William Coleman, editor of the *Evening Post*.[13]

Neither Cooper nor Joanna left any personal record of their marriage. Two of his professional contemporaries made statements about it but with no corroborating details. Durang said, "Mr. Cooper married in early life a lady of this country, which proved a very unhappy union."[14] Noah Miller Ludlow, the southern manager with whom Cooper became involved later, made a similar comment.[15] Certainly, Joanna's illness in the face of Cooper's driving theatrical career must have given the couple a great deal of difficulty and sadness.

The Park Theatre was darkened for one night of mourning prior to the beginning of a winter break. During the interim Cooper had to fulfill an engagement in Boston, where he was scheduled to make a joint appearance with Fennell. William Clapp said that their performance together proved to be "one of the most exciting on record, and created the greatest enthusiasm not only in this city, but throughout the country." When they alternated the parts of Iago and Othello in two performances of *Othello*, Robert Treat Paine said, "'In the part of *Iago* our unequivocal preference went along with Mr. Cooper, *per totum agmen*. In the conduct of the scenes his subtle honesty to *Othello*, his imposing assurance to *Roderigo*, and his deadly malignity in soliloquy, were more deeply imbued with discrimination, 'form and pressure.' The colors were applied with a bolder pencil, and the lines were traced with a stronger character. Nature has denied to Mr. Fennell the use of such powerful means, as Mr. Cooper can employ prodigally, without exhausting them. In the economy of the stage art and situation, Mr. Cooper was wonderfully superior. Yet, if we drop the curtain, and consider the exhibition as a mere didactic exercise of recitation, Mr. Fennell does not halt behind his antagonist.'"[16]

After successfully completing the Boston run, Cooper returned to New York. He reopened the Park Theatre on February 29, playing Charles Surface in Sheridan's *The School for Scandal*. He also began preparations for the culmination of the season to present the spectacle of *Cinderella*, designed by Holland. Promoting the theatre in his *Salmagundi*, Washington Irving made much amusement about the plans for the extravaganza: "Several expert rat-catchers have been sent into different parts of the country to catch white mice for the grand pantomime of CINDERELLA.... Great pains and expense have been incurred in the importation of one of the most portly pumpkins in New-England; and the publick may be assured there is now one on board a vessel from New-Haven, which will contain Cinderella's coach and six with perfect ease, were the white mice even ten times as large."[17]

During the rehearsal period for *Cinderella* the orchestra members became noticeably delinquent, so Cooper began a policy of deducting pay for absences. However, on the first of April, opening night, a large audience had already assembled when the conductor, James Hewitt, was informed that none of his musicians would perform unless all the money they had forfeited during rehearsals was returned to them first. Hewitt rushed to report the state of affairs to Cooper, but Cooper simply asked him if he could play the music himself. Hewitt assured him he could, having practiced it for the past three weeks. Straightway Cooper went onstage to inform the audience of the situation, offering them refunds on their tickets or the continuation of the performance to the accompaniment of a single violin. The audience had come to see the show and quickly accepted the violin. In an interim of a few days Cooper hired new musicians for the production, which ran for thirteen nights.[18]

In the summer of 1808 Cooper arranged for Stephen Price to buy a share of his interest in the Park Theatre and become his co-manager. This was an excellent move for the long-term interest of the theatre. Price was not an actor, nor was he a playwright — he was a well-known businessman who had graduated from Columbia College and practiced law. "King Stephen," as Washington Irving dubbed him, was the first professional theatre manager in America and would have a long career both at the Park and in England, where he managed Drury Lane for a time.

Taking over the finances of the theatre, Price relieved Cooper of much of the burden of management, not always to the good pleasure of the actors. In his memoir, giving a generally favorable view of the managers under whom he had worked, James Fennell recalled, "One solitary instance of what I thought injustice occurred on the part of Mr. Price, of Newyork"; going on to say, "had Cooper engaged me I should have had no cause of complaint, but he was absent."[19] Durang also said of Cooper, "All his instincts were those of a man of principle. His benevolence was expansive and silent in action: his truth undoubted."[20]

It was at this time that Cooper met Mary Fairlie, a friend of Washington Irving's. Nineteen years old, Mary was a celebrated young belle and wit of New York society. Irving exchanged long letters of gossip with her and sketched her in his *Salmagundi* as "miss SOPHY SPARKLE, a young lady unrivalled for playful wit and innocent vivacity, and who, like a brilliant, adds lustre to the front of fashion."[21] Mary's father, Major James Fairlie, had been aide-de-camp to Baron Von Steuben during the Revolution. A noted wit himself, he had distinguished himself among his fellow officers by causing their dignified Commander-in-Chief to laugh out loud. Washington Irving said that "at the return of peace," George Washington was sailing a boat on the Hudson when he "was so overcome by the drollery of a story told by Major Fairlie of New York, of facetious memory, that he fell back in the boat in a paroxysm of laughter."[22] Mary's mother, Maria Yates, was the daughter of the Chief Justice of the Supreme Court of New York and descended on her mother's side from one of the oldest Dutch families in New York, the Van Nesses.

In a letter Irving wrote to his friend Joseph Gratz in Philadelphia, after returning from that city with Cooper,—"having experienced several minutes' delay on the road, to the great annoyance of Cooper, who travels watch in hand[,]"—he described "a sort of crazy party at Mary Fairlie's, where we went to take tea in a sociable humdrum manner, but scarcely a dozen of us had assembled together before a fiddler made his appearance. Had it been the D----l himself (not meaning to speak irreligiously) he could not have thrown us in a greater uproar. In a word there was dancing and romping and playing the fool until one o'clock, to the great discomposure of my gravity and decorum."[23] The following season in a letter to another friend, Irving spoke of Cooper's "laying close siege to Mary" but predicted that he could never win her.[24]

The event of the first Cooper-Price season, 1808–09, was the stage debut of Master John Howard Payne, already noted for his periodical, *Thespian Mirror*. Still a boy of sixteen at the time, Payne was small for his age and according to Dunlap, looked even younger.[25] On October 4 he wrote his father about a disappointing audition he had had with

Cooper: "'Mr. Cooper, whose opinion I have asked, and before whom I have recited Anthony's oration and Brutus and Cassius' conversation respecting Julius Caesar, without pointing out a single fault, discourages me entirely. He says that after infinite study and labor I may possibly succeed—*as a youth*. Opposed to this, I have the favorable judgment of all others who have heard me; and if a determination is to rest on the opinion of any individual, I should refer it to Mr. Fennel [*sic*].'"[26]

The young Payne is reminiscent of the sixteen-year-old Cooper, who had approached Stephen Kemble so boldly not many years before at Edinburgh. On February 24 he was presented to the public at the Park Theatre as Young Norval in *Douglas*. As self-willed as Cooper, but surrounded by family and well-wishers, at first he had an easier time than Cooper. William Wood recalled that on returning to America from a trip to England in October 1809 he found Payne "in the full tide of popular favor at Baltimore,"—One gentleman paid a check for fifty dollars for a single ticket to see Payne perform, in addition to a liberal sum for a box to accommodate his family.[27]

Soon, however, as biographer Gabriel Harrison explains, Payne's "vanity" got him in trouble: "The boy was flattered beyond judicious limits. No one bade him beware of vanity, and vanity became one of the elements of his character throughout his life. Therefore it made no matter how well Mr. Payne may have been treated, or how highly his talents were appreciated, he always seemed to think and act as if he was not receiving his full deserts." He cites the example of the boy's rudeness to Stephen Price, who had loaned him Cooper's costumes "to set him off" at his debut, saying, "His arrogance toward that venerable manager upset all prospects of success in this country[.]"[28]

On tour Payne also acted in Philadelphia, Richmond, and Charleston, but thereafter, finding himself shut out of New York, went off to England. He enjoyed some success abroad, but soon gave up the stage in favor of his literary career. Best known as the author of the song "Home, Sweet Home!" he also wrote a play, *Brutus; or, The Fall of Tarquin*, in which Cooper appeared at the Park and on tour to great success.

In Philadelphia in 1810 Stephen Cullen Carpenter, earlier associated with Charleston, began a new journal, the *Mirror of Taste and Dramatic Censor*. In his opening issue in January he published a seventeen-page biography of Cooper with an engraving of his portrait as Hamlet painted by Sully. This, like similar first-issue coverage by Payne in the *Thespian Mirror*, and Buckingham in *The Polyanthos*, illustrates the initial impetus which Cooper's appearances provided to the incipient artistic and literary scene in the new nation.

Carpenter also wrote a series of reviews of Cooper's appearances that season. His Macbeth, he said, "takes the lead of all the actors that have ever appeared in this country; and is in our judgement preferable, in many parts, to either Kemble or Cooke; far, very far, superior to Holman."[29] Of his Mark Antony in Shakespeare's *Julius Caesar*, he remarked that while uneven, in Act 3, scene 1, "We have never seen any thing in histrionic excellence to surpass, few to equal it."—

We mean when ... after the assassination of Caesar, he returned to the senate house, and, dropping on one knee, hung over the mangled body: his attitude surpassed all powers of description. Then when after gazing for a time in horror at the corpse, with his hands clasped in speechless agony, he looked to heaven, as if appealing to its justice, and again turning to his murdered friend, exclaimed—

Oh mighty Caesar!—
 —Dost thou lie so low?
Are all thy conquests, glories, triumphs, spoils
Shrunk to this little measure?—Fare thee well.

All the conflicting passions, and excruciating feelings which Antony can be supposed to have felt on that awful occasion—astonishment, fear, suspicion, grief, tender affection, indignation, and horror seem rising in tumultuous confusion in his face, and glared and flashed in his eyes.

Mr. Cooper as Hamlet. From an engraving by Edwin, after a work by Thomas Sully. Reproduced for the first issue of *Mirror of Taste and Dramatic Censor* 1: 1 (January, 1810). Harvard Theatre Collection, Houghton Library.

And in "the speech in which he shakes the conspirators by their bloody hands, and, like a consummate, artful politician, postpones the indulgence of his grief and indignation for the accomplishment of a higher purpose," he commented, "he was not excelled by Barry himself [Spranger Barry, famous Irish actor in eighteenth-century London]."[30]

That season one theatre-goer wrote a letter to the editor of the *Mirror of Taste* descrying the unruly behavior of the audience on two separate occasions when he went to see Cooper perform:

> The manager, or the magistrates, or somebody is greatly to blame about the playhouse. I brought my family to the pit to see that great actor, Cooper, play Zanga [Edward Young, *The Revenge*, 1721]. We sat in the pit the whole time the blackguards were throwing down scraps of apples, nutshells in handfulls, and what is worse something I can't well name — some about me said that brandy or strong grog was thrown down. It might be so once. —but it was not exactly that which fell on me and my family. Since then, I went to see him in *Macbeth,* and left my wife and daughter at home for fear; and the fellows above were as bad as before — and had I not luckily kept my hat on I should once have got my head broke with a hard heavy hickory-nut that was thrown with all the force and spitefulness as if the person wanted to hurt somebody very severely.... On the night the *Revenge* was performed, even while Mr. Cooper was engaged in a most interesting scene, a boy, not in mean clothes either, stood up at the front corner of the gallery, roaring out and speaking as loud as he could to some one on the opposite side. Yet this, were it not for the time it happened, was to the surrounding tumult, as a dying sigh to the roar of a northwester.[31]

At the end of his sketch on Cooper Carpenter noted that he was "one of the most dutiful and generous of sons to an amiable mother, whose old age he cheers with punctual bounty, and by the most constant and pious filial reverence and affection." He also mentioned Cooper's sister, "a lady of high personal endowments and great goodness. She was early married to Mr. Perreau of Calcutta, a gentleman who stands as high in the opinion of the world as any man in India."[32] In late spring it was announced that Cooper would make another trip to England. It was generally assumed that he was going in order to recruit actors for the Park; but there was a private reason for the trip—his mother, Grace Mary Cooper, had died on March 21. Godwin recorded going to her home both the day before and the day after her death and attending her funeral on the 25th.[33]

"This Glorious Son of York"—1810

Whatever his purpose, as it turned out, it was on this second return to England, in 1810, that Cooper made his most dramatic and influential move as a manager. Meeting George Frederick Cooke again, by arduous pursuit he persuaded the famous British actor to make an American tour.

Again, Dunlap, though sometimes inaccurate or fanciful, tells the basic story of Cooper's adventure in capturing Cooke for the American market.[34] According to Dunlap, in crossing the Atlantic he stopped in Ireland before going on to Liverpool, arriving there on July 7. Dunlap said that when he got off the ship, he read in a Liverpool newspaper that Cooke was to act Richard the Third at the Theatre Royal there that evening, so he went to see him, going backstage after the performance to renew his acquaintance with the great actor. Dunlap is likely in error about the timing of this meeting, since, as Cooke biographer Don Wilmeth documents, Cooke did not appear for a summer engagement in Liverpool until July 24.[35]

It is also likely that upon his arrival in England, Cooper first went to London to see his family, going on to Liverpool later in the month. When he did go backstage there to see Cooke, at first Cooke could not place him, but after Cooper reminded him of the times they had spent in each other's company in 1803, Cooke recollected the younger man and went on to inquire of him what he was doing in England. Cooper explained that he was on his way to tour the Continent and see Paris for the first time, but while he was in England was planning to engage English actors for the American theatre.

During that backstage meeting in Liverpool, Cooke voiced his dissatisfaction with his situation in England. In the fall of 1808 Covent Garden had burned down, and during the following summer Kemble had seen to the building of a large, pretentious new building modeled after the Temple of Minerva in Athens. In this structure the size of the popular galleries was reduced to accommodate twenty-six private boxes, and to add to the insult, the backstairs to the boxes enabled the entry of prostitutes, which outraged the public morality. With the necessary increase in ticket prices for the pit and box, the hiring of a popular foreign singer, Madame Catalani, at seventy-five pounds a night, focused the public ire. A class war brewed, harking back to the hostility engendered by the Licensing Act of 1737. London had always been a theatre-going town, and it was that law, now completely outmoded, that had restricted all legitimate drama to the two patent houses, effectively monopolizing theatrical activity.

On the opening night of the new house, with a production of *Macbeth*, a mob stormed in to claim the seats. When Kemble opened his mouth to begin, they set up a clamor. Hoots, cat-calls, and demands for the old ticket prices drowned out all of the actors' words throughout the performance. Each night the riots continued, and on the sixth night a ludicrous O. P. dance developed; audience members shouted out "O. P." and then ceremoniously pounded the floor with feet or sticks. The "Old Price Riots" became a *cause célèbre* throughout London, continuing for upward of two months. Scribbled on walls and shouted by newsboys, "O. P." appeared on a medal, on caps, fans, handkerchiefs, and waistcoats. Ultimately Kemble, who was the center of the attack, had to capitulate completely and reinstate the old prices.[36]

During the riots, Cooke remained in public favor himself, although all performances were disrupted, and unlike some of the other actors, he supported Kemble. Right after the settlement, however, he appeared onstage drunk, and on another evening failed to appear at all. With this, the public and press turned on him with vicious attacks, and while he got through most of the rest of the season, he failed to appear for scheduled performances in early June.

Cooper had to leave for London the day after his meeting with Cooke, but in response to the interest he had expressed during the course of their conversation, told him he would consider the possibility of arranging a tour for him to America and would talk it over with James H. Dickinson, the Boston manager, who was currently in London. As a result, on August 5, he wrote Cooke a letter from London offering him an engagement to act at New York, Boston, Philadelphia, and Baltimore, for ten months, at a salary of twenty-five guineas a week, twenty-five cents a mile for travel, plus benefits in each city, and his transatlantic passage fare as well.

Cooper received no answer from Cooke, who had apparently walked out on an acting engagement at the town of Preston, by-passed his commitments to act at Cheltenham and Hereford, and "buried himself" at Blackpool, a little town on the Irish Sea. Their next encounter took Cooper by surprise. He himself had an engagement of twenty performances at the Theatre Royal in Liverpool,[37] and on September 10 when he went offstage during a performance of *Richard the Third*, the stage door was opened for him by the enigmatic Cooke, who had been watching from backstage. They parted after the performance with no talk of any consequence, but the visit, continuing their friendship, would have raised the spectre of the American offer.

Cooke remained in Liverpool at a small tavern behind the theatre, tempting death with violent spasms from drinking, and wasting his money on a group of low-life theatrical companions. Every day a post-chaise was on order to take him back to London, but day after day he found it inconvenient to depart. A fellow actor at Covent Garden, Joseph Munden, who was in Liverpool recovering from a bad case of gout, had promised their manager, Harris, that he would try to accompany Cooke back to London personally to ensure his return. On an appointed day, October 2, Munden "hobbled" to Cooke's room, where he found Cooke dressed, but sitting by an empty brandy bottle unwilling to budge. Munden finally "left him 'alone in his glory.'" In his *Memoirs* he blamed Cooke for his "accomplished hypocrisy" and "the villainy of his conduct" toward Harris.[38]

Seeing Cooke's situation, with the interest he had indicated, Cooper was more than ever determined to make arrangements to get him to try his luck in America. Wary of approaching him directly in Liverpool, where the citizens were well aware of the famous star's presence, instead he set a man to watch him and report if he actually decided to take off for London. Several days passed, until one evening Cooper's man hurried up to him at a dinner he was giving for some friends, giving him the startling report that Cooke had suddenly decided to take the chaise and was at that moment posting toward London.

Cooper no sooner got the news than he took quick leave of his guests and rode off on horseback to overtake the post-chaise. His athletic dashes between Philadelphia and New York stood him in good stead, and he was able to catch up with it when it halted to let Cooke out to offer an elderly lady a ride. At that point Cooper rode up and asked Cooke why he had not replied to the offer he had sent him and if he had changed his mind about wanting to go to America. Cooke replied that he had expected to see Cooper, but that Cooper was always on horseback or in a post-chaise: "'here to-day, there to-morrow, and next day no one knows where. One might as well try to catch Will-o'-the-wisp; you may be seen, but its always moving.'" Then he affirmed, "'I have no engagement, and only wish to go up to London to settle some business, play one night for them, then bid a long adieu to Black Jack [John Kemble] and all the rest of them.'"

Cooper knew that if Cooke went back to London, he would never get away. He therefore emphasized to his prospective catch that if he wanted to go to America, he should not go back to London at all. Through a long series of unnerving encounters, he finally got him in the coach heading for London, but shortly had it turn around to speed back toward Liverpool. However, he also knew that if he went back into the town of Liverpool, the people there would prevent Cooke's departure for America as well. So he planned to presume on the hospitality of a casual friend, Mr. Tawbuck, who lived five miles out of Liverpool, to board Cooke for a day or two until a ship's passage was available, persuading him to stop there by assuring him that Tawbuck had an excellent stock of Madeira. Cooke finally agreed and was soon in a state of senseless inebriation, ordering Tawbuck around under the illusion that he was an innkeeper.

The next morning Cooper made a trip into Liverpool to arrange Cooke's transatlantic passage and buy some items necessary for his comfort aboard ship. Coming back and seeing him sober after a sound night's sleep, he asked him to affirm in Tawbuck's presence that he had no contract or debts in England and that it was his own decision to go to America, which Dunlap said Cooke willingly reiterated. In keeping with the feverish confusion of the whole project, at the last minute, the captain of the ship, which was scheduled to depart at two o'clock on October 4, sent word that because of a favorable wind, he would push off anchor three hours early. Cooper managed to rouse Cooke from bed, hire a coach and four, and speed him off just in time to board the *Columbia* before it got under way. The adventure was not complete without a customs officer who said Cooke lacked the proper papers. After some altercation, on the captain's advice Cooke offered the officer money, which he was easily persuaded to accept in place of a passport.

On the first day or so at sea Cooke drank brandy in such large quantities that he became violently ill. In that state he fought the captain, cursed Cooper, and wailed over the loss of his "dear native land." But when he finally recovered, the ship's supply of hard liquor had all been drunk up by the other passengers, so he had to be content with Essence of Lemon, which Cooper had wittingly provided for him. After more than six weeks at sea, with only the plain food of the ship for his diet, Cooke arrived in New York in better health than he had enjoyed for years.

When the news of Cooke's secret departure got out in England, it caused a furor. The newspapers published the story, together with the accusation that Cooper had abducted Cooke. To answer the complaints against him, from Liverpool on October 7 Cooper wrote a cordial letter of denial to the London papers, asserting that he had been negotiating a contract with Cooke since about August 6, "completed on the 3rd inst in the moment of perfect sobriety, and entire understanding of all the arrangements." The letter appeared in the *Monthly Mirror*, together with a reprint of a letter Cooke had written to Harris Sunday, September 30, to assure the manager he and Munden had booked their return to London on the following Tuesday morning's coach. The reporter concluded: "The writers are worthy of *any part of America!* Mr. Cooke was engaged to Mr. Harris, and owed him eight hundred pounds. All this Mr. Cooper knew as well as Mr. Cooke, and—and—but they are both transported, and let justice be satisfied."[39]

Both contemporaries and theatre scholars have pored over and debated the various accounts and details of Cooper's *coup de théâtre* in hiring Cooke for America. Opinions differ about how much Cooke did or did not have to drink at the chief points in question; where he had it; when Cooper conceived the idea, before or after he went to England; who was guilty. Biographer Arnold Hare points out that Cooke was habitually inclined to escape difficulty, and deduces that with his health weakened and his second marriage failed, the idea of touring America had appealed to him.[40] Dunlap, saying his account "was narrated by Mr. Cooper with an air of frankness, which, together with his character, leaves no doubt upon the mind of the writer[,]" asserted, "That Mr. Cooke was engaged to Mr. Harris at the time he embarked for America, is certain; but it is equally certain, that Mr. Cooper did not know of such engagement. Mr. Cooke, at the time, declared himself unengaged and perfectly free, and persisted in the assertion after his arrival in America. I speak of my own knowledge."[41]

Cooke indeed had some sort of contract with Harris. As Don Wilmeth documents in his account, engagements for Cooke, on September 15 and 29, and one for October 6, are on the Covent Garden salary lists;[42] so before he ever left England he had violated his contract by failing to appear. If Cooper did not know this, he made little attempt to find it out, particularly in view of Cooke's obvious reluctance to return to London. If he did know it, his own long-time attitude toward the London management would have offered him a degree of self-justification—after all, his own associations had been with the radicals in London, and his close friends had suffered unfair reprisals and repression.

One evening in Philadelphia before Cooper returned from England, Cooke, loose from drink but not intoxicated, told Dunlap that "Cooper had inveigled him into an agreement when he was drunk," but went on to admit "that he was drunk tho' not entirely so when he went on board ship, that he would have return'd to be sure but he was ashamed to return after having gone so far."[43] What is certain is that Cooke was flawed and Cooper knew it, as he had written Godwin as early as 1800. In London he had shamed himself onstage by appearing under the influence of alcohol on notable occasions for which he had been thoroughly excoriated in the press. When Cooper came upon him he was licking his wounds and absorbing himself in brandy. Cooke was thus vulnerable to Cooper's lure, and Cooper undoubtedly felt he was fair game. Observing that Cooke arrived in America "minus a wardrobe" and on fairly loose terms of contract, Charles Durang concluded that Cooper most probably used strong persuasion on Cooke but congratulated him on his "Yankee ingenuity and cleverness of business talent."[44]

Dunlap said that when Stephen Price heard from Cooper in England that Cooke was on the sea bound for New York, he exulted "again and again" with Richard the Third's opening words, "' Now is the winter of our discontent made glorious summer by this son of York[.]'"[45] Without Cooper the Park Theatre season was lagging badly. In September Price had called in William Wood for a starring engagement, and Fennell was booked for six nights but got sick during the course of the short engagement. On Wednesday, November 21, Cooke made his American debut as Richard the Third and was received with wild acclaim. Twenty-two hundred people crushed into the theatre that night to see the famous actor from England; the receipts were $1,820.[46]

"A Hearty Welcome"—1811–12

Meanwhile Cooper made his first trip to Paris. Luck was with him! As legend has it, it was in Paris, presumably on this trip, that he played a card game for unusually high stakes "with a stranger from Philadelphia" and won a house on the banks of the Delaware River in Bristol, Pennsylvania.[47] The last week of January he wrote back to a friend in England, "I shall very soon leave England earlier by far than I expected. Cooke is doing wonders in New York."[48] On February 6 he departed Brussels to meet his ship at Portsmouth to return to America.

Aboard the *Magdelen* he wrote back to Godwin: "[S]hould I have it in my power, by any means that occur to me or that you may suggest to advance your interest here you will oblige me by commanding my services. You will not expect to derive much information or amusement from my letters, particularly from one written in the midst of salt beef with coarse biscuit, & surrounded with filth & discontent, so will not meet with disappointment in reading this struggling scrawl."[49] March 22 he arrived in New York, where the large receipts from Cooke's performances enabled him to send an advance check of a hundred pounds sterling to Godwin, with the good news, "Cooke is doing wonders he is at present playing at Philadelphia—I play here Monday night & expect to receive a hearty welcome from my fellow citizens. Your son, Thos. A. Cooper."[50]

Monday night, April 8, 1811, Cooper opened at the Park Theatre as Hamlet. The receipts, which totaled $1,270,[51] indicate that the welcome was indeed "hearty." The next evening he played Macbeth. In the bloom of success, now that he was back from Europe, he began to pursue Mary Fairlie in earnest. When Washington Irving saw his intention, Irving, who had introduced him to Mary, revealed some latent prejudice toward his theatrical pal, as well as a bit of jealousy. He wrote to his friend Henry Brevoort, "Among the other turtles who were pairing at this convocation was old Satan and Mary Fairlie. It would have amused you to see Cooper playing softness and suavity."[52]

While Cooper was still in England, incensed by the Americans' habit of comparing his performances to Cooper's, Cooke had poured out a steady flow of insulting remarks about him to Dunlap: "'I'll show these fellows what acting is, they talk of their Cooper their Idol, their Wooden God. Haven't I stood the trial with John. What is your Cooper?'"[53] At the end of his New York engagement, however, playing Cato in Addison's play for his benefit, Cooke had gone onstage drunk and totally unrehearsed. He had proceeded to halt, repeat, use speeches from other plays, as well as invent incoherent phrases. It was a performance to put all of Cooper's failures in the shade, and he would never completely recover the New York public.

In March, accompanied by Dunlap, Cooke had gone on loan to Warren and Wood to play for twenty nights at the Chestnut Street Theatre. People in Philadelphia stood in line all night to get seats to see the famous actor from England. Much scuffling for tickets led to near riots, and in the morning people blocked up the stage door on Carpenter Street to see Cooke's coach arrive for rehearsals. The receipts for the engagement amounted to $8,809.16.[54]

When Cooke heard that Cooper had returned to America and was making his reappearance on the stage in New York, he began to reproach him bitterly. At that point Cooper's scene designer, Mr. Holland, made a trip to Philadelphia and reported to Dunlap in private that Cooper said "he dreads to meet Cooke—justifies Prices [sic] system of treating him*— that Harris, Kemble &c were incensed to a great degree at him for sending Cooke away & repuls'd all attempts at explanation. That Cooper is conscious of using undue means to get him off—rails at him as an old worthless drunkard—says he would not undergo again for *any sum* what he did for that purpose."[55]

It was on April 20 that Cooper made the trip to Philadelphia to join Cooke. That evening when he went backstage to pay his respects to the British star, Dunlap said that Cooke was "first a little strange but soon got over it."[56] That evening over supper he agreed to extend the Philadephia

---

*Price invited Cooke to stay in his home, but confined him to his room when he got drunk.

engagement four more nights to play with Cooper, and Dunlap pointedly noticed, "[t]wo days previous to playing with Mr. Cooper, and during the whole time of their playing together, Mr. Cooke was as perfectly abstemious as any man living. In vain is his beloved port wine set before him, ... To keep himself in order to play in his best style by the side of Mr. Cooper, was a motive sufficient at this time to counteract all those falsely called *irresistible* propensities[.]"[57] In Philadelphia Cooper played Othello to Cooke's Iago, Beverly to his Stukely in *The Gamester*, and Jaffier to his Pierre in *Venice Preserv'd*.

In describing their joint *Othello*, Durang observed of Cooke's style that he "made no gesticulations, but elicited all his acting through the expression of the face. He often made a thrilling point without seeking to do so. He never, *seemingly*, courted applause, but, like all actors, he sinisterly sought it, and when he got it, he became animated, and was sure to improve upon it by increasing his electrifying strokes. He kept close to quietness and whispers—in these traits his merits consisted, and all was accomplished without any apparent effort."

Of Cooper's performance he remarked: "Mr. Cooper's peculiar qualities were most happily adjusted for the Moor. He had figure, voice and graceful action. He infused into the part all that *orientalism* of character, which the poet of Avon has so richly clothed with similar sentiment of beauteous poetry. He entered into the grandeur of *Othello*—his expression—his

George Frederick Cooke as Iago. Large mezzotint engraving by G. Ward, after a painting by James Green, 1801. The Hampden-Booth Theatre Library, The Players, NYC.

soul, with the most perfect *abandon*. It may be said, at this time, Cooper's *Othello* was a perfect performance."

Then he explained how Cooper's characterization was brilliantly offset by Cooke's subtle counterpoint: "Cooke's *Iago* was a continual reaction of quiet, yet vigorous points—vigorous, not from any overcharged acting, but from the unique expression of the passions, so well, so powerfully delineated in the features, and the excellent emphasis in his readings, with his modulation of voice. There was no effort; there seemed no acting; yet the performance was the most elaborate effort of art. It looked like nature—but it was nature directed by the most skilful playing. It was the philosophy of acting."—

> When Cooper would roll off one of his fine speeches, with all the charms of musical combination, and the audience was on the point to "applaud it to the very echo, which should applaud again," Cooke, with one of his intensely powerful looks, and half lines in reply, would, like a flash, turn the whole intended plaudits from *Othello* upon himself. He filched the plaudits from Cooper, the audience so felt; but Cooke's powers impelled the diversion in his favor, toppling Cooper in an *instant* from his towering height to an oblivious position, with only the sympathies of his audience.

In playing with Cooke, Cooper relished both the challenge and the profits, not hoarding these either, spending the money while advancing the way. Durang said, "Mr. Cooper regretted not having played more counter-parts to Cooke. But, the difficulty was to select a play where two such equal characters could be obtained, as Cooke was very confined in his great efforts."[58] Cooke was a supreme artist, but by this time his acting was confined to a handful of roles. In those in which his brilliance shone, some said he exceeded even Garrick and Macklin, but at fifty-three years of age he was dissipated and notoriously unreliable. Cooper on the other hand, in the prime of life, continued to play the whole range of tragic and comic roles, and in years hence would have new roles and successes, extending himself to further venues.

Despite Cooke's misgivings with regard to his recent failure in New York, Cooper succeeded in getting him to return with him to appear together there as well. On May 8 in New York they acted *Othello*. This was Cooke's first appearance on the New York stage as Iago, and the receipts to the house were $1,620.[59] Cooper neither begrudged Cooke the attention he received, nor feared the comparison. When played by a star, Iago is in fact a better part than that of Othello, the heroic Moor tricked into jealousy over the matter of a handkerchief. Only recently Cooper had won the critical notice in Boston for his Iago rather than his accustomed role of Othello, and his popularity was not diminished by Cooke's appearance. However, the advent of Cooke afforded the American public the chance to gain a degree of perspective in their assessment of Cooper's acting.

Cooke had intended to return to England after completing his ten-month contract with Cooper. Fate held him, however, for in June of 1811 he took a third wife, Mrs. Violet Mary Behn, the daughter of the proprietor of the Tontine Coffee House. Built on Wall Street by stockbrokers, this public house served as a marketplace for ships, slaves, and real estate, and Cooke had boarded there soon after his arrival in New York.

Independent of Cooper, Cooke continued to make starring appearances the following season. The day after Christmas a terrible fire burned down the Richmond Theatre, killing 71 people; it had been held open in the hope that Cooke would appear there, but he had decided to go to Boston instead. The well-known Virginia congressman, John Randolph of Roanoke, wrote Cooper a letter from Washington referring to the disaster, which caused a drop-off in theatre attendance in all the cities: "Could you promise me the pleasure of seeing you this winter in this vast and desolate city, as it is the whim to call it, it would very much enhance the gratification which your letters never fail to afford. I should like, too, to hear some intelligence of your theatrical campaign—of the future doing of Mr. Cooke ... a great part of my inducement to visit New York is now taken away: for, after the late dreadful occurrence at Richmond, I should hardly be able to look on any theatrical spectacle with pleasure."[60]

In the spring of 1812 Cooper produced a new play, *Marmion*, a dramatization of Sir Walter Scott's poem of that name [1808] by an American, James Nelson Barker. With the author's concurrence he had announced it as British to counteract the ludicrous snobbery in the New York audience toward American plays, a prejudice which helps explain Cooke's wild success when he was first advertised in America.

That spring was the end of Cooke's second season in America, and expecting to sign a renewal contract with Harris at Covent Garden, he had booked his return passage to England for June 5. However, the imminence of war with Britain caused an embargo which prevented his departure; war between the United States and Britain was formally declared on the eighteenth. During the ensuing conflict *Marmion* was often repeated. Durang said, "The injuries which *King James* recites to England's ambassador, *Lord Marmion*, in the 4th act, as received by Scotland from his country, assimilated so closely to those received by the United States, that the scene was always unboundedly applauded."[61]

Increasingly infirm, Cooke died in New York on September 26, 1812, at the age of sixty-seven. He was buried in the Strangers' Vault at St. Paul's Chapel, a short walk from the Park Theatre. In an elaborate two-step, Cooper had gone to Drury Lane to take Kemble's place in 1803, had met Cooke and acted with him; and in 1810 had appeared again, right after the Old Price Riots had humbled Kemble, spiriting Cooke away to the New World, the most famous actor who had ever played there. For Cooke's part, his acclaimed tour of America proved to be the crowning stroke of a long career in the theatre; the natural style of acting he carried forward from Garrick, well-suited to the new society in the new century. Cooper had thus extended the pattern of starring he was developing in the far-flung young country and completed the transplantation of the British theatrical tradition to American soil.

Fourteen

The American Roscius— 1812–19

In the spring of 1812 Cooper moved up Broadway to number 350. Good friends as well as partners, he and Stephen Price established themselves in elegant adjoining houses on "Park Row," at the northeast corner of Broadway and Leonard Street. The young literary set, Washington and Peter Irving, Henry Brevoort, James Kirk Paulding, Henry Ogden, lounged about the Park green room when they were in town, and the managers entertained at home with lavish dinners replete with wine, wit, and gambling. Making more money than any actor before him, Cooper maintained a cavalier demeanor. One day, seeing a cartload of hay on Broadway, he bet Price the proceeds of his upcoming benefit that he could pull the longer straw; when Price won and the benefit cleared $1,200, he summed it carelessly: "'I've lost two hours' acting.'"[1]

Past Park Square, down at 41 Cortlandt Street, the Fairlie mansion was a gathering place for the fashionable world, the Livingstons, the Hoffmans, Gouverneur Morris, who had replaced Jefferson as American Ambassador to France; where such distinguished foreigners as the French diplomat Talleyrand, and Joseph Bonaparte, once King of Spain, were also frequent visitors.[2] Major Fairlie's friend John Pintard later wrote a characteristically dour letter to his daughter Eliza Davidson recalling Fairlie's wife Maria. In a description reminiscent of contemporary London society, he said that in its heyday before the steamboat she "reigned Queen of Rockaway," the stylish Long Island beach resort, "at the head of a very dissipated, drinking, gambling circle composed of commedians & bon vivants[,]" adding, "I was often invited to go on Sat^y to carouse all Sunday, but had resolution to decline."[3]

The great lady had been delighted to entertain Cooper, New York's star, at tea or whatever, but she made it no secret that she and her husband did not approve of his interest in their daughter. They considered it unspeakable that he would propose marriage to Mary. Not only was he an actor, he was also a widower some thirteen years older than she was. In truth, Maria Fairlie was not inclined to think anyone deserving to marry into her family, and she had too powerful a personality not to impose her will. Neither of her two sons ever married and only two of her three daughters. At twenty-three, Mary, "[t]he elegant, the sylph-like, the all-admired[,]"[4] married the thirty-six-year-old Cooper anyway, and Maria Fairlie never forgave either one of them.

Even Cooper's intimates looked askance at the marriage, which opened a door to society generally closed to his profession. Irving does not seem to have been romantically attached to Mary, but he was an ardent admirer and life-long friend of "the fascinating Fairlie," as he designated her. After the wedding, which was on June 11, 1812, he wrote to Brevoort: "The marriage has at last taken place between Mary F_____ and Cooper. They were married at his new house—Neither Mr. nor Mrs. F were present, nor any one excepting King Stephen [Price] and his spouse—after the ceremony was performed Cooper attended her home and left her—and two or three days after they set off for Baltimore.... The old Major was worried into a kind of half consent. That is to say, if the girl could not be happy without it, why, he supposed it must take place. Cooper has been applying for a Lieut Colonelcy or a Majority in the army; but I believe has not succeeded. I was told yesterday that they had returned home again. Such is the end of a dismal courtship and the commencement I fear of an unhappy union."[5]

Cooper took his bride to "Carolina" for a honeymoon,[6] probably enjoying the opportunity to introduce her to his friends in Charleston. On their return to New York, the couple settled down in time to prepare for the upcoming theatre season. Cooper's own frequent and widespread activity as an itinerant star, plus the appearance of Cooke, had made the public insatiable for stars. He had written John Philip Kemble in December offering him $5,000 pounds sterling for a year to play in Boston, New York, Philadelphia, and Baltimore.[7] In the process of concluding the negotiation, however, the war came, and Kemble declined to cross the Atlantic. Cooper and Price had to be content with Joseph George Holman instead, with whom they had also been in correspondence. Holman agreed to come anyway; his career was on the decline in London, so he had more to gain than Kemble by making the trip to America.

Two days after Cooke's death, on September 28, Cooper and Price presented the British star, whom Cooke had replaced at Covent Garden, in his New York debut as Hamlet. On the rise in London when Cooper was struggling in the provinces, Holman had been ideally suited for the

William Dunlap, American, 1766–1839. *Mrs. Thomas A. Cooper*. Oil on canvas, 74 × 62 cm. ©The Cleveland Museum of Art, gift Mrs. J. H. Wade, 1916.997.

part of the young romantic lead. From the time of his arrival in America, however, it was painfully obvious that he was past his prime. His daughter Agnes, who came to play opposite him, in some measure held the New York audience, but by mid-October Cooper found it necessary to add his own name to the bills for most of the Holmans' performances. He acted Pierre in *Venice Preserv'd* to Holman's Jaffier and Miss Holman's Belvidera, Iago to Holman's Othello and Miss Holman's Desdemona.

During the War of 1812 Cooper was totally an American in his sympathies. He even organized a volunteer corps of Park Theatre employees whom he would drill regularly in Park Square.[8] In the late summer when he was in the midst of a performance in the Boston theatre, news came that the U.S.S. *Constitution* under Captain Hull had captured the British frigate *Guerrière* off the Grand Banks of Newfoundland August 19. Elated, Cooper suggested to the manager, Snelling Powell, that he stop the performance to announce the victory. A naturalized citizen himself, Powell agreed, and when the audience heard the news, everyone called for the National Air, which was "repeated again and again amid prolonged applause."[9]

The following season, on September 24, Cooper and Price illuminated the front of the Park Theatre to celebrate the naval victory of Commodore Perry over the British in Lake Erie.[10] Again on October 23 they joined with City-Hall, Tammany Hall, Washington Hall, and others in the neighborhood for a grand illumination for General William Henry Harrison's victory near Detroit.[11] Nevertheless the war hurt American theatre business appreciably. Also, that fall a direct threat to the Park Theatre materialized in the form of a rival company. Some of the actors at the Park had become dissatisfied with the dictatorial nature of Price's management. Price not only controlled the Park Theatre, but also farmed his stars out to the theatres in other cities, and was fast obtaining a monopoly of the whole network of theatre activity; he could set salaries, cast roles, hire and fire at will.

In November the musician Charles Gilfert and Mr. and Mrs. Twaits left the Park to form a separate company, which they called the "Theatrical Commonwealth." Using a space in the circus building at Broadway and Anthony Street, they proceeded to take a number of well-known performers with them, including the Holmans and John Bernard. The result of the rivalry was that neither theatre could attract a sufficient audience night-in-and-night-out to meet costs. Fortunately for the Park, however, Cooper himself out-balanced any single attraction at the rival theatre. The reviewer in the *Columbian* said that not in even one character was Holman a match for Cooper, "whose voice can in fact almost 'with the thunder vie[.]'"[12]

In December, upon the death of Mrs. Twaits, the Commonwealth closed, and in January of 1814, financial difficulty forced the company to migrate to Philadelphia for the spring. Some of them returned to the Park, but Twaits returned to reopen the other theatre, enlarged and refurbished as "the Anthony Street Theatre." He managed to finish out the season there, though sadly, his asthma turned to consumption in the process, and he died shortly afterward, still in his twenties.

Meanwhile, despite Irving's prediction and the difficulties of the theatre business, the Coopers' home life was flourishing, the marriage an extremely happy one. On May 5, 1813, their first child was born, a daughter whom they named Mary Grace, for Cooper's mother. The next year, on September 2, they had a son, James Fairlie, named for Mary's father, who soon began to join the company at Cooper and Price's. In town that fall to perform at the Park, William Warren said on Sunday September 18 he had dinner at Price's, and "in the evening Commodore Decatur—Mr. Cooper and Commodore Lewis came in also Major Fairly [*sic*]."[13]

When Irving and Brevoort were in town they would stay at Mrs. Bradish's boarding house, which produced an amusing Portuguese companion, Dennis Sampayo. Irving wrote to Brevoort, who was with Dennis and the Coopers at Rockaway: "Dennis is full of business He has to bustle out to your sisters—then to Mrs. Coopers then home & then the lord knows where.... He mentioned as a great mark of Mrs. Coopers politeness that she told him on their ride up, 'Dennis, (if) don't be bashful or constrained, if you feel sleepy take a nap whenever you please.' We all assured him that such vast indulgence could only be in consequence of his having made himself wonderfully agreeable.... Dont omit to keep him at his studies of Shakespeare—he hints that Cooper begins to be a little jealous of his dramatic powers."[14]

The following year Irving went abroad. On December 28, 1815, from England, he wrote Brevoort about having seen the new London star, Charles Mayne Young, successor to Kemble at Covent Garden: "I am delighted with Young, who acts with great judgement discrimination & feeling. I think him much the best actor (I have seen) at present on the English stage." Educated at Eton, the son of a stylish London doctor, Young had remained in the provinces until he was thirty. Only a year younger than Cooper, in London he had the career Cooper, also a doctor's son, might have had without the extraordinary fate that molded Cooper.

Irving went on to say, however, that he did not think Young was Cooper's equal as an actor: "I have not seen his [Young's] Macbeth which I should not suppose could equal Coopers. (but) In fact in certain characters, such as may (found classed) be classed with Macbeth, I do not think that Cooper has his equal in England. Young is the only actor I have seen that can be compared with him[.]" He projected, "I cannot help thinking if Cooper had a fair chance, (& would) & the public were to see him in his principal characters, he would take the lead at one of the London theatres." But admitted, "[T]here is so much party work, managerial influence & such a widely spread & elaborate system of falsehood & misrepresentation connected with the London theatres, that a Stranger who is not peculiarly favoured by the managers, or assisted by the prepossessions of the public stands no chance." Then he recalled, "I shall never forget Coopers acting in Macbeth last spring, when he was stimulated to exertion by the presence of a number of British officers. I have seen nothing equal to it in England. Cooper requires excitement, to arouse him from a monotonous, commonplaced manner he is apt to fall into—in consequence of acting so often before indifferent houses. I presume the (return) crowded (theaters) audiences which I am told have filled our theatres this season, must bring him out in full splendour."[15]

As the war drew to a close, Cooper was indeed coming into the most profitable years of his career. In every city he played he could fairly well command his price. On January 30, 1815, he opened a twelve-night engagement in Philadelphia. While he was there, on February 8, Andrew Jackson's forces won the Battle of New Orleans, the crowning American triumph in the capital of the new territory. Once the news reached

Philadelphia, to celebrate the victory and the war's end, the Chestnut Street Theatre was specially illuminated the thirteenth, and Cooper appeared as Alexander the Great.[16]

As starring on the road was becoming increasingly lucrative, national capitalism on the rise, Cooper found himself less and less involved in the management of the Park Theatre. That spring he decided to give up his partnership, which was soon taken up by Edmund Simpson, an acting protégée from England who had served him as stage manager; Simpson would be a popular actor and lessee of the Park for many years.

After a summer of touring Cooper made his reentry to the Park stage in November as Hamlet. In Philadelphia in January he cleared $400 each night of a twelve-night engagement, plus an additional $300 at his benefit.[17] The star made slightly more than the theatre management, but the theatre clearly stood to profit by the star's visit. On June 14, 1816, Mary gave birth to another daughter, Elizabeth Priscilla, named for Cooper's sister. Priscilla would grow up to become her father's co-star.

In Baltimore that October Cooper first acted Bertram in Charles R. Maturin's play of that name, a violent drama in which he had a decided success. When he played the role in Boston in November, the critic for *Boston Weekly Magazine* remarked on the noticeable departure he made from his accustomed classical, to a more natural style, to achieve the extremes of passion:

> We had thought heretofore that Mr. Cooper was not so happy in the display of mental conflicts of this elevated order, as he is allowed to be in expressing those gentler emotions of the soul, that require the graces of unimpassioned elocution. In his performance of "Bertram," however, he soared far beyond his usual tamely elaborate elegance, and assumed a more fiery, impassioned, and yet natural tone of acting than we ever recollect observing in any of his preceding performances; none of which, we think, ever afforded an example of those powers he here exhibited, of painting, in the most vivid colours, the transports of hatred and revenge; the mutations of which, from the frenzied denunciations of madness, down to the sullen torpor of despair, were so apparent in Mr. C's performance of this fiendlike character, as even to shock the feelings; it was too naturally painful to be pleasing.[18]

The reviewer noticed that he was bringing increased maturity and more natural movement to his familiar roles as well. Of his Hamlet he remarked, "His soliloquies in particular were distinguished by a chastened and pathetic eloquence.... The scenes with the Ghost were marked by the display of a natural and unaffected terror, beyond comparison superior to the artificial starts—the etiquette of uncovering the head—the graceful extension of the arms, and the studied elegance of posture which we have not only observed in the attempts of others, but in the past performances of Mr. Cooper himself[.]" And he said Cooper "bestowed" upon the character of Duke Aranza in Tobin's comedy, *The Honeymoon*, "his usual brilliancy and interest."

Boston had been hard hit economically, first by the 1807 Act of Embargo prohibiting trade with Britain, and then by the subsequent war. As a result Boston theatre audiences had become thin, and the quality of the resident company had steadily declined. The critic for the *Weekly* declared the company who supported Cooper to be "totally incompetent to assist with common decency, in the representation of any single play of celebrity." He accused the manager of hurrying Cooper in and out with a tight three-week engagement to keep his actors from suffering the comparison, finding it "impossible to destroy the attachment, which a refractory public still persist in testifying for the American Roscius, and that line of characters, which he alone saves from oblivion[.]"[19]

At the end of the engagement when Cooper acted Benedick in *Much Ado About Nothing* the critic expressed "surprise that this should be his first appearance here in a character, in which he appeared to as much advantage, as in almost all those, which he considers his favourite parts." He went on to assert, "In his hands, the witty and accomplished Benedick shone with as chaste and brilliant a lustre, as histrionic talent ever bestowed upon a comic character." And said the masquerade scene "was conducted with infinite life and humour; and the bye play of the arbour scene was only exceeded by the felicity, with which he afterwards represented the insipient love of the entrapped Benedick." The two very different roles of Bertram and Benedick he pointed to as "shining evidences of the versatility of Mr. Cooper's talents, and of his ability to display, with equal excellence, the boisterous conflicts of tragic passions, and the vivacious humour of elegant comedy."[20]

In March 1817 Cooper gave two performances of Bertram at the Park Theatre in New York and offered a performance of King Lear in Shakespeare's tragedy of a father and his three daughters. He returned to the Park for one night at the end of the season to appear for the occasion of a visit by the new U.S. President, James Monroe. On June 11, after meeting with the Mayor at City-Hall and the State Society of the Cincinnati, Monroe was entertained at "a sumptuous dinner" at Merchant's Hotel on Wall Street; attendance included Cooper's father-in-law Major Fairlie, at that time President of the U.S. Bank; also Vice President Daniel Tompkins, New York Governor Clinton, General Scott, and numerous other distinguished officers. The following evening Monroe 'honor[ed]" the

Theatre with his presence," and the managers presented Cooper in *Macbeth*, followed by the company chorus singing, "Rise, Columbia, Brave and Free."[21]

That same June, on the twenty-third in London, John Philip Kemble took leave of the stage in the role of Coriolanus. Cooper had appeared in the first New York production of *Coriolanus*, Shakespeare's tragedy of character—the brilliant soldier, in defiance of his proud mother's ambition, unable to parry to Roman politics.[22] Some twenty years later, in 1819, when he performed the role in Boston, the reviewer for the *Galaxy* commented: "We confess it is in Coriolanus, more than in any other character, that we are pleased with Mr. C. His person, his voice and manner, are well adapted to display the fiery and unbending nature of that proud Patrician, and the towering grandeur of Roman majesty."[23] And concluded, "What modern performer can boast of filling so wide a range of characters as Mr. C.? In almost all of those of an heroic cast, we can pronounce without hesitation, (now that Kemble has retired,) that he has not an equal. And when we consider his great merit in others, to which, he is not perfectly adapted, is it too much to say, that he is probably the first actor of the age."[24]

That year, 1819, Cooper moved his family from New York City to the home he had acquired on the banks of the Delaware River in Bristol, Pennsylvania. On the Old Post Road between New York and Philadelphia, Bristol was a convenient mid-way point for touring. Since its beginning it had been connected by ferry boat to Burlington, New Jersey, and the location on the river, with regular steamboat service to Philadelphia later on, made it both accessible and picturesque. Founded by Quakers, substantial industrialists eventually developed the town, home to families such as the Landreths of the Landreth Seed Company; the Grundys of the Bristol Worsted Mill; and the Dorrances of the Campbell Soup Company. Nearby "Bath Springs" had made Bristol famous as a health resort when Philadelphia was the capital of the country, and in its heyday the town numbered prominent government figures and foreign ambassadors among its residents. Once the U.S. Capital moved to Washington, however, Bristol lost much of its glamour, as well as its population, so the news that Mr. Cooper, the famous theatrical star, was bringing his wife and three children to live at 722 Radcliffe Street stirred the waters.

Radcliffe Street is an elegant residential avenue running along the river, the eastern border of the original town. When the Coopers moved into their new home, they adorned the rooms with Gobelin tapestries and chair coverings he had acquired at an auction in London; with titles such as "Art and Nature in Africa" and "Art and Nature in Europe," they were said to have been ordered by Marie Antoinette for Lafayette.[25]

Cooper Home at 722 Radcliffe Street, Bristol, Pennsylvania. Courtesy the Grundy Foundation.

There in Bristol the American star welcomed many of the actors Price brought from England. The comedian Charles Mathews wrote his wife about a visit: "On Sunday last I received a summons from Price, to follow him to Bristol, seventy miles from New York. I arrived there on Monday evening, and found him at Cooper's house, where I was made very welcome. He is away until next Saturday; but Mrs. Cooper and Mrs. Price made me very comfortable. They are both very charming women. Cooper's house is after my own heart, delightfully situated on the banks of the Delaware."[26] The same age as Cooper, Mathews first appeared in New York in 1822 in Holcroft's *The Road to Ruin*. In meeting him, William Wood recalled how he spoke of "his early days of wandering and privation; in which Cooper more than once was a fellow sufferer." He remembered Cooper's performance of Penruddock in Wales when he was still a boy as "the best juvenile attempt he had ever witnessed."[27]

Fifteen

A Rival

A New Vogue—1819-20

In the fall of 1819 Washington Irving, having heard that the young romantic British star, Edmund Kean, of Drury Lane Theatre, was planning his first American tour, and Charles Young was on leave from Covent Garden, wrote Cooper a letter from London advising him that the time was perfect for his own reappearance in London:

> I write in haste and therefore will at once come to the point. If you have any notion of visiting England now is your time—Kean is making preparation to visit America & intends sailing in the course of the Autumn— Young is not engaged at Covent Garden—he has left it for at least a year—on a friendly understanding with Mr. Harris, the motive is to increase the public interest in him on a reappearance—There is a sad dearth of Tragic talent here—Covent Garden opened with *Charles Kemble in Macbeth!* At the end of the play he was complimented with applause from some friends & hisses from a few of the *grieving judicious.* MacReady cannot be foisted upon the public for the first line. Should you come out there can be no question of your making an advantageous arrangement with Harris—and should you do the things I have seen you do in my time I know no man here that can stand before you—If you come you should do so at once—you will be like a god send to the poor tragic muse also who is absolutely in a State of widowhood.

Irving ended his letter with a salutation to Mary: "Give my most affectionate remembrances to Mrs. Cooper and tell her that a diligent study of her Species in various parts of the world I have come to the conclusion that she is one of the finest specimens I have met with."[1]

At this point Cooper was too immersed in his American career to take Washington Irving's advice. Instead, he was developing a new vogue in contemporary Roman roles, which, like Coriolanus, were well-suited to his demeanor and temperament. In the fall of 1819 he first appeared in

Mr. Cooper as Leon. From an engraving by Edwin, after a drawing by C. R. Leslie. Harvard Theatre Collection, Houghton Library.

New York in the title role of John Howard Payne's play, *Brutus; or, The Fall of Tarquin*, a tragedy set in Rome during the occupation of the Tarquins. The noble Roman, Lucius Junius Brutus, is disguised as a mad jester at the Tarquin court, and the rape of the Roman gentlewoman Lucrece by a Tarquin prince incites him to lead a successful rebellion against the usurpers. The tragic turn occurs when Brutus' own son, Titus, who is in love with a Tarquin princess, fights against him with the enemy; Brutus suffers the agony of having to condemn Titus to death by the axe.

Remarking, "The genius of Mr. Cooper is always powerful, and he never fails to do himself honour where there is strong passion tearing the heart," the *Mirror* critic described his use of natural physical mannerisms to convey the passion of Brutus, "the agonized father, struggling between patriotism and paternal affection."—"The trembling restlessness of the hands—the toying with his robes—the firm pressure of the lip, that would conceal the emotions he cannot restrain—and the flinging forth the arms in the 'agony of grief,' as he excuses his weakness ... all but renewed evidence how well Mr. Cooper can perform, and how cordially our audience can admire his performances."[2]

In Boston Cooper opened a two-week engagement in December with a premiere of *Brutus*. "Dramaticus" in the *Gazette* compared his enactment of Brutus disguised as the jester to his Leon [*Rule a Wife and Have a Wife*], affording a description of the physicalization of his popular comic role: "We were particularly interested with Mr. Cooper's delineation of the feigned madness of Lucius Junius, because it was the prototype of nature, and because it recalled to our mind, his inimitable execution of the simplicity and awkwardness of Leon; a part which in his hands, has often afforded us unmixed gratification. The peculiar bent of his elbows, and knees, the blank and unmeaning expression of his visage. ..."[3]

The *Galaxy* critic in Boston also described his success with the "affected idiocy" of Brutus in Act One of the play, "his hand raised to conceal his face from the view of the tyrant, and that face speaking volumes[.]" Of the last act he commented, "His sudden starting from his seat on the tribunal, and his abrupt address to the Romans, indicating a fear, that the powerful feelings which agitated his breast, would lead them to suppose he would swerve from his purpose, was in every respect true to nature. Indeed, his whole performance, his attitudes so noble, and apparently unaffected, and which a sculptor might have studied with advantage, altogether afforded a rich feast both to the soul and to the eye."[4]

Back in New York, on November 4, 1820, Cooper appeared in the title role of another new play, *Virginius*, by the Irish playwright James Sheridan Knowles. Kean's British rival, William Charles Macready, had created the role in London the previous season. Like *Brutus*, the play is an historical drama about a Roman father and his child, but in this case the father, the brave centurion Virginius, is driven to kill his virtuous daughter Virginia to save her from the lustful tyrant Appius Claudius. The heroic values coupled with the domestic milieu made it particularly appealing to the nineteenth-century American audience.

Some of the critics in New York objected to Cooper's alteration of the text; in order to heighten the final tragedy, he joined the last two scenes of the play. He was accused of violating propriety as well when he strangled Appius Claudius on stage in full view of the audience, and he killed Virginia with a sword rather than the historically correct butcher's knife as directed in the play. But he knew how to create effect; the public was captivated. The critic for the *New-York Mirror* wrote that Cooper "was made for such characters, and cannot choose but play them well. Nature, indeed, has done so much for him, that he were unpardonable to be less excellent than what he is. Had our celebrated and much lamented countryman West [the painter Benjamin West], attempted to centre in one figure all that we have read and all that we can conceive of Roman greatness and magnanimity, he could not have chosen a better model than the person of Cooper. When taste and genius are the moving principles of such a form, what external results have we not a right to expect!"[5]

Kean was booked to open in New York later that month, but even before his arrival, critics had begun to choose sides, some loyal to the classical ideal of Cooper, others ready to espouse the radical innovation of Kean. It was a controversy not only over two individual performers, but also over two different styles of acting; and it was a contest involving national allegiances. The celebrity of Kean drew much interest, but there was a strong desire on the part of many Americans to protect Cooper, their own American-made star, against the onslaught of the foreign genius.

The natural son of a hawker in the environs of Drury Lane Theatre, Kean had grown up in that area of London and had had a meteoric rise to fame on the Drury Lane stage beginning in 1814. He had been engaged to make his American debut at the Park Theatre, but on May 21 the Park burned down and the company had to move to the old Anthony Street Theatre, so Kean made his first appearance there instead, on November 29, in the character of Richard the Third.

Fate placed Kean in a theatre originally developed by renegades from the Park; and twelve years younger than Cooper, his youth and fame posed the first serious threat to Cooper's supremacy in America. In contrast to Cooper's formal grace, Kean's movements were sudden and startling, his fits of passion shocking. Acting in his own natural style after Cooke, he had made a stunning debut at Drury Lane as Shylock, Shakespeare's Jew in *The Merchant of Venice*, and his best parts were the dark ones: Iago, Richard III, Sir Giles Overreach [Philip Massinger, *A New Way to Pay Old Debts*], Barabas [Christopher Marlowe, *The Jew of Malta*]. Of scarcely medium height, however, he lacked the requisite deportment for the noble figures which Cooper suited to perfection, and Cooper's current emphasis on the classical roles would showcase the difference.

Just prior to Kean's arrival, on November 18, an essay signed "Crito" appeared in the *Evening Post* in New York attacking Cooper's alteration of the text of *Virginius*, as well as the artificiality of his acting style: "Every actor who attempts to *declaim* the character of Virginius himself must fail to give it the effect intended by the dramatist; ... it is entirely foreign to nature for a distracted father, ... to stand regulating the position of his arms, body and feet, and poising his words [.]"[6]

On the day of Kean's debut, the twenty-ninth, *The American* retorted: "I do not intend to enter into any discussion as to the truth of Mr. Cooper's readings, or the substitution of a sword for a knife in the sacrifice of Virginia—I choose rather to consider the general spirit of the piece, and those feelings of indiscriminate detraction which characterize every line of it. Its object is apparent.... Mr. C. must be believed to be *too* dignified and stately, before the pantomimic starts and lounging walk of Mr. K. can demand applause. Mr. C.'s commanding figure—clear, or *since Crito admits it, fine* voice, and graceful gestures, must be destroyed, that he who wants them all, may be held up as nature's favoured child."[7]

On November 30 in Boston the *Galaxy* reviewer also wrote a special piece to rebuke what he called Crito's "virulent, and ... malicious, attack[.]" In the same vein as the response by *The American*, he pointed out, "The object of Crito is, probably, to convince the friends of Mr. C. (and by his friends we mean a large majority of the play-going people of the United States) that he is no actor, and that they have been for fifteen or twenty years most miserably deceived." He went on to assert, "The reputation of Mr. Cooper is built of indestructible materials and will resist the battering of much more powerful foes than Crito; its foundation is laid too deep in the affections, passions and emotions of the human heart, to be *uprooted* by the feeble efforts of such 'groundlings;' its superstructure is too bright and glittering to be sullied by the pestiferous breath of spite and envy; and its owner, we should hope, has too much of manhood in him to whine or fret for the lashing of such 'puny whipsters' as Crito."

In addition, the paper carried an essay on "The Histrionic Art," which is in effect a defense of the classical intent inherent in Cooper's style. The author states, "It is only in the Theatre, that any image of the real grandeur of humanity—any picture of generous heroism and noble self-sacrifice—is poured on the imaginations, and sent warm to the hearts, of the vast body of the people.... There, are the deep fountains of hearts, long encrusted by narrow cares, burst open, and a holy light is sent in on the long shaken forms of the imagination[.]" Referring to Shakespeare, and the stories of Coriolanus and Cato, he goes on to reflect on the "transitoriness which is necessarily connected with the living grace which belongs to no other order of artists."[8]

The last week of November Cooper had begun his accustomed engagement in Boston, offering his popular Shakespearean roles, as well as Virginius. The *Galaxy* reported, "An audience, more numerous and respectable than any that had been before assembled in the theatre the present season, witnessed with great delight the performance of Mr. Cooper in Hamlet on Monday evening."[9]

It was at this time that the leading Boston editor, J. T. Buckingham, also stated definitively: "Macbeth is Mr. Cooper's *chef d'oeuvre*. He is perfectly identified with the character. The *dagger scene*, which he plays in a style altogether his own, is one of the sublimest efforts of histrionic genius. The terrible agonies of his mind, which proclaim their existence with 'most miraculous organ,' are too powerful to be long the object of attention. In the latter part of the play, after Macbeth has 'supped full of horrors,' the moral reflexions are given with such exquisite beauty and feeling, that we almost forget the crimes of the murderer, and pity the wetched victim writhing with the tortures of his own conscience."[10]

From a painting of *Thomas A. Cooper as Macbeth*. Oil on canvas, 8½ × 11¼. Museum of the City of New York, gift William P. Stephens, Esq. 39.239.4.

On December 8 the *Galaxy* critic reviewed Cooper's premiere performance of *Virginius* saying the playwright should be grateful for the improvement by the actor. He also noted "the tenderness with which he assured Virginia that he *would not leave her*," remarking, "There was much of natural playfulness and feeling in Mr. Cooper's manner of drawing from Virginia the confession of her love, and of his bestowing her hand on Icilius."[11]

Seeing Macready in the part during his American tour in 1826, the southern manager Noah Miller Ludlow commented, "I saw Mr. Macready perform *Virginius* in one of his tours through the United States, and at a time when he was in the prime of life, and when he had performed it often enough to have matured any conception of the character which he might have formed. But I did not like his rendition of it; it was too cold and lifeless; it lacked the tender, loving, fatherly beauty of Cooper in scenes with the daughter[.]"[12] Cooper and his daughter Priscilla would later act the play together.

In December Cooper opened a six-night engagement with Virginius in his first appearance at the Walnut Street Theatre in Philadelphia. Earlier that year in April, right before the Park Theatre burned down, the Chestnut Street Theatre had also burned to the ground, with all of its effects, scenery, wardrobe, gasworks, pianos, music and play library.* The managers, William Warren and William Wood, had no insurance, but despite the heavy losses, they determined to open the next season by leasing the old Olympic Theatre, built as a circus, renaming it for the street on which it stands. Today the Walnut Street is the oldest acting theatre in America, and the only one where Cooper performed that is still in existence.

"A Triumph to Cooper"—1820-21

At the end of the year Cooper set up a direct challenge to Kean by booking an engagement at the Anthony Street Theatre right after Kean left. Although considered bad judgment even by his defenders, it was a characteristic challenge on his part. In January heated exchanges ensued in the press involving theatrical and editorial interests, as well as a multitude of letters to the editor from private citizens. The *American* compared Cooper as "the tragic muse in good health and her sober senses," to Kean, "the same lady, ... labouring under an attack of the palsy or a visitation of St. Vitus[,]" accusing Kean of bringing his claque of "*bravos*"

---

*The Park Theatre would reopen September 1, 1821; and the Chestnut Street on December 1, 1822.

with him.¹³ In the *Evening Post* "A Philadelphian" retorted, "[T]he editor of the 'American', and five or six gentlemen, whose names I can mention, all professed and devoted admirers of Mr. Cooper, took their places in the *pit* on the evening of the representation of 'Macbeth', and that among other 'vociferous demonstrations of pleasure' *that party was distinguished by the frequency and loudness of their 'bravos.'*"¹⁴

Another letter in the *Evening Post*, from "A New-Yorker," viewed Kean's style as born of his defects: "Mr. Kean had little or no grace of gesture, therefore his predecessors were cold, stiff and stately. He had no voice, (or, as the Examiner uncourteously says, one 'between an apoplexy and a cough,') and therefore their recitation was too measured and continuous." He admitted Kean to be "a man of talent" but at his best in parts requiring "no tumult of passion," where "the sweetness of the lower tones of his voice break most agreeably on the ear." He ended by highlighting Cooper's "powerful and musical voice" and fine person, contrasting him with the great British stars: "Garrick was below the middle size, while Kemble had a tremulous, perhaps a whining voice." Adding, "To a cultivated taste Mr. Cooper adds an enunciation most clear and distinct."¹⁵

Kean became the subject of private as well as public theatrical debate, and Cooper partook. Remembering how he "preferr[ed] with a few familiar friends to … enjoy a segar, and unrestrained conversation[,]" John B. Irving said that when he was in Charleston, after the play the star habitually retired to his dressing room in the old theatre on Broad Street to change his costume for gentleman's dress, then "invariably repaired" to the private rooms of the manager, Charles Gilfert. Irving described Gilfert as "a consummate man of the world" who gathered "that famous clique, every member of which was a celebrity."—the painter, John Jarvis; belles-lettres scholar Isaac Harby; the poet Dr. Farmer; et al.¹⁶ On one such occasion when the talk turned to Kean, Irving recalled Cooper's rising from his chair and raising his hand to make his point, saying, "'No impression I ever received from a play or an actor, approached the effect produced by Kean, as Sir Giles Overreach in the play of *A New Way To Pay Old Debts*.'"¹⁷

He took the opposite view of Kean's Othello, as James Murdoch recalled: "One day, in a company of gentlemen (at his residence on the banks of the Delaware, Pennsylvania), where the merits of Mr. Kean's acting were being discussed, the tragedian Thomas Cooper suddenly exclaimed with great animation, 'Othello! Othello! Why, gentlemen, Kean cannot come within a mile of Othello. His snarling, snappish speech and his gusty flights of vehement passion are all very striking and effective; but, gentlemen, they are directly opposite to the physical and intellectual forces of Othello.'" He referred to the text: "'This is clearly indicated by the conscious deliberation and dignity of the language in which Shakespeare has presented the character. Mr. Kean is not susceptible of the full force of the mighty and tumultuous passions which stormed and seethed in the heart of the unhappy Moor, a man whose life-experiences were all in the camp or on the battlefield—a mode of life which teaches men, by the force of unyielding discipline, to control their passions. But let the curb once snap, and the dread gulf yawns for the victim of blind and ungovernable rage.'" Concluding, "'I grant you Othello was impulsive, but it was the majestic passion of a roused lion conscious of power. Shakespeare's words tell us what kind of passion inflamed the Moor ... it was 'as broad and general as the casing air[.]'"[18]

John Wesley Jarvis, American, 1781–1840. *Thomas Abthorpe Cooper*, c. 1810. Oil on wood, 86.2 × 66.5 cm. ©The Cleveland Museum of Art, gift Mrs. Benjamin Thaw, 1918.173.

In an essay on Cooper, Isaac Harby, a distinguished critic of the drama, commented: "Mr. Cooper's forte is in the deep, the terrible, the strong and overwhelming passions of the soul ... when he lets loose, as it were, the very flood of passion.... It is in those workings of the soul, when anguish shakes her—when she labours to escape out of some terrible and trying situation, in the scene of *Coriolanus* with his wife and mother as suppliants—in *Othello*, where *Iago* first poisons his mind with jealousy, *Sir Edward Mortimer* [Geo. Colman, Jr., *The Iron Chest*], in the trial scene."[19]

Boston welcomed Kean in February, and he played a successful premier engagement. In late May, however, despite the manager Dickinson's insistence that the season was virtually over, Kean got him to agree to a return engagement in Boston, which proved to be his downfall. After two nights that were poorly attended, on the third night, finding that there were only twenty people in the audience for his Richard the Third, he refused to play. The affront to the American public resounded. Kean was condemned not only in Boston, but in New York and Philadelphia as well. He subsequently wrote an explanatory letter published in the *National Advocate*, but throwing the blame to the management, it was bereft of an apology and did not serve him well.

Major Fairlie's friend John Pintard wrote to his daughter about the incident. Beginning, "You have been charmed with Mr. Cooper, an excellent actor," he went on to describe Kean's departure from Boston "in dudgeon, execrated for his ingratitude." And commented, "[H]ow soon are his Laurels tarnished, for this capricious air will follow him & render him unpopular wherever he goes, at least in America. He can return, rich, & execrate the Yankees [for] penuriousness & want of taste. This conduct will be a triumph to Cooper, whose friends regard him far superior to Kean. Novelty & the eclat with w^h the latter commenced his debut on the Am[erican] Boards were highly favorable to him, [b]ut good critics did not approve his style of acting w^h aimed too much at originality & did not accord with the spirit of his characters."[20]

Kean made preparations to return to England, but before he left, taking the part of Britain, he paid homage to his great spiritual predecessor, George Frederick Cooke, by arranging for removal of his remains from the Strangers' Vault at St. Paul's and reinterment in a grave in the churchyard; he also saw to the erection of a marble monument to his memory, a site for theatrical pilgrimage ever since.[21]

Sixteen

A New Venue—1820–25

The 1820–21 season produced two more rivals to Cooper's one-man rule. On November 27 a young Philadelphian, fourteen-year-old Edwin Forrest, made his first professional appearance at the Walnut Street Theatre. He played the role of Young Norval in *Douglas* and was immediately hailed as a second Cooper. The following summer the twenty-five-year-old British tragedian, Junius Brutus Booth, Sr., made his first appearance in America at Richmond, Virginia. Like Kean, Booth was best known for Richard III and Sir Giles Overreach and generally played in a limited repertoire. Although he had won fame in England, in 1817 venturing a joint appearance as Iago to Kean's Othello, he had been roundly vanquished by Kean and dismissed by the London critics as an imitator of Kean. It was three years after that defeat that he left his wife while she was out of the country visiting relatives, to elope with a young Covent Garden flower vendor who was already pregnant by him; in setting out for America, they intended to stay. Bringing the romantic acting style with him to the new country, as Cooper had the classical, by chance Booth encountered Cooper at the lodging house where he stayed near Richmond, and from then on the two actors maintained a friendly acquaintance on the road.

In the spring Cooper, the quintessential American, had headed out as always, leading the way to the new territory. While Kean was still on tour in the East, he gave his good faith to the Southern manager, James H. Caldwell, to make a first appearance in New Orleans. A British-born comedian, Caldwell had emigrated from England in 1816, and soon after, turned manager, with plans to instigate a regular season of English-speaking theatre in New Orleans,[1] which previously had only French. An old-world gentleman himself, he attempted to upgrade the personal standards of the audience, getting rid of drunkards in the pit and advertising, "'Peanuts are proscribed.'"[2] He also introduced gaslight to the city.

With George Wilmot riding behind him, Cooper traveled to New

Orleans in a covered wagon long enough to sleep in, journeying through Indian villages along the way. He carried candles and salt and pepper to season the game he would kill, camping out perhaps "on some of those battle grounds in the Creek nations, or at the beautiful confluence of the Coosa and Talapoosa, and the Old Hickory Trees[.]"³

In New Orleans on March 23, Cooper opened an engagement of sixteen performances with *Macbeth*. Among the roles he played, including Othello, Hamlet, Virginius, and Pierre, two were in plays that had never been performed in New Orleans before, *Julius Caesar* [Antony] and *Rule a Wife and Have a Wife* [Leon]. He was also the first major star to appear in the western territory of the United States, so Caldwell raised the price of attendance from one dollar to a dollar and fifty cents.

The increase in ticket fees caused a public furor; people sent heated letters to the Editor of the *Louisiana Gazette*. "Old Price" wrote: "For a long time it has been reported that Mr. Cooper, the celebrated tragedian, was coming to New Orleans. Public expectation was excited. All classes of society determined, if he did come, to go to the Theatre. At length Mr. Cooper has arrived, and curiosity is raised to the highest pitch—every countenance is lighted up—every person is pleased—all are anxious to see Mr. Cooper perform, and all are rejoicing that they shall have an opportunity of gratifying their desire. But in the very midst of this hilarity and joy, *upon this extraordinary occasion*, is heard the demand of the manager for *One Dollar and Fifty Cents! One Dollar and Fifty Cents!*"⁴

One, calling himself "Many," said he understood from "a particular friend" of Mr. Caldwell that the price increase was calculated to "'prevent the greasy Kentuckians, and the rabble from leaning over the backs of the boxes to the great annoyance of the Ladies.'" He rejoined, "If this is fact, we hope Mr. Caldwell will avow it, so that the public may give him credit for his politeness, and no longer accuse him of extortion[,]" and warned him of the smoldering fury:

> [L]et him not suppose, because there was no disturbance on the night of Mr. Cooper's first appearance, that the public may be imposed on, and that they will be imposed on, and that they will submit without resistance. No, we can inform Mr. Caldwell that their indignation against him was only restrained by their respect to Mr. Cooper. A large proportion of those who were at the Theatre on Friday evening, were ripe for revolt. It would have required but a single puff to have blown the spark into a blaze. The frequent calls from different parts of the house of "O. P. *The Manager, Mr. Caldwell*," were strong indication of the spirit and feeling which predominated among the multitude.... [W]e venture to predict, that the feeling of indignation ... will be manifested on some future occasion, when not prevented by the presence of Mr. Cooper.⁵

Another letter, from "Macbeth," referred to the Old Price Riots at Covent Garden when the manager had had to yield. This writer viewed the excuse of "*increased expenses*" for importing the star as "very lame," since he presumed Caldwell would profit all the more.[6]

As it turned out, Caldwell did not yield to the old price demand; respect for Cooper prevailed. In fact, his engagement proved to be so popular that it was extended eight more nights; Cooper received the extraordinary sum of $3,333.33 for the 16 nights alone, and Caldwell said they averaged $700 a night for the 24.[7] The next year, joining the development of a new American section just above the French Quarter, Caldwell began building the American Theatre on Camp Street. He later estimated that his success as a manager began with his first engagement of Cooper:

> [I]mmediately after my emigration to New Orleans, in 1819, I conceived the idea of drawing our great tragedian, Cooper, to share with me in an engagement, the liberal support of this glorious people. I succeeded, and from that day the drama assumed a tone which has spread through the whole valley of the Mississippi. From that day I have wielded the tinsel sceptre, and commanded to the South and West, every distinguished member of the profession, who has sought these shores, even in the face of death, as too many thought it was, to visit this (as they termed it), yellow fever city. Mammon and fame led them on; and season after season, I introduced them to crowded and delighted audiences."[8]

Following Cooper's first appearance in New Orleans, in the fall of 1821 Price reopened the Park Theatre with the addition of the comedian Joe Cowell from Drury Lane, who later published a book of recollections. Cowell related a story about playing one of the three witches for Cooper's Macbeth soon after his arrival. With his customary star demeanor, Cooper failed to acknowledge Cowell's presence. Instead, at a rehearsal he took so much time rearranging the staging of the witches to his own best advantage that Cowell became enraged; he finally decided to ignore the directions and play his witch for Cooper just as he had for Kean at Drury Lane—though admitting, "I couldn't but admire the man's splendid talent."

Cowell said he knew that Cooper had arranged for him to appear on his nights and also "administered to [his] vanity" by waiting every night after his own performance to watch him in the farce, but in his distant way, Cooper continued to ignore him personally. So one night in the green-room during a performance of *Virginius*, when the star came up to the mirror to adjust his toga, Cowell happened to be sitting right in the way, and instead of moving aside deferentially, tilted his head and said,

"Booh!" Soon thereafter Cooper was inviting him to dine, and Cowell became a frequent visitor at Cooper's home in Bristol.

Cowell remarked that in Bristol, "the luxuries attendant upon affluence were so regulated by good taste that Cooper never appeared to such advantage as when at home. His family was numerous and very interesting." Fond of entertaining, the Coopers were also adding children to their family year by year. One after another, four more daughters arrived, Olivia, Julia, Virginia, and Louisa. Priding himself on discipline, Cooper told Cowell that while they were still quite young, if they started to cry, he would throw water in their faces to cure them.[9] Soon after moving to Bristol he had bought the lot next door, and built a second home, number 800, for the children, their nurse and a governess; connected to 722 by a covered walkway, they called it "the White House."[10]

Cooper returned to New Orleans for a second engagement in 1822. There on February 13 he premiered what would be one of his most stunning successes, another Roman role, Damon in *Damon and Pythias* by John Banim, which had opened in London the previous season. Set in Syracuse, the play is a classical melodrama in which the virtue of true friendship motivates the action of heroism. Damon, a philosopher and senator, is condemned to death for his opposition to the tyrant Dionysus. To enable him to obtain a six-hour stay of execution to go home to take leave of his wife and son, Damon's friend Pythias stands in for him as a hostage. While Damon is with his family, a well-meaning servant kills his horse to prevent his return to be executed, but Damon races back on foot to save Pythias, arriving at the last moment to take his place under the ax. In the end Dionysus is so struck by the friends' mutual devotion that he pardons Damon.

Durang described Cooper's "physical and mental" enactment of the part of Damon, a mingling of the classical and the romantic:

> He stood before the entranced auditory a splendid statue of the agonized *Laocoon*. It was a classical conception. We never saw a combination of physical and mental acting more ably illustrated by any eminent performer. Cooper's entrance in the last scene of the play, exhausted, tottering, and falling prostrate before the scaffold—his shriek at hearing the voice of *Pythias*—the convulsive embrace—the enfeebled, worn-out man, but unsubdued spirit, mounting the scaffold with recuperative energies at the call of "*Damon*" by *Dionysus*, were all consummate strokes of art and nature, originally conceived by Cooper—not so done by any foreign artiste. He did not borrow from Macready. The catastrophe so painfully developed, yet so philanthropically concluded was a *chef d'oeuvre* of dramatic delineation.[11]

On his way back north in April, Cooper stopped in Louisville, Kentucky, where he performed for six nights to "invariably crowded" houses, accepting his earnings of about $1,200 in produce, rather than risking a significant loss in exchanging western for eastern money.[12] He also played a first engagement in Cincinnati where the young Sol Smith was acting as stage manager. Smith recalled an untutored girl's late arrival for Cooper's performance in *Othello*. Having never set foot inside a theatre before, the young woman saw an empty seat onstage among the senators and went up to claim it just as Cooper delivered a line referring to Desdemona, "here comes the lady." Smith said this caused such confusion that the audience broke out clapping, and the actors, including Cooper, joined in the general amusement as well.[13]

In the fall of 1823 Cooper took his performance of Damon to New York. In the *Mirror*, Theodore S. Fay remarked, "There is something so elevated in the acting of this gentleman—... He seems to have been created to personify the noble characters of times gone by. His figure—his face—his very voice breathes forth the high-toned grandeur of Roman greatness. In portraying the overwhelming passions of a noble soul, I believe he stands unrivaled." Fay devoted three full columns to a description of the portrayal—the farewell with his young wife: "the agonizing efforts ... to relate his news ... he tears himself from her—gives a long, last, broken-hearted look ... and then rushes to relieve the danger of his friend"; with his servant: "the stern and bewildered urging, 'Where is my steed?'—the flash of suspicion ... all the agonizing emotions of his soul ... 'Almighty gods!'—the picture of mute despair ... a monument in mute fury—Many of the audience rose on their feet. I heard several exclamations of astonishment, and he dragged off the struggling Lucullus, amidst loud and reiterated thunders of applause."[14] The young British actor/manager, Francis Courtney Wemyss, who had come to America the previous year, said he saw Cooper only in these later years, but that "even then, his performance of Damon ... was a masterpiece of art, ... Nothing on the stage ... ever surpassed this. It was painfully true to nature, ... This was the conception of a master-mind. For my own part, after witnessing it, I always wished to leave the theatre that nothing might break the charm for the evening."[15]

In September 1823 the reviewer for the *National Advocate* noted, "The principal attraction of the Theatre is Cooper in his great Roman characters, Virginius, Damon and Brutus"; reflecting, "[I]t is a fortunate event that these plays have been written at a period when something new was desirable for Mr. Cooper ... they are parts peculiarly adapted to his person and physical powers." They also represented the classic principles of independent liberty and virtue at the heart of the new American republic. Pointing out that the "mellowness" of these characters, "corresponds with the ripened years and matured experience of Mr. Cooper, and which in a young man would be awkward and inappropriate[,]" the reviewer went on to notice, "There are strong points also in these parts which impress themselves so forcibly ... that Mr. Cooper bursts those icy bonds which check and crib his genius, and all is pathos, softness and effect,— it is nature prostrating the barriers of art."[16]

For his benefit in Washington on February 7, 1825, Cooper played Damon to "a numerous and splendid audience[,]" which included President James Monroe and his friend from the Revolution, the visiting Marquis de Lafayette; also Secretary of State John Quincy Adams and General Andrew Jackson. Mr. and Mrs. Barnes appeared at the end of the play to sing a comic song, followed by Cooper's recitation of Dryden's "Alexander's Feast."[17]

Seventeen

Turning Tide

An American Tragedian—1825-28

In 1825 Cooper and Mary were living well, enjoying life among the local gentry and entertaining a brilliant circle of friends. With his nephew Prince Murat, Joseph Bonaparte, who had an estate at Bordentown, would come sailing down the Delaware in a barge bedecked with flags and four oarsmen for an afternoon in Bristol.[1] That year in Philadelphia Cooper added a new role to his repertoire, the melancholy eccentric Jacques in Shakespeare's *As You Like It*, and it was remarked that "[t]he humors and quaint reflections of *Jaques* [sic] well accorded with the peculiarities of Cooper."[2] In Boston in March his benefit produced a great House[,]" and his engagement was "unexpectedly extended two nights" for reappearances in two of his current offerings, *Selim* [William Dimond, *Bride of Abydos*, after Byron's poem] and *Gaius Gracchus*, another play by Sheridan Knowles, author of *Virginius*.[3]

Meanwhile in London, characteristically involved with alcohol and low life, Kean's vulgar correspondence with his married mistress had been publicly exposed by a lawsuit brought against him by her husband, a Drury Lane shareholder. January 24, 1825, hounded by the press and hooted off the Drury Lane stage, in late September Kean returned to America. Hoping for better luck there, he was bitterly disappointed, for the American press had picked up the cry. November 14 at the Park Theatre in New York, which was packed to overflowing, continuous hissing drowned out every word of his performance of Richard the Third. In the Boston theatre, pelted with nuts and pieces of cake and shouted "Off," Kean had to be smuggled out of the theatre, never to return to that city.

In 1826, before Kean left, his chief British rival, William Charles Macready, thirty-three years old, made his first appearance in America. Durang thought Macready best, not in Shakespearean roles, but "in more original parts with a native talent ... the misanthropes of Byron and

Kotzebue, as *Werner* and *The Stranger*." He was the first actor to move beyond the habitual focus on dramatic climax to emphasize total production standards, but he was not comparable to Cooper in such a role as Damon, nor his equal in Macbeth, according to Durang:

> We must perforce aver that we did not think that his [Macready's] dagger scene, in the second act [*Macbeth*] was equal to Cooper's. There was a beauty of horror ... in Cooper's idea and acting in this celebrated scene. Macready did not start at once at the ideal dagger, as if he saw it tangible to the eye. But he kept his sight constantly on the "painting of his fear," recoiling and advancing to the dread object of his struggling excitement, till he reached the possession of the real instrument by drawing his own weapon. In this, Macready displayed much art and original thought, but its execution was not agreeable. There was something very unpleasant in the sudden transitions of voice, attitude, and expression of feature. Those harsh, guttural [*sic*] exclamations so grating to the musical ear, the peculiar distortions of his face and body so frequent in his bursts of passion, were positive asperities that annihilated the agreeable tints of the picture.[4]

It was that same year, 1826, that Stephen Price went to England to run Drury Lane Theatre, when the management of Robert Elliston failed. At the time Kean was still under contract to Drury Lane, and in December, having overcome the initial public opposition to his second tour in America, he returned to London with some success and some money, having most likely expected to take over Drury Lane himself. He acted for Price through the summer, however, but in the fall quarrelled with him and left to go over to the rival theatre at Covent Garden. Although Kean's personal scandal had shut the door forever on his lifelong desire, to be accepted as a gentleman by London society, he had been received back onstage in London as a returning prodigal.

Left without a star, Price contacted Cooper to fill the void. Apparently without much hesitation, Cooper agreed to go. While naturally inclined to help a friend, the offer must also have spoken to his own lifelong desire, to be accepted as a star in the country of his birth.

Before leaving for England, Cooper made a farewell appearance in Philadelphia as Macbeth, and at the conclusion of the performance appeared before the curtain to address the audience. Referring to "the almost unvarying patronage that has attended my career through that long period, first bestowed on me by your fathers, and since continued by you; more than half of whom, now present (I presume) at the distant period, to which I refer, had not come into existence[,]" he pointed out, "I came to America before I had completely arrived at manhood. I may, therefore, be truly said to have passed my whole life of utility among you. What a generous public has awarded to my exertions, has remained in the country, by the means of an almost uninterrupted residence, and the culture of a large family, with which I have been blessed." He went on to express gratitude to his public and bid them *"Adieu!"*[5]

On November 14, 1827, Cooper made his last appearance before leaving the country in New York. He was now fifty-two, and with all the years of exertion, had passed his physical peak; also, the new style of acting was in full vogue in London. However, based on his most recent performances, the *Enquirer* held out high hopes for his success: "Mr. Cooper has already appeared in *Virginius* and *Damon*, and will perform once more previous to his departure for England. We saw him on Saturday, in *Damon*. If he shall, in London, exhibit the same masterly personation, we will answer for his most entire success." Noting his occasional lapses—"Mr. Cooper has played so long to a New-York audience, and is so sure of their good will, that he sometimes suffers himself to fall into a careless style of acting. This is one of the freaks of great talent.... We have seen Mr. Cooper indulge in this kind of capricious relaxation,"—he went on to emphasize the excellence of the Damon performance: "[W]e have seen him, too, rise again, as on Saturday, to the highest pitch of the art."

The writer pointed out that Cooper's strength would be his uniqueness: "In London, Mr. Cooper, will have the distinguishing merit of great originality. He is not like *Young*, a mere imitation of John Kemble, nor like *Macready*, a partial imitator of Kean. Nor does he like Kean, and Macready, rely for effect on any species of trick and quackery. He is the most unaffected and simple actor on the stage. He makes to himself an *ideal* of the character, and goes directly forward, in conformity to that ideal, without seeking to catch applause by the paltry artifices of the profession." As for his style, he predicted, "The old school of criticism will admire his acting. With those by whom Kemble's style was regarded as dramatic perfection, he will be a favorite. The younger *amateurs* will prefer Mr. Kean, and possibly, Macready." Concluding, "But we are convinced of one thing, that the London audiences, when they shall have seen Mr. Cooper in his best characters, and shall have learnt that our American tastes have been formed and fashioned on his performances, will forever cease to allude to those tastes with sarcasms or sneers."[6]

The *New-England Galaxy*, which ran a reprint of Cooper's farewell and the remarks by the *New-York Enquirer*, defined the two-fold challenge he would face: "The taste of the present race of critics is formed upon a model altogether different from his style of acting; and a host of national and political prejudices will be arrayed against him." But then asserted, "Nevertheless, we think he has patience and firmness to conquer them all." And added their own "hearty wish for a pleasant voyage, a happy issue, and a safe return. Such a wish we tender him with all our heart."[7]

Sometime in the late fall Cooper left for England. In a letter to their son James, who was at Christ's Church School in Cowneck, New York, preparing for West Point entrance exams, Mary Cooper expressed anxiety concerning her husband's transatlantic voyage: "I have never seen the notice you speak of the *Throne's* having arrived in London. I am very anxious just now to hear from your dear father. All I have heard is that the vessel was spoke by the *Napoleon* when not many days sail from Liverpool. Still the danger of the coast of England in this inclement season fills me, in spite of myself, with apprehension. The moment I receive a letter, the next day at the furthest, I will send you notice of it."[8]

By the time that letter was written, Cooper had already arrived safely in England. His wife's sense of danger proved more on the mark with regard to the professional backlash that greeted him in London. This was his first return to England since he had left in 1810 amid public outrage for absconding with Cooke when he and Price were joint managers of the Park Theatre. Price had further incurred the wrath of the inbred London theatre world by presuming to take over the management of Drury Lane, one of the Royal Theatres; the other managers had every intention of putting him out of business. Moreover, London was still smarting from the insults Kean, their reclaimed star, had sustained in America. When the English press and public learned that Cooper was on his way to England to act at Drury Lane, they began gathering their forces to take revenge on Kean's purported rival. As Durang surmised, "poor Cooper was the first victim of repute from Yankee land that fell in the way, and he was sacrificed *sans* grace."[9]

On December 17 Cooper opened his engagement at Drury Lane as Macbeth. The house was full, but in the very first scene the audience began to laugh at the three witches, and from then on the performance was jinxed. In the second act after the murder of Duncan, when Cooper spoke the line, "Wake Duncan with thy knocking! I would thou could'st."—the first and second galleries began an "uproar" of laughing and hissing which was taken up by the pit and boxes.[10] *The Age* explained:

> [C]ertain speeches, very ludicrously spoken by an underling, put the audience in a quizzing humour, which got Mr. COOPER somewhat unfairly treated. The laugh once raised, was readily turned by some persons who seemed unfriendly, and others who evidently relished nothing so well as a row, against the hero of the evening, and he really was not

heard with attention enough to enable us to pronounce any decided opinion about him. He made a few new and very good points, which more favourable hearers would have taken up strongly, and praised him for; but they passed off unheeded. He is by no means a young man, but his person is still exceedingly good.—His style and manner of acting is indeed too much in the spirit of the POPE and HOLMAN school; but its constraint and exaggeration on Monday evening may be, we should presume, attributed to the depressing causes at which we have already hinted.

Uncharacteristically, Cooper seems to have been swept away by the animal magnetism. The reviewer said he "was ill, but declined making any fuss about it;" and as the evening proceeded, "was frightened, and tried to cover his fears by a sort of swagger which spoiled his acting."[11] Describing the debacle, the critic for the *Standard* said once the clamor began, "Many of his *hits* thenceforward drew forth nothing but laughter, and he appeared to have lost confidence; so much so, that in the latter part of the play he reeled and staggered on the stage, scarcely knowing what he was about." That critic pronounced the performance "a total failure[,]" saying Cooper's pauses were "more intolerable than even those of Kean or Macready." And concluded, "He will not do." More fairly, however, he noted, "the tumult … almost rivalled an O.[ld] P.[rice] row[.]"[12]

As put in an attack in the *Morning Herald*, Macduff "had to kill *Macbeth* three times before he would yield, and seemed actually at a loss how to dispose of him, as *Macbeth*, the more he fought and was wounded, became the more lively, and at last became so infuriated as to seize his sword with both hands to knock his antagonist down." The reviewer remarked, "This scene was laughable in the extreme, and when *Macbeth* at last fell, the laughter, hissing, and cries of 'Off, Off!' were such, that the tragedy could proceed no further, and the curtain dropped." Commenting that the play was "burlesqued by Mr. Cooper," whom he described as "a strong-built, athletic-looking man, with a countenance bearing a striking resemblance to that of the celebrated Talma," he blamed the manager for having "exposed an actor of long standing to great insults, and created a disturbance in the house which has had no equal since the O. P. rows."[13] Even the afterpiece was not allowed to continue, despite repeated attempts by the singers, until at last, the stage manager Mr. Wallack, responding to the audience's demands, came out to announce an opera for the following evening.[14]

At the beginning of Cooper's career in Edinburgh, when he forgot Malcolm's last lines in *Macbeth*, the curtain fell early and Kemble fired him. This time it was Cooper himself who declined to appear again, and his scheduled performance of Othello was canceled. Stephen Price fought to maintain his managership of Drury Lane through one season and lost everything he had in the venture. When he gave up his lease on the theatre, by an act of bankruptcy he was granted a legal discharge of his debts by a British court. However, true to style, he proceeded to regain his losses and eventually paid off all of his debts with interest. Cooper had no hope of seeing the money Price owed him, but eventually Price paid him a thousand pounds.

Any human being would have been stung by the bitter blow Cooper suffered at the hands of the British public and press, and certainly he must have been. Seen metaphysically, however, he was a famous figure, and as such, embodied the transition between the British and American theatres, and this was the final *coup de grace*. As Durang put it, "Cooper was truly an American tragedian, made here, and so recognized at home and abroad, yet as such was atrociously persecuted at London in the year 1827[.]"[15]

Cooper's American public was outraged by the English insult to their great actor and laid the blame for his failure in London entirely to English prejudice against Americans. With this in mind Mrs. Duff's promoters billed her as an import from Dublin rather than America when she crossed the Atlantic to appear in London a year or so later.[16] The theatrical rivalry continued when the young native-born American star, Edwin Forrest, met with hostility from the followers of Macready on his second British tour in 1845.

Before leaving England Cooper dined with Godwin in January in the company of Mary Shelley and John Howard Payne and went over to Paris briefly. Although he is in a list of guests at a tea on Godwin's birthday March 3,[17] it is not likely that he attended — by mid–March he was back in America. On the 18th he made his first reappearance on the American stage at the Federal Street Theatre in Boston, the city that had banished Kean.

Having given up the idea of addressing the audience prior to the performance, instead he wrote a letter concerning his defeat in London to J. T. Buckingham, editor of the *Boston Courier*, who published it the day of his opening:

> [T]o the joy that I feel at once more meeting you, I have a superadded sentiment of the warmest gratitude for your kindness. When I make bold to tell you explicitly that I did not deserve the indignity, with which I was treated on the occasion of my appearing in Drury Lane Theatre last December, I am confident of your belief for two reasons; my character is generally so well known to you all that you will not suspect

me of falsehood; and, secondly, my word must find corroboration in your understandings, for you would insult them and the good sense of your fathers to believe that, for more than twenty years, you have been heaping favors upon a rank, impudent, and incapable imposter. The treatment I met with could only be merited by such a one. Pity for my incapacity would have attended an ill-judged attempt to gain the critical favor of a London audience; a contemptuous dismissal from their bar of taste might be merited by an impudent and forward person insisting upon a right to their favor; none but a felonious impostor detected and unmasked in an attempt to steal away their understandings, could deserve the hissings and hootings that pursued me almost throughout, and, at the conclusion, the joyful shouts and exultations that rung over me, as over a prostrated enemy. Of course I made no second attempt. The doing so, if not absolutely admitting the justice of the sentence as far as it went, would have been virtually acknowledging the legitimacy of the tribunal; and most assuredly that cannot be a legitimate critical tribunal, which could permit extraneous causes to influence its rewards—or treat an incapable or even a contemptible effort as the act of a wicked and atrocious foe.

The experience had taken a personal toll, so, in addition to their "kindness" he said, "I have to crave something more from you, your indulgence."—

Yes, your *patient* indulgence; for, veteran as I am in the profession, and familiar in the character I am about to assume, my situation is a very new one. To do justice to himself, an actor's mind must be free from any personal feelings, so that his whole force may be concentrated into one single point. All co-operating circumstances that at this moment surround me prevent that desirable state of mind. I therefore, absolutely, and without affectation, request your indulgence for my deficiency. I request it in recollection of times gone by: I request it as a countryman; I hope to be permitted to call myself so, and not in flattery.

Referring to his own "pretensions," Cooper noted that the assault he suffered had forced him at last to recognize fully and finally that he was an American: "The first air I breathed, as a man, was on American ground. From the time, now thirty years since, that I swore allegiance to the American government and constitution, I have always considered and called myself an American, whenever a proper occasion called upon me to do so.—Both here and in Europe, when on different occasions I have been abroad, I have never travelled without an American passport in my pocket. On all grounds, this night, I request your *indulgence*. In London sentence of death has been passed upon my pretensions, and exulting fury attended my execution. My body is exempted from that sentence, and a kind of Irish commutation has taken place. I am banished home."[18]

Cooper received $2,000 for performing six nights in Boston, and the audience gave him a standing ovation at each performance. Edwin Forrest joined him for the last four nights, and they played *Othello* together, alternating the roles of Othello and Iago. The program proved so popular that they went on to play it in Philadelphia and New York; the arrangement was agreeable and profitable to both: Cooper the King, Forrest the heir apparent. On April 23 Cooper played Othello for his benefit at the Park Theatre, with Forrest as Iago, bringing in $1,800.[19]

In May they fulfilled an engagement at the Bowery Theatre under the management of Charles Gilfert, closing on the twenty-first. As it happened, however, the Bowery burned down five nights later, and having expected to return there for eight more performances, the disaster proved to be a waymark for Cooper. He went on to finish the season in Providence, but there, as the lower classes had begun attending the theatre, those who had originally supported it stayed away "except on very rare occasions," such as this last engagement of Cooper, "when there was a large assemblage of his old friends, many of whom had not witnessed a play since his former visit to Providence, several years previous."[20]

Back in New York that fall, with the opening of a new season, it was apparent that the generational tide had fully turned there as well. On August 20 Gilfert opened the Second Bowery Theatre and hired the 22-year-old Forrest at fifty dollars a week as a stock actor, but did not engage Cooper. Intending to promote Forrest as an attraction on his own, Gilfert declined to pay the high price imperative for the established star. The Bowery would be known as the democratic theatre in contradistinction to the aristocratic Park, which had attracted the whole public audience in the earlier part of the century.

The youngest son of an improvident immigrant father, who died when he was thirteen, Forrest had grown up with scant formal education, doing odd jobs to make money. A puny boy, he became fascinated by the circus, which led him to take up gymnastics. Through this pursuit he gradually developed an impressive strength, with bulging muscles in his chest, arms, legs, and neck, as well as a powerful voice, which proved to be his chief assets for a stage career. Since he was essentially untutored, he was more limited in his interpretive ability. He studied his parts very diligently, but relied on logic to work out characterizations and was never able to achieve heights of imagination or spiritual insight. As a handsome young actor he began by following Cooper, but on Kean's second tour, he played with Kean in Albany and received his encouragement. This was a formative experience which liberated the young actor to create his own style from a fusion of the two, a passionate democratic naturalism, and his powerful physical presence and earnest intent made him effective and popular with the American audience, one of their own.

Success and Sorrow—1828–33

Since the fall of 1827 Noah Ludlow and Cooper had been corresponding about the possibility of forming a partnership to run theatres in Mobile, Cincinnati, and Pittsburgh, with the idea of promoting the financing of new theatres in the latter two. Despite the support of certain of Cooper's friends and admirers, however, it became apparent that theatrical activity in those cities was not sufficient to justify the building of second theatres. Ludlow said that he and Cooper "met at the house of his [Cooper's] father-in-law, Judge Fairly [*sic*], ... discussed the subject ... and came to the conclusion we would let matters rest then as they were[.]"[21] As an alternate plan they decided to lease the Chatham Garden Theatre in New York, which had developed out of a summer entertainment parlor built in Chatham Gardens in 1824.

Among the first performers at the Chatham Theatre were Joseph Jefferson, Sr. and his son. The first theatre in New York to be lit by gasjets, for a time after its inception it looked as if the Chatham would become a rival to the Park. Ticket prices by that time had been significantly reduced, and young working class men in New York began attending the Chatham regularly. However, the manager, Barrière, died in 1826, and that October, after much delay, the new Bowery Theatre opened and began to draw the workers crowd. Although Henry Wallack and a number of others made attempts to keep the Chatham going, it was up for rent in 1828 when Cooper and Ludlow took it over.

Ludlow employed the actors to make up the company, including some performers from his southern and western companies and some, "strangers to me, but known to Mr. Cooper[.]" Although they were ready by mid–August, Ludlow said that he took the advice of Cooper to hold off the opening until September to allow a sufficient interlude after the opening of the Bowery, set for August 20. On September 15 Cooper opened the theatre as Duke Aranza in Tobin's *The Honeymoon,* and Ludlow reported that the great star "played with all the spirit and graceful dignity of his earlier days. In his assumption of the rustic he was plain, hearty, and manly; in his mingling with the peasantry, he was social, without losing sight of his rank; and in his last scene was, every inch of him, a grand duke." According to his agreement to star in the first fortnight of the season, Cooper proceeded to play most of his old favorites, including Virginius, Damon, and Leon; and for his benefit the twenty-fifth made his last appearances as Penruddock and Petruchio.[22] Ludlow was elated to find that "Mr. Cooper's friends turned out in considerable numbers," saying, "in point of quality I fancy that the Chatham Theatre seldom held as many of the *élite* of the city before or since."

At the end of the two weeks Cooper followed his usual schedule, leaving New York temporarily to act in Philadelphia and Baltimore. This came as a surprise to Ludlow, who had apparently expected him to stay with the theatre as resident star throughout the season. According to Ludlow, when he objected, Cooper told him he would see Mr. and Mrs. Hamblin in Philadelphia and engage them for the Chatham Garden during his absence; but if he did, he has left no word of it himself, and the Hamblins did not appear. Without a star Ludlow's company was unable to compete with Forrest at the Bowery, so they had to close down the theatre at the end of October.[23]

Meanwhile Cooper set out on an extended tour of the South and West, his first since his return from England. In reward for all his years of touring, the national audience received him with adulation in every city he played—Baltimore, Washington, Charleston, Savannah, Augusta, Mobile, New Orleans, and Cincinnati. He proved to be at his best again when he performed Macbeth on his home territory. A critic at a performance in Charleston reported that in the scene in Act Two after the murder of Duncan, which had been his undoing in London, his "'effect upon the audience was electrical.'"—

> The deed appears so to have congealed the mental powers of the murderer that Macbeth, as personated by Cooper, walks across the stage, backwards with his eyes fixed upon the door of the chamber in which the king and *guest* should have slept—his countenance like marble—his looks—wild—his gait bewildered—finding his way from the horrid scene 'without his eyes'—until the touch of Lady Macbeth recalls him to recollection, and he starts, as it were, into life and thought with a universal tremour and exhaustion of frame.[24]

In New Orleans in March Cooper appeared as Pierre in *Venice Preserv'd* to the Jaffier of Junius Brutus Booth and the Belvidera of Mrs. Sloman. The critic for the *Advertiser* said, "Seldom has an audience in America had a chance of witnessing so much histrionic excellence concentrated on a single piece[.]" He described Mrs. Sloman as "unquestionably a first-rate tragedian, probably the best, for a female, that has appeared on an American stage since the days of the peerless Mrs. WIGNELL [Mrs. Merry]."[25]

Since his early years there, New Orleans had become a teeming city, as Cooper described it in a letter he wrote to his daughter Mary Grace. He told her he had to "share such disagreeable accommodation—a small room in a crowded hotel –" commenting, "[W]henever I have been here before I have always had private furnished rooms –it is absolutely dangerous to pass the streets at night scarcely a week passes without two or three assassinations at early hours & in very publick places—"[26] On the final night of his engagement he appeared as Macbeth to Mrs. Sloman's Lady Macbeth, and the reviewer, predicting a full house, remarked, "It rarely happens in any country that such an actress as Mrs. SLOMAN appears on the stage with such a performer as COOPER."[27] The engagement was extended four more nights.[28]

Cooper could still provide a living for his family by touring, but he and his wife were growing increasingly concerned about the future. The whole family was awaiting confirmation of Jim's appointment to West Point. His mother wrote him that she had received a letter "from my great correspondent, Matt Van Buren," who was currently acting as advisor to President Andrew Jackson, and said that his father would "see Old Hickory himself" when he went on to Richmond.[29]

It was the following summer when they received the news of Jim's acceptance. Cooper responded with a letter of congratulations mingled with fatherly exhortation: "You must feel too much gratification yourself to run the risk of losing the 'mens sibi conscia recte' by carelessness, inattention or bad conduct. But this ought to be sufficient. *Aut Caesar aut nihil.*" In reply to Jim's request for a writing desk, he said he was sending his own, "newly repaired and fitted up."[30] In the letter she wrote to Jim, his mother, in speaking of career choices, warned him against the theatre: "The *stage* I trust you never have thought of—Your own father's example would deter from that—and yet how few actors have ever arrived at the height and respectability he has attained—but pleasing a capricious public taste must be the very worst species of slavery—It is a profession which depends upon the slightest accident to be destroyed. I could write a volume on this point—but I am sure it is unnecessary."[31]

Later in the fall the first real sadness came to the Cooper family when Mary Cooper's father died October 10. On tour in the East, Cooper had to inform his wife of the news in a letter, which he sent to Bristol by an associate, asking him to "prepare her in some measure for the content."[32] She was expecting the birth of another child, but she journeyed to New York for the funeral, and Cooper left the theatre in Boston to join her. It was a large public funeral with New York's leading citizens in attendance. Major Fairlie had served as Clerk of the Supreme Court of New

York for many years, so the courts were adjourned the day after his death to honor him. He had also been a distinguished Revolutionary War veteran, a founding member of the Order of the Cincinnati, and the Order directed their members to wear a badge of mourning for thirty days.[33]

From New York in December Mary wrote Washington Irving, who was living abroad, to tell him about her father's death. In speaking of her loss, she said, "His wit, humor, and vivacity continued to the last; and advance of years only seemed to make him more mild in temper and more tenderly affectionate in his disposition. My children were his children, and his presence in our house was a fete. Twice a year we were so favored." She told Irving she had none of the old gossip, "You and I have both outgrown the age of fashion and folly here." Instead she described her children for him. "Priscilla[,]" she said, "is the genius (there must be a genius in the family) she is just past fourteen, but as tall as I am. She is all talent[.]"[34]

Mary had remained in New York for several months to take care of her mother, and the strain told on her own health. When she returned home to Bristol, she gave birth to a son, Stephen Decatur, but the baby died almost immediately. The following year she had another son, William Gaston, but he too lived only a few weeks.

During the 1830–31 season Cooper acted for a fortnight in New Orleans, playing the unaccustomed character role of Sir John Falstaff in *King Henry IV* to great success, as well as Cardinal Wolsey in *King Henry VIII*.[35] When he appeared again in Philadelphia, Durang, who served as prompter, commented, "Cooper's declining days were now visible ... yet he displayed much of his original vigor and strong musical voice in *Damon, Virginius, Zanga*, etc. All those characters of a middle age he still portrayed with pleasing and graphic effect."[36] On July 18 at the Walnut Street Theatre a performance of *Othello* was advertised as the "LAST NIGHT OF THE GRAND CONCENTRATION OF TALENT. MR. COOPER, MR. BOOTH, MR. BURTON and MRS. DUFF on the same evening."[37] In June, however, Cooper had found it necessary to write a note to Nicholas Biddle, President of the Bank of the United States, to ask for a loan of a thousand dollars.[38]

In the fall of 1831 Mary Grace, by then 18, went with her father on his annual tour to take care of his costumes, recording in her diary, "Sewed at Papa's dress for Richard III until night."[39] As usual Cooper had lined up performances in the major cities, but his wife's health was failing. In the spring Washington Irving, who had just returned from Europe, ran into him in downtown Philadelphia. He invited Irving to go home with him to Bristol for the afternoon, which he did, and wrote a letter about the visit to his brother Peter who was still in Paris:

> This morning I was seated at breakfast at the public table of the Mansion House, when Cooper entered to take his repast. I recognized him instantly; indeed, he retains much of his shape and look, though the former is a little squarer and heavier. I immediately accosted him. He took his seat beside me, and we had an interesting dish of chat. He was on the point of starting for his home at Bristol, and invited me to pay his wife and family a visit, and return in the afternoon steamboat. So said, so done. I took my seat beside him in a light, open carriage, with a tall stripling in the uniform of a cadet of West Point, whom he introduced as his eldest son, and who had much of his mother's countenance. I found Mary Fairlie in a pretty cottage in the pretty town of Bristol, on the banks of the Delaware. She was pale, and thinner than I had expected to find her, yet still retaining much of her former self. I passed a very agreeable and interesting day there....
> ...After dining with them, I got on board a steamboat that was passing at five o'clock, and was whisked up to this city in an hour and a half.[40]

Mary soon became seriously ill, and the strain of anxiety and responsibility weighed heavily on Cooper. He developed respiratory trouble that forced him to cancel several of his appearances. On January 29 he acted Iago to Forrest's Othello at the Park Theatre in New York, his last appearance on that stage.[41] At the time William Dunlap came across him on the street. Observing that Cooper was so changed he "scarcely knew him. A red bloated face, red nose, feeble walk, attenuated limbs," Dunlap reflected, "Probably we never meet again."[42]

On March 19, 1833, Mary Fairlie Cooper died, aged forty-four. That day, in the midst of his mourning, Cooper sat down at his desk and wrote a letter of desperation to Charles Ingersoll, a lawyer in Philadelphia whom he had once assisted as a nineteen-year-old with literary ambition by introducing him to Godwin.[43] Explaining that his professional season had "been interrupted by repeated attacks of fever, and incapacity from an accident & Mrs. Cooper's severe indisposition—" he confided, "Mrs. Cooper, after inexpressible suffering for 6 months, now lies dead in the house & surrounded by worn out, sobbing, & groaning children. I know not which way to turn myself to do what under the circumstances are necessary in decency." Then he asked Ingersoll for a loan pursuant to the sale of his real estate: "I have nothing that I can dispose of but real estate, consisting of my present residence (which I had previously advertised for sale) & some back lands and undivided estate in New York. Under all these circumstances, I have ventured to make an appeal to you for loan say of $500."[44]

A couple of days later John Pintard wrote his daughter about Mary's death: "It made me melancholly [*sic*] to read yest^y the death of Mrs. Mary Cooper on the 19th inst. the eldest daughter of my once old friend Major Fairlie. She married Cooper the Tragedian & lived with every luxury on an elegant embellished seat at Bristol opp° Burlington.... She lost a few months past her only Sister Louise who died at her house where her unfortunate mother still resides." In a second letter he described Mary as "a lady of refined cultivated mind & great sensibility, very amiable & friendly in her intercourse" and said plans were afoot to arrange benefits "for the relief & support of that veteran of the stage, T. Cooper who is s^d to be destitute."

A sour observer, Pintard judged Cooper's profligacy: "No actor in the U.S. has ever rec^d in his prime more substantial remuneration than Cooper. Between the several Theatres he has cleared $20,000 a year for several years. Prodigal & dissipated he spent in luxurious living this ample income. Major Fairlie told me at the time he married his daughter, He [*sic*] considered Cooper worth $80,000, w^h he advised him to anchor to ride by in old age. This & all his earnings appear to be exhausted.... He kept open house at his seat every Sunday[.]"[45]

Always on the move, early on Cooper had adopted a careless disregard for the money he made, neither by temperament nor persuasion prudent about the future. A liberal republican since his time with Godwin, as he later wrote in an informal letter to his son James, he was anti–Whig, and opposed to the establishment of a national bank and all the capitalistic policies which he saw as "mak[ing] us subservient to the monied aristocracy of Great Britain."[46] Had he been conservative, he could indeed have retired from the theatre a wealthy man. In 1831 Charles Mayne Young, the classical actor of his age in London, who was no match for Kemble or Cooper according to Washington Irving, retired in London well off with a respectable reputation intact. Instead, Cooper's favorite pastime was gambling, which had cost him a considerable sum over the years, and he had poured out money for the entertainment of his family and friends; fine dresses for his daughters; horses; servants; and priceless furnishings for his two homes. Having grown up impoverished to work hard, he had also given away generous sums to both friends and strangers.

Durang said that Cooper was always quiet about his acts of charity, but that "[i]n his days of prosperity, the carpenters, scene-shifters, prompters, property-men and tailors, at the expiration of his engagements, were always made joyful by a donation of a liberal kind." Reflecting that Cooper "possessed affections, with all the peculiarities of his queer austerity—... which lend grace to this life," he also described his anonymous generosity to the impoverished and neglected widow of a fellow actor.[47]

In another such instance James Murdoch said he was told that once when Cooper was on the street in Charleston, he saw someone's household goods out on the sidewalk for auction, so "[h]e stopped and asked some questions, by which he found the sale was of a widow's furniture distrained for rent. He stopped the sale, handed the auctioneer the amount of the landlord's claim, with the costs, and went on his way."[48]

EIGHTEEN

"The Father of the American Stage"—1833–36

As the news of Cooper's distress spread, Ingersoll and other prominent citizens and fellow actors in Philadelphia and New York began to arrange a series of complimentary benefits in the major cities. The proceeds from the benefits were to make up the "Cooper Fund" for the support of his children. While Cooper made preparations to sell one of his houses in Bristol, the committee for the Fund met at the Adelphi Club in Philadelphia to fix a date for the benefit there and plan the program. Charles and his daughter Fanny Kemble, who had come to America on tour the previous fall, volunteered their services, as did all the foremost actors in Philadelphia. Ticket prices were set at $2 each with no distinction between the pit and boxes, and the committee solicited contributions over and above the ticket fee.

The Philadelphia benefit took place on June 10, 1833. Cooper acted Pierre in *Venice Preserv'd* supported by Mr. and Miss Kemble as Jaffier and Belvidera. Mr. T. D. [Thomas Dartmouth] Rice, the American blackface entertainer, added his famous "Jim Crow" song to the bill. Unfortunately, the weather was extremely hot and a great many people were out of town for the summer, so despite the appeal to the public and the quality of the performers who had donated their services, the receipts from the benefit were unexpectedly low.[1]

Contrary to his prediction, Dunlap did see Cooper again, a day or so after the benefit, and recorded in his diary, "Meet Cooper (T. A.) He says the benefit here netted 1800 dollars but has ruined him & if he cannot arrange something for his relief ... he must advertize his furniture this afternoon. I made him promise to call on me for advice & assistance if anything is done for him in New York. O! it is melancholy!"[2] Cooper had written Charles Ingersoll again the end of March repeating his intention to sell one of his houses, as well as furniture: twelve classically painted chairs, two settees and Pier tables "made by Finlay of Baltimore ... commissioned all to match—all in perfect preservation[,]" a grand piano, a "very handsome" hanging lamp, etc.[3]

In succeeding weeks the contributions of friends raised the Philadelphia Cooper Fund to $2,500,[4] but disappointed in the receipts and with only the interest at his disposal, Cooper could see that he would have to look elsewhere to provide for his family; his six daughters were all still dependent on him.

Before Mary died she had encouraged Priscilla to go on the stage if necessary to help her father out, as Priscilla explained in a letter to her brother.[5] That summer she broached the subject to her father, but at first he was opposed. Cooper had always protected his daughters from theatrical life, which he, like any gentleman of his time, considered unsuitable for young ladies of breeding. However, as he looked at their situation, he began to recognize that although she was only seventeen, Priscilla was mature and sensible enough to maintain her character as a lady despite the heady atmosphere of stage life. In early September he therefore contacted Dunlap, saying that he considered his daughter Priscilla "as an Actress, *a la mode de* Miss Fanny Kemble."[6] Fanny had gone on the stage in 1829, when her father Charles Kemble was managing Covent Garden, to save him from bankruptcy.

In the late summer Cooper began coaching Priscilla in one or two roles. Then he went to New York to plan a Cooper Fund benefit there. He wrote Edwin Forrest a letter on October 2, saying: "I propose when these benefits are over, to play a few nights in various places to take my leave of the stage, it would be desirable that I should be set at liberty in that respect as soon as possible—circumstanced as my family is, I fear I cannot, consistently with propriety leave them alone for any length of time."[7] In New York he was disappointed to find himself caught in a rivalry between the Park Theatre and the Bowery. His situation made it mandatory to have the benefit as soon as possible, so he had made plans for early November; and considering the Park his home, had expected to have the benefit there. However, Simpson and Price, who had recently returned from Europe, said they could not offer him a booking until December 18, and despite the history of their mutual involvement, refused to accommodate him. He had to take Dunlap's advice and accept the use of the American Theatre, the Bowery, instead, which this time was offered to him at his convenience, on November 7.

Five days before the benefit, the *New-York Mirror* carried a biography of Cooper closing with a statement that he "has contributed to the innocent pleasure of thousands, and has done more than any one man in his profession to elevate the taste of his adopted country."[8] The play for the benefit was *The Honeymoon* with Cooper's traditional role, Aranza, acted by the Bowery manager, Thomas Hamblin, with William Wallack as Rolando. Following the play Miss Wheatley sang a song, the Woods played an olio, and Mrs. Barnes recited Collins's "Ode on the Passions." Then Hamblin spoke a poetic address written by Samuel Woodworth, founder and first editor of the *Mirror*: "'The king comes here to-night!' He who could wring/Our hearts at will, was 'every inch a king!'" The last lines of the address were spoken by the stage manager, Mr. Farren, to introduce Cooper. It was reported that when he first came onto the stage, "shouts and cheers so overcame the veteran that, after bowing his acknowledgments, he was obliged to retire to wipe his moistened eyes and gain his usual voice before he entered on the difficult task of reciting Dryden's splendid ode ["Alexander's Feast"], which was received as usual with the loudest demonstrations of delight."[9]

Suitably, New York came through for Cooper. The benefit there brought in $4,500, said to be the largest testament ever given in Europe or America to a retiring star. The *Mirror* published a list of the receipts for famous theatrical benefits, calculated in dollars, to show that Cooper's had outdone them all: Kean's at Drury Lane [3,277.77], Talma's at the Théâtre Français [2,602.50], a benefit for Dunlap at the Park Theatre [3,194.50], and one for John Howard Payne on his return from Europe [4,200].[10] Cooper sent the New York papers a letter of thanks, singling out George P. Morris, editor of the *Mirror*, with whom he had not been previously acquainted.

Before the benefit Dunlap had written Cooper saying that Colonel Morris advised him that "if his daughter was ready & willing and her appearance on ye Stage determined, now was the time (for him & her sisters)[.]"[11] Taking this lead, three months after his final bow to the New York stage, Cooper reappeared February 8, 1834, in an engagement with Forrest at the Bowery Theatre. On the seventeenth he took a benefit at which he introduced Priscilla to the New York audience, as Virginia in Sheridan Knowles's tragedy. Forrest, who had offered his services, was set to play Virginius at Cooper's request, but at the last moment, Priscilla, understandably nervous, told her father she would feel better if he were to play the part with her himself. When this was "hinted to" Forrest, Forrest immediately consented to give up Virginius to Cooper and take the subordinate role of Dentatus instead.[12]

New York theatre-goers crowded the house to see "Cooper's daughter" and waited anxiously for her first entrance. The moment came when Cooper as Virginius in his powerful voice said to his servant, "Send her to me, Servia." Priscilla appeared from the wings—"tripping toward him with affectionate smiles, Virginia saluted him with the lines, 'Well, Father, what is your will?'" It was reported that "a great shout of joyous approbation rose from the entire audience; the action of the play was suspended for a few minutes, and the eyes of both the parent and his child were filled with tears."[13]

In the review of Priscilla's debut, the *Evening Post* showed a warm regard for the feelings of the young lady:

> The Bowery theatre was crowded last evening and a feeling of the utmost kindness was manifested towards the diffident maiden of whose first public effort they were to be the judges. No female possessing that degree of sensitiveness and modesty which is the invariable accompaniment of genius ever made a very successful first appearance. Those who succeed very well at first, are not apt to continue successful long.... One scene last evening was particularly affecting—it was that in which Virginius describes what a treasure his daughter had been to him ever since her mother's death—how she had been "his sweet companion, pupil, tutor, child," and with what anxious and mingled feelings he had watched over her and directed her education. The perfect and touching applicability of the language to the real circumstances of the widowed tragedian and his motherless girl drew tears from many an eye.[14]

Priscilla was just seventeen and had presumably received only a small amount of tutoring in a couple of roles. How much natural dramatic talent she actually had was yet to be seen. Her only motive for going on the stage was to help her father, and her courage was rewarded by the generous public reception she received in New York. Privately, when Maria Fairlie heard the news that her granddaughter was to appear on the stage of the Bowery Theatre, she refused to receive the Coopers at her home, although she later expressed regret for her "worldly pride" when she wrote about it to her sister-in-law.[15]

From New York the Coopers traveled to New Orleans, where Edwin Forrest was arranging another Cooper Fund benefit at the American Theatre. For weeks in advance the *Advertiser* had been publicizing the "Grand Dramatic Festival for the Benefit of T. A. Cooper and His Children." On April 2 the paper carried a notice signed by over thirty prominent citizens of New Orleans "desirous of giving public testimony of their high sense of the talents of a Tragedian," recognizing him as "the veteran Father of the American Stage,"—"to whose constant and unremitted exertions, during years gone by, they owe many a delightful hour, while present at his masterly representations of the noblest and most exalted points of human character [.]"[16]

Miss Cooper as Helena in Shakespeare's *A Midsummer-Night's Dream*.

An article on the 10th attested to the high artistic standard Cooper had set for the United States through all the years of touring. Beyond the bounds of a personal career, his had come to embrace the cultural leadership of the new nation:

> To those acquainted with the history of Mr. Cooper, and who can bear testimony to his uniform zeal and devotion, for upwards of thirty years past to the best interests and prosperity of the American stage, no appeal need now be made in his behalf. They know that to him, more than to any man living, are the people of the United States indebted for the present elevated state of the American Drama; that to his indefatigable exertions and exalted talents, do they owe that refined taste, and chaste and correct style which so eminently prevail throughout our theatres; and to him, in fine, is due a large debt of gratitude, not only for his unwearied and successful struggles in attempting to erect a standard calculated, at once to benefit the literature and morals of the country, but also for some of the most exquisite emotions which the human heart can know—emotions excited and called forth by his splendid impersonations of the "varied progeny of the tragic muse," and of those lofty qualities and ennobling relations, which the magic power of his genius has so often made to pass in review, and each as it passed, to exercise its thrilling and soul subduing influence."[17]

An announcement the day of the performance, April 14, bespoke his personal appeal: "He, from the commencement of his arrival amongst us, identified himself with our feelings and interests."[18] That evening among a variety of entertainments, the third act of *Othello* was presented with Cooper as the Moor and Forrest as Iago. The final offering was *Virginius*, in which Cooper introduced his daughter to the New Orleans public; Forrest delayed a first trip abroad in order to appear as Dentatus.

The Coopers were welcomed with warm affection by the citizens of New Orleans and received complimentary notices. The receipts of the benefit, though not high, only $1,636.73,[19] increased the Cooper Fund sufficiently to ease Cooper's present situation, and he was happily gratified. Cooper and Forrest proceeded to fulfill a two-week engagement, closing on the twenty-fourth with a repeat performance of *Virginius* with Priscilla.

The following season Cooper returned to New Orleans, as he would as late as 1836, when the 19-year-old American-born debutante, Charlotte Cushman, would come under his powerful influence. Turning from a failed operatic career to the stage at James Caldwell's suggestion, she had the opportunity, not only to observe Cooper in his great roles, but also to play with him onstage, in *Rule a Wife and Have a Wife*.[20]

At the time, James Rees, "Colley Cibber," attended Cooper's benefit in *Macbeth*. Recalling, "It was in the zenith of his fame, when the name of Cooper stood foremost among the histrionic aspirants of the day, that I listened enraptured;"—again this critic recognized the high skill and true distinction of Cooper's art:

> [N]ow, even now, the master-spirit appears, and like some sterling old painting, its beauty still bespeaks the master, though its colors are somewhat mellowed by the hand of time, his every movement now is grace, every action and attitude show the finished actor, and we turn with sorrow from the too mechanical movements of those around him, to admire still more the model they should study. Cooper *has been great*, and is so still; age has not dimmed the fire of his eye, nor destroyed the energies of his mind; giant-like, he moves along in all the majesty of his collected strength. Years have rolled on since last I saw him; what he was then cannot be written; what he is now can be seen and heard. His Macbeth, as played the other evening, has no equal on this side of the Atlantic; we doubt if even now it can be excelled on the other.[21]

Epilogue

1835-49

In the fall of 1835 Cooper returned to New York briefly to appear in a benefit for Thomas Hamblin at the Bowery Theatre on November 24. Probably neither he nor Priscilla realized then that his performance that night as Antony in *Julius Caesar* would be his final appearance before the New York audience. He had performed for them for more than thirty-seven years and had outlasted most of his contemporaries. Mrs. Merry, the great actress with whom he had first appeared on the New York stage, was long since dead. Hodgkinson, Fennell, Warren, Cooke, and Kean, all were gone.

A month after turning eighty, on April 7, 1836, William Godwin died; near the end of his life he had seen Parliamentary reform begun and regained a measure of the respect he deserved. That August his daughter Mary Shelley, by then a widow of many years, wrote to Cooper to ask his help in editing her father's papers.[1] Cooper had, however, saved none of Godwin's letters, though he had continued to send him money over the years, but invited Mrs. Shelley to visit him in America.[2]

During the 30's the Coopers toured together regularly in a varied repertoire, including among others *Othello*, *The Honeymoon* and *The Gamester*. They played four times in Charleston, where Cooper played Benedick to his daughter's Beatrice in *Much Ado About Nothing*, and Mercutio to her Juliet in *Romeo and Juliet*. Of a final performance of *Much Ado* there in 1838, a reviewer asserted that Cooper, "if we allow for the absence of that buoyancy which belongs to an earlier period of life, showed no diminution of that power of varied expression which has always characterized his performances. Into the soliloquy where he first learns the love of **Beatrice** for him there was thrown the sympathizing influence which thoroughly identifies the performer with the character he performs. The gradations from the very first revelation of the fact that he was adored, to the moment that the idea has been realized to his mind that he was really beloved by her who had made him the mark of her too trenchant wit, were marked by consummate judgment and effective personation."[3]

It was probably in 1837,[4] on one of their tours to Richmond that Priscilla received the attention of Robert Tyler, son of the former Governor of Virginia, John Tyler. After seeing her act Desdemona, Robert went backstage to ask Mr. Cooper's permission "to pay his addresses." From then on he pursued Priscilla, writing her passionate love letters from Williamsburg.[5] Priscilla continued to travel with her father, but in the fall of the following year, closing an engagement on October 29 at the Pearl Street Theatre in Albany, the Coopers made their last appearance together on record in *Much Ado*.[6] Priscilla subsequently accepted Robert Tyler's proposal, and on September 12, 1839, they were married at St. James' Episcopal Church in Bristol.

At the beginning of his career in America, Cooper had written to Godwin, mingling Miltonic words with Shakespeare, "Whether 'the drizzling mists, and congregated vapours,' which lowered over and obscured the early day of my existence, *have* dispersed, so as to leave a bright meridian; or whether the evening of my life will be glowing and serene I am equally ignorant."[7] Despite the passing of his fame, the later years did prove to be "glowing and serene." The month after Priscilla's wedding, in October, Mary Grace Cooper married Frederick Raoul of Charleston. The Raouls bought their son and daughter-in-law an estate at Mt. Meigs, near Montgomery, Alabama, where a group of South Carolinians had moved to cultivate the rich cotton land. At Longwood, the plantation they built there, Cooper would spend a number of comfortable winter months surrounded by his children, grandchildren, and friends.

In August, 1840, Priscilla and Robert took his father with them to visit Cooper in Bristol. At the time Tyler was William Henry Harrison's running mate for President of the United States on the Whig ticket. Cooper himself was a Jacksonian democrat, however, and Priscilla wrote Mary Grace, "Pa and Mr. Tyler agree about as much as oil and water." Nevertheless, good humor prevailed, and it was at this time, with the support of the family, that Cooper made his final decision to leave the stage and sell his home in Bristol.[8]

Harrison was subsequently elected President, but he died right after taking office. As a result, in April, 1841, John Tyler acceded to the Presidency, the first Vice-President to do so. His swift decision to interpret the Constitution broadly, to assume the office of President and not just the duties, set a significant precedent.[9] Unfortunately, his wife, Letitia Christian, was already suffering ill health, but she joined him in Washington, and Robert and Priscilla did so as well. Robert took a position in the Land Office. The following fall Mrs. Tyler died in the White House, and since his two grown daughters already had homes of their own, the President asked Priscilla to assume the duties of First Lady.

After taking office Tyler arranged a political appointment for Cooper as military storekeeper at the Frankford Arsenal in Philadelphia with the rank and pay of a captain of infantry. The first actor to have a U.S. government appointment, Cooper was reported to be minutely assiduous and punctual in his duties at the arsenal.

From a portrait of Thomas Abthorpe Cooper by Gilbert Stuart, oil on wood panel, ca 1820. Palmer Museum of Art, the Pennsylvania State University, gift Friends of the Palmer Museum of Art, 80.54.

Later President Polk appointed him to the more lucrative post of inspector in the New York Custom House. A reminiscence in New York described him in those later years: "A portly old gentleman with rubicund face and silvery hair, clothed in summer in an entire suit of white, with an eyeglass hanging jauntily from his neck and a certain indescribable air of high-breeding about him, was often observed in the neighbourhood of Wall Street by many who little imagined that in his person was once concentrated all the matchless elegance of the tragedian Cooper."[10]

After President Tyler remarried in 1844, Robert and Priscilla were free to leave Washington for Philadelphia, where Robert became Clerk of the Superior Court. They eventually moved with their young children to live out in Bristol; and after 1846, when Cooper retired from the post in New York, he divided his time between the Tylers in Bristol and the Raouls in Alabama. The winter of 1848 he was ill much of the time he was in Alabama; that same winter the Park Theatre burned down in New York. His trip back to Bristol in the spring left him worn out, so his daughter Julia Campbell came from New York to help Priscilla take care of him. On Saturday, April 21, 1849, at age seventy-three, Cooper died quietly in the afternoon at the Tylers' home.[11] He was buried beside his wife in the churchyard of St. James' Episcopal Church in Bristol.

Cooper is significant both as the chief transitional figure between the British and the American stage and as a seminal figure in the development of the American theatre. Born in England, he was the first major star to come to America as a young man and build his fame in the new country. Hired for the Chestnut Street Theatre in Philadelphia, it was in New York City, which would become the center of America's commercial theatre, that he made his fame. He went on to develop the itinerant star system as the primary American theatrical model, and initiated the importation of the great British stars as well.

Touring indefatigably throughout the vast new nation, his performances were understandably uneven, but with true heights of imagination and insight, his best were repeatedly described as "electrifying" and "dazzling," particular scenes referred to as "masterpieces." He also offered a broader repertoire to the American audience than any of his contemporaries, the first major star to travel to Charleston, the Southwest territory and New Orleans. A patriarch in the new country, Cooper's grandeur in the classical repertoire created a legacy for American actors, conveyed directly to the two first major American-born stars, Edwin Forrest and Charlotte Cushman, and in later years he took his daughter Priscilla as his co-star. The length of his eminence beginning in the Federal Period, the standard of cultivated excellence he maintained and spread throughout the young country, and his stature as a gentleman, justify his designation as *The Father of the American Stage.*

Chapter Notes

The letters by Thomas Cooper herein cited, when not otherwise indicated, are from the *Abinger Papers*, as are all those by his mother, Grace Mary Cooper, and his sister, Elizabeth Priscilla Cooper.

Preface

1. Charles Durang, "The Philadelphia Stage" (*Philadelphia Sunday Dispatch*, 1854), 3, Ch. 29: 91.
2. Thomas Cooper to James Fairlie Cooper, December, 1838, Harvard Theatre Collection, Houghton Library.
3. William Wood, *Personal Recollections of the Stage* (Philadelphia, 1855), 409–24.

Chapter One

The primary manuscript source for all direct quotations of Cooper in Chapter One is the letter he wrote to William Godwin from "the City of Washington," September 1–9, 1800. Secondary sources for this chapter, in addition to those cited in numbered notes, include: Washington Topham, "The Benning-Maguire House E Street and Neighborhood," *Records of the Columbia Historical Society* 33–4 (1932), 110–11; Mary Augusta Kennedy, *The Theatre Movement in Washington 1800–1835*, unpublished Master's thesis, Catholic University of America, 1933; "Washington City and Capital" in *American Guide Series*, Federal Writers' Project, Works Progress Administration (Washington D.C.: U.S. Government Printing Office, 1937), 143;

Kenneth R. Bowling, *The Creation of Washington, D.C. The Idea and Location of the American Capital* (Fairfax, Virginia: George Mason University Press, 1991), 235 ff.

1. *Letters of Mrs. Adams, the Wife of John Adams* (Boston: C. C. Little and J. Brown, 1840), 2: 240–1.
2. Wood, *Recollections*, 411–12.
3. "Diary of Mrs. William Thornton 1800–1863," *Records of the Columbia Historical Society* 10 (1907), 177.
4. John Clagett Proctor, "Old Historic Theaters and Concert Halls," *Sunday Star* (Washington, D.C.), December 20, 1931.
5. *Centinel of Liberty, or George-Town and Washington Advertiser*, August 22, 1800.
6. Thornton, *Diary*, 182–3.
7. Allen C. Clark, *Greenleaf and Law in the Federal City* (Washington, D.C.: Press of W. F. Roberts, 1901), 258–60.
8. Wood, *Recollections*, 423–4.
9. Sir Joshua Reynolds, *Discourses on Painting and the Fine Arts, Delivered at the Royal Academy* (London: Jones and Co., 1825; reprint ed., New Haven and London: Yale University Press, 1988), 240.
10. Francis Courtney Wemyss, *Twenty-Six Years of the Life of an Actor and Manager* (New York, 1847), 1 [of 2], 75. See also William Wirt, "Essay on Manner," *The Old Bachelor* (Richmond: The Enquirer Press, 1814, reprint ed., Delmar, N.Y.: Scholars' Facsimiles and Reprints, Inc., 1985), 31: 204–5.
11. Lael J. Woodbury, "The American Theatre's First Star: Thomas Abthorpe Cooper," *Theatre Annual* 15 (1957–8), 13–14; Fred Belton, *Random Recollections of an Old Actor* (London: Tinsley Bros., 1880), 151.

12. Wood, *Recollections*, 56–7.
13. *Ibid.*, 57.
14. *Ibid.*, 56.
15. *Centinel of Liberty*, August 26, 1800.
16. *Ibid.*, August 29, 1800.
17. Thornton, *Diary*, 185.
18. *Centinel of Liberty*, September 5, 1800.
19. Thornton, *Diary*, 188.
20. *Centinel of Liberty*, September 5, 1800.
21. Thornton, *Diary*, 192–4. Allen C. Clark (*Greenleaf and Law*, 259) states the closing date incorrectly as September 13.
22. Aloysius I. Mudd, "Early Theatres in Washington City," *Records of the Columbia Historical Society* 5 (1902), 68.

Chapter Two

1. The baptismal record is the primary source for Cooper's birth date, which is so stated there. Approximately a hundred years after his death, one of Cooper's great-granddaughters, Priscilla Goodwyn Griffin, had a tombstone placed at the Coopers' gravesite in the churchyard of St. James' Church, Bristol, Pennsylvania; Cooper's birth year is incorrectly inscribed thereon as 1776, and Mary Fairlie Cooper's birthdate, October 20, 1788, is omitted.
2. Author unknown. *Abinger Papers*: Dep. c. 607/3.
3. Signed at Dacca, the will is on file in the India Office Library, India Office Records, 197 Blackfriars Road; London SE1.
4. Mary Shelley, *Memoirs*.
5. There is a full inventory of Dr. Cooper's personal effects in his will.
6. William Godwin, *An Account of the Seminary That will be opened On Monday the Fourth Day of August, At Epsom in Surrey, For the Instruction of Twelve Pupils in the Greek, Latin, French, and English Languages* (1783, reprint ed., Gainesville, Fla., 1966), 2.
7. Godwin to Holcroft, August 5, 1788, in C. Kegan Paul, *William Godwin: His Friends and Contemporaries* (1876, reprint ed., New York, 1970), 1: 54. A family friend of the Shelleys, Paul had permission to publish what he selected from Godwin's correspondence from Godwin's grandson, Sir Percy Florence Shelley (1819–1889).

8. William St. Clair, *The Godwins and the Shelleys The biography of a family* (New York and London, 1989), 56.
9. William Dunlap, *Diary of William Dunlap* (New York, 1930) 1[of 3], 229.

Chapter Three

1. Wood, *Recollections*, 410.
2. Godwin, *An Account of the Seminary*, 22–43.
3. Dunlap, *Diary* 1: 222–3.
4. Paul, *Godwin* 1: 64.
5. Godwin, *Journal: Notes on Tom Cooper his studies and temper 1790–91, Abinger.* Dep. b. 229/2. Chap. 3 quotations of Godwin (except in letters) are from this source.
6. B. Sprague Allen, "William Godwin and the Stage," *Publications of the Modern Language Association of America* 35, new series 28 (1920), 365.
7. Grace Mary Cooper to Elizabeth Priscilla Cooper, ca. 1791.
8. Cooper to Godwin, [1790]; Mary Shelley, *Memoirs*.
9. Godwin to Cooper, April 19, 1790.
10. Cooper to James Marshal, November 3, 1790.
11. Edmund Burke, *Reflections on the French Revolution* (1792, reprint ed., London: J. M. Dent Sons Ltd., 1951), 9.
12. Paul, *Godwin* 1: 17.
13. Dunlap, *Diary* 1: 223.
14. Grace Mary Cooper to Godwin, March 1, 1793, Winchester Street.
15. Elizabeth Priscilla Cooper to Godwin, February 27, 1793, Denbigh.
16. Elizabeth Priscilla Cooper to Godwin, November 14, 1792, Denbigh.
17. Godwin to Dyson, March 21, 1792, *Abinger.* Dep. c. 607/3.
18. Dunlap, *Diary* 1: 229.
19. Dunlap, *History of the American Theatre* (1832, rep. ed., New York, 1963) 1[of 2], 342.

Chapter Four

1. Dunlap, *American Theatre* 1: 342.
2. James Edward Murdoch. *The Stage, or Recollections of Actors and Acting from an Experience of Fifty Years: A Series of Dramatic*

Sketches (1880, reprint ed., New York, 1969), 90.
3. Dunlap, *Diary* 1: 223-9
4. Cooper to Godwin, July 27, 1792, Edinburgh.
5. Cooper to Godwin, July 28, 1792, Edinburgh.
6. Cooper to Godwin, August 6-7, 1792, Newcastle.
7. Cooper to Godwin, August 1, 1792, Edinburgh.
8. Cooper to Godwin, August 6-7, 1792, Newcastle.
9. Cooper to Godwin, August 11, 1792, Newcastle.
10. Cooper to Godwin, August 13, 1792, Newcastle.
11. Wood, *Recollections*, 414.
12. See illus., page 205. There is also a Gilbert Stuart portrait of Cooper in the Hampden-Booth Theatre Library, The Players, NYC.
13. Cooper to Godwin, August 15, 1792, Newcastle.
14. Cooper to Marshal, August 16, 1792, Newcastle.
15. Cooper to Godwin, August 24, 1792, Newcastle.
16. Dunlap, *Diary* 1: 224.
17. Elizabeth Priscilla Cooper to Godwin, October 27, 1794, Oak Hill.

Chapter Five

1. Grace Mary Cooper to Godwin, March 1, 1793, Winchester Street.
2. Cooper to Godwin, March 1, 1793, Portsmouth.
3. Cooper to Godwin, March 21, 1793, Portsmouth.
4. Dunlap, *Diary* 1: 139.
5. Cooper to Godwin, April 8, 1793, Portsmouth.
6. Cooper to Godwin, March 21, 1793, Portsmouth.
7. Cooper to Godwin, April 8, 1793, Portsmouth.
8. Cooper to Godwin, July 13, 1793, Winchester.
9. Cooper to Godwin, July 19-21, 1793, Winchester.
10. Cooper to Godwin, July 13, 1793, Winchester.

11. Cooper to Godwin, October 18, 1793, Southampton.
12. Cooper to Godwin, November 20, 1793, Southampton.
13. Cooper to Godwin, October 18, 1793, Southampton.
14. Dunlap, *American Theatre* 1: 347.
15. Cooper to Godwin, November 20, 1793, Southampton.
16. Cooper to Godwin, January 12, 1794, Chichester.
17. St. Clair, 85.
18. Dunlap, *Diary* 1: 290.
19. St. Clair, 130.
20. Wood, *Recollections*, 411.
21. Cooper to Godwin, October 21, 1794, Stockport.
22. Cooper to Godwin, October 28, 1794, Stockport.

Chapter Six

1. Cooper to Godwin, January 20, 1795.
2. Elizabeth Priscilla Cooper to Godwin, August 1, 1792, Edinburgh.
3. Cooper to Godwin, July 25, 1795, Exeter.
4. Thomas Holcroft, "The Actor, No. V," *Westminster Magazine*, August, 1780.
5. Murdoch, *The Stage*, 87.
6. William Winter, *Other Days Being Chronicles and Memoirs of the Stage* (New York, 1908), 28.
7. Washington Irving to his brother William Irving, Jr., October 26-9, 1805, London, in *Letters*, ed., Ralph M. Aderman, Herbert L. Kleinfield and Jenifer S. Banks, 1 [of 4] (vol. 23 of *The Complete Works of Washington Irving*, Boston: Twayne Publishers, 1978), 212.
8. Cooper to Godwin, August, 1795, Exmouth.
9. "Life of Mr. Cooper," *Mirror of Taste and Dramatic Censor* 1: 1 (January 1810), 38.
10. "Retrospect of First Appearances. Mr. Cooper," *Monthly Mirror* 1 (December 1795), 45-50.
11. Ibid., *Monthly Mirror* 1: 113-17.
12. Ibid., *Monthly Mirror* 2 (May 1796): 39-41.
13. *Oracle and Public Advertiser* 19:144, October 23, 1795.

14. *The London Times*, October 20, 1795.
15. *The London Times*, October 27, 1795.
16. *The London Times*, November 2 and 3, 1795.
17. Wood, *Recollections*, 412.
18. *The London Times*, December 1, 1795.
19. *Monthly Mirror* 1: 121-2.
20. Joseph Norton Ireland, *A Memoir of the Professional Life of Thomas Abthorpe Cooper* (1888, reprint ed., New York: Burt Franklin, 1970), 95.
21. Dunlap, *Diary* 1: 225.
22. Durang 1, Ch. 28: 55.
23. *Monthly Mirror* 2: 122.
24. Cooper to Godwin, March 26, 1796, Bath.
25. Elizabeth Priscilla Cooper to Godwin, May 13, 1796, Brompton.
26. Durang 1, Ch. 28: 55.
27. Thomas Holcroft to Cooper, September 3, 1796, reprinted in Dunlap, *Diary* 1: 255-6.
28. Dunlap, *Diary* 1: 256.
29. Archibald Hamilton Rowan, *Autobiography* (1840, reprint ed., Shannon, Ireland: Irish University Press, 1972), 252-3.
30. Dunlap, *Diary* 1: 229.

Chapter Seven

The primary manuscript source for all direct quotations of Cooper in Chapter Seven is a letter he wrote to William Godwin from Philadelphia, April 1, 1800.

1. John B. Irving, "Reminiscences of a Tragedian" Part 7, *Home Journal*, January 2, 1858.
2. William Warren, *Journal*, October 18, 1796, Channing Pollock Theatre Collection, Howard University.
3. Ireland, *Memoir of Cooper*, 1.
4. William Dunlap, *American Theatre* 1: 301-2.
5. Durang 1, Ch. 28: 53.
6. John B. Irving, "Reminiscences of a Tragedian" Part 2, *Home Journal*, August 29, 1857; "Dr. Irving's Reminiscences of the Charleston Stage," *South Carolina Historical and Genealogical Magazine* 52: 3 (July 1951), 167.
7. Warren, *Journal*. Entry, Tuesday November 8, 1796, records their arrival in Baltimore at Evans-Indian Queen Tavern at 3 P.M.; November 11 Warren says he played the character of Tempest in *The Wheel of Fortune*, noting, " I was very well received. Cooper plays Penruddock—his first appearance[.]" Durang notes [1, Ch. 27: 51] that in his *History of the American Theatre* Dunlap mistook the date of Cooper's American debut: "*En passant*, we will here mention an error of Mr. Dunlap's. He states that Mr. Cooper's first appearance in America was at the Chesnut street theatre [*sic*], in the character of *Macbeth*. We quote from Mr. Warren's diary—which has been kindly placed at our disposition by Mrs. Anna Marble, daughter of Mr. Warren, and widow of the late lamented Daniel Marble, the American comedian." David Ritchey, ed., *A Guide to the Baltimore Stage in the Eighteenth Century: A History and Day Book Calendar*, (Westport, Conn. and London: Greenwood Press, 1982), 34, also states incorrectly: "Although these performers arrived in October, Baltimore audiences did not have an opportunity to see them until May[.]"
8. Wood, *Recollections*, 413.
9. Christopher J. Thaiss, "Shakespeare in Maryland, 1752-1860" in Philip C. Kolin, *Shakespeare in the South Essays on Performance* (Jackson, Mississippi, 1983), 59-60.
10. See Richard Butsch, *The Making of American Audiences From Stage to Television, 1750-1990* (Cambridge, 2000), 32-43.
11. Wemyss, *Twenty-Six Years* 1: 73.
12. By 1805 when the New Theatre on Chestnut Street was enlarged to accommodate 2000, only 900 were box seats.
13. Paul Leicester Ford, *Washington and the Theatre* (New York: The Dunlap Society, 1899), 45; Proctor, "Old Historic Theaters and Concert Halls," *Sunday Star*, (Washington), December 20, 1931.
14. *Gazette of the United States, & Philadelphia Daily Advertiser*, December 10, 1796.
15. Durang 1, Ch. 20: 36.
16. Charles Beecher Hogan, ed., *The London Stage 1660-1800; A Calendar of Plays, Entertainments & Afterpieces Together with Casts, Box-receipts and Contemporary Comment Compiled from the Playbills, Newspapers and Theatrical Diaries of the Period* (Carbondale, Ill., 1968), Part 5: 3 (1792-1800), 1588-9. See also Genevieve Richardson, "Costuming on the American Stage 1751-1901: A Study of the Major Developments in Wardrobe Practice and Costume

Style" (Ph.D. dissertation, University of Illinois, 1953), 32.
17. Durang 1, Ch.18: 33; 3, Ch.105: 338.
18. *Gazette of the United States*, February 3, 1797.
19. Stephen Cullen Carpenter, "Life of Mr. Cooper," *Mirror of Taste and Dramatic Censor* 1: 1 (January, 1810), 41–2.
20. Durang 1, Ch. 29: 56.
21. Cooper to Godwin, April 1, 1800, Philadelphia.
22. Dunlap, *American Theatre* 1: 352.
23. Durang 1, Ch. 27: 51.
24. *New York Gazette*, September 12, 1797, in George C. C. Odell, *Annals of the New York Stage* (1927–49, reprint ed., New York, 1970), 1: 460.
25. Dunlap, *Diary* 1: 160.
26. Durang 1, Ch. 29: 56.
27. *Ibid.* 1, Ch. 28: 55.
28. Ireland, *Memoir of Cooper*, 15.
29. Durang 1, Ch. 15: 27–8.
30. *Ibid.* 1, Ch. 28: 53.
31. Dunlap, *Diary* 1: 212.

Chapter Eight

The primary manuscript source for all direct quotations of Cooper in Chapter Eight is the same as in Chapter Seven, his letter to William Godwin from Philadelphia, April 1, 1800.
1. Oral Sumner Coad and Edwin Mims, Jr., *The American Stage*, vol. 14 of Ralph Henry Gabriel, *Pageant of America, A Pictorial History of the United States* (New Haven, 1929), 51–3; Dunlap, *American Theatre* 2: 12; Odell, *New York Stage* 2: 6.
2. Dunlap, *American Theatre* 2: 14–16.
3. Dunlap, *Diary* 1: 225–7.
4. *Commercial Advertiser*, February 28, 1798.
5. Dunlap, *American Theatre* 2: 16.
6. *Commercial Advertiser*, March 2, 1798.
7. Dunlap, *Diary* 1: 227–31. See also Durang 1, Ch. 28: 55. Charles Macklin acted on the eighteenth-century British stage for almost seventy years, famous for his portrayal of Shylock in Shakespeare's *Merchant of Venice*. By his extensive coaching of young actors, he was influential in the legacy of British acting style and technique.

8. Wood, *Recollections*, 243.
9. *Commercial Advertiser*, March 5, 1798.
10. Dunlap, *American Theatre* 2: 19.
11. Dunlap, *Diary* 1: 228.
12. Dunlap, *American Theatre* 1: 190.
13. Dunlap, *Diary* 1: 234–5.
14. Dunlap, *American Theatre* 2: 20–2.
15. William Dunlap, *ANDRÉ A Tragedy in Five Acts* (1887, reprint ed. with an introduction by Brander Matthews, New York: Burt Franklin, 1970), "*Preface*" (April 4, 1798), xxxii.
16. *Commercial Advertiser*, February 2, 1799.
17. *Commercial Advertiser*, April 26, 1799.
18. Charles E. L. Wingate, *Shakespeare's Heroes on the Stage* (New York and Boston, 1896), 24.
19. *Commercial Advertiser*, May 2, 1799.
20. *Commercial Advertiser*, May 4, 14, 17 and 27, 1799.
21. "Records of the First and Second Presbyterian Churches of the City of New York" (published for the New York Genealogical and Biographical Society, 64 Madison Ave., NYC), 15 (1884), 33.
22. Dunlap, *American Theatre* 2: 81. A version of the Kotzebue play was running in London at the time; Dunlap got his title and the names of the characters from the English bill.
23. *Commercial Advertiser*, December 12, 1798.
24. Dunlap, *American Theatre* 2: 125.

Chapter Nine

1. *Commercial Advertiser*, November 28, 1799.
2. *Commercial Advertiser*, December 5, 1799.
3. Thomas Holcroft, "The Actor, No. V," *Westminster Magazine*, August, 1780.
4. *Commercial Advertiser*, December 11, 1799.
5. Ford, *Washington and the Theatre*, 62.
6. *Commercial Advertiser*, January 1, 1800.
7. *Commercial Advertiser*, January 13, 1800.
8. Cooper to Godwin, April 1, 1800, Philadelphia.
9. Dunlap, *American Theatre* 2: 124–5.

10. Cooper to Godwin, April 1, 1800, Philadelphia.
11. Durang 1, Ch. 34: 68.
12. *Port Folio*, January 17, 1801.
13. Cooper to Godwin, [n.d.], in reply to Godwin's of December ?, 1800.
14. Cooper to Godwin, September 1–9, 1800, City of Washington.
15. Durang 1, Ch. 44: 88.
16. Wood, *Recollections*, 414.
17. *Port Folio*, February 5, 1801.
18. *Port Folio*, February 14, 1801.
19. *Port Folio*, February 26, 1801.
20. *Port Folio*, March 28, 1801.
21. *Port Folio*, April 4, 1801.

Chapter Ten

1. Dunlap, *Diary* 1: 54–5.
2. Durang 1, Ch. 34: 68.
3. Dunlap, *American Theatre* 2: 148.
4. *Ibid.*, 151.
5. *Ibid.*, 154–9; Odell, *New York Stage* 2: 121.
6. Durang 1, Ch. 63: 135.
7. *New-York Evening Post*, December 10, 1801.
8. *New-York Evening Post*, December 26, 1801.
9. *New-York Evening Post*, December 17 and 26, 1801.
10. Dunlap, *American Theatre* 2: 160.
11. *Morning Chronicle*, October 21, 1802.
12. Register of Baptisms in the Parish of Trinity Church, New York 1: 542.
13. Kenneth Garlick and Angus Macintyre, ed., *The Diary of Joseph Farington* (New Haven and London, 1979), September 24, 1802, vol. 5 [of 17], 1876.
14. Cooper to Richard Brinsley Sheridan [n.d.].
15. *Morning Chronicle*, December 27–8, 1802.
16. Durang 1, Ch. 62: 134; Dunlap, *American Theatre* 2: 166–7.
17. *Morning Chronicle*, January 10, 11 and 12, 1803.
18. *New-York Mirror*, November 2, 1833.

Chapter Eleven

1. William Godwin, *Journal*, March 7 and 9, 1803, *Abinger*, Dep. e. 206 Folio 30.
2. *The London Times*, March 8, 1803.
3. *The London Times*, March 18, 1803.
4. *The London Times*, March 22, 1803.
5. *Monthly Mirror* 15 (March 1803): 191.
6. Elbridge Colby, ed., *Life of Thomas Holcroft* (1925, reprint ed., New York, 1968) 2 [of 2]: 253–4.
7. *Ibid.* 2: 302, n.1.
8. Cooper to Godwin, [n.d.], in reply to Godwin's of December ?, 1800.
9. William Dunlap, *The Life of George Frederick Cooke* (1815, reprint ed., New York, 1972), 1[of 2]: 298–318.
10. Wood, *Recollections*, 419–20. The great Georgian letter-writer, Sir Horace Walpole, referred to Roscoe as "'the best historian and poet of this age.'" (W. S. Lewis, ed., *Horace Walpole's Correspondence* (New Haven: Yale University Press, 1937), vol. 15 [of 48], 328.
11. Wood, *Recollections*, 99.
12. *Ibid.*, 420–1.
13. *Manchester Townsman*, December 28, 1803.
14. *Manchester Mercury*, January 3, 1804.
15. *Manchester Townsman*, January 10, 1804.
16. *Manchester Townsman*, January 24, 1804.
17. *Manchester Townsman*, January 16, 1804.
18. *Manchester Townsman*, February 14, 1804.
19. *Manchester Townsman*, February 23, 1804.
20. R. J. Broadbent, *Annals of the Manchester Stage, 1735–1845*, 3 vols., Manchester [n.d.], 304.
21. *Manchester Townsman*, February 14, 1804; *Gore's General/ Liverpool Advertiser*, January 26, 1804.
22. Dunlap, *Cooke* 1: 341–6.
23. *Port Folio*, March 3 and 31, 1804; *Morning Chronicle*, March 6, 1804. The *Literary Magazine and American Register* ran a reprint: 1, 6 (March 1804), 431–4. As advance publicity for Cooper's first tour of the South the sketch also appeared in *Repertory*, April 9, 1805; *Richmond Enquirer*, August 15, 1806, et.al.
24. Dunlap, *American Theatre* 2: 210–12.

# Notes—Chapter Twelve

Chapter Twelve

1. Durang 1, Ch. 48: 100.
2. *Morning Chronicle*, November 17, 1804.
3. *Morning Chronicle*, November 19, 1804.
4. *New-York Evening Post*, November 20, 1804.
5. *Morning Chronicle*, November 29, 1804.
6. *Morning Chronicle*, December 1, 1804.
7. *Morning Chronicle*, December 4, 1804.
8. David B. Ogden to William Meredith, November 30, 1804, New York, *Meredith Papers*, Historical Society of Pennsylvania.
9. *Morning Chronicle*, December 8, 1804.
10. *Morning Chronicle*, December 1, 1804.
11. Noah Miller Ludlow, *Dramatic Life As I Found It* (1880, reprint ed., New York, 1966), 73–4.
12. *Scrapbook of Anna Warren Marble* (Chicago, 1853), Channing Pollock Theatre Collection, Howard University.
13. Dunlap, *American Theatre* 2: 213–14.
14. William W. Clapp, Jr., *A Record of the Boston Stage* (1853, reprint ed., New York, 1969), 82–4.
15. *Independent Chronicle*, April 22, 1805.
16. Letter to Eloise, June 19, 1817, London, reprinted in Gabriel Harrison, *John Howard Payne His Life and Writings* (1885, reprint ed., New York, 1969), 72–3.
17. Dunlap, *American Theatre* 2: 216–23.
18. John Bernard, *Retrospections of the Stage* (London, 1830), 1 [of 2]: 28–9.
19. John Bernard, *Retrospections of America* (1887, reprint ed., New York/London, 1969), 268. Spranger Barry was an Irish actor who acted at Drury Lane with Macklin and Garrick, becoming Garrick's rival when he went over to Covent Garden in 1750.
20. George O. Willard, *History of the Providence Stage, 1762–1891* (Providence, 1891), 33–4.
21. *Port Folio* [newly issued as a monthly] 1: 3 (March 1809), 265.
22. Charles Blake, *Historical Account of the Providence Stage* (1868, reprint ed., New York, 1971), 147.
23. *Polyanthos* 1 (January 1806), 73–86. Like Cooper, Buckingham had lost his father as a boy; after making his way as an apprentice to a printer, he had founded the daily *Courier*.
24. *Polyanthos* 1 (February 1806), 212.
25. *Polyanthos* 1 (February 1806), 210.
26. *Polyanthos* 1 (March 1806), 279–80.
27. *Thespian Mirror* 11 (March 8, 1806), 91 and 12 (March 15, 1806), 99.
28. *Thespian Mirror* 1 (December 28, 1805); 4 (January 18, 1806), 25–7; 5 (January 25, 1806), 33–5.
29. *Thespian Mirror* 11 (March 8, 1806), 88.
30. *Thespian Mirror* 14 (May 31, 1806), 112.
31. Coad and Mims, *American Stage*, 62.
32. William Dunlap, *History of the Rise and Progress of the Arts of Design in the United States* (1834, reprint ed., New York, 1965), 1[of 3]: 322–3.
33. Durang 1, Ch. 62: 133.
34. *Ibid.* 1, Ch. 63: 135.
35. *Richmond Enquirer*, April 11, 1806.
36. *Charleston Courier*, April 21, 1806.
37. John B. Irving, "Reminiscences of a Tragedian" Parts 3 and 4, *Home Journal*, September 5–12, 1857.
38. *Monthly Review and Literary Miscellany of the United States* [also called *Monthly Register and Review*], 1 (1806), 334–5.
39. *Monthly Review* 1: 329–31.
40. John B. Irving, "Reminiscences of a Tragedian" Part 2, *Home Journal*, August 29, 1857.
41. Woodrow L. Holbein, "Shakespeare in Charleston, 1800–1860," in Kolin, *Shakespeare in the South*, 98–9.
42. *Ibid.*, 88.
43. *Virginia Gazette*, June 4, 1806.
44. *Richmond Enquirer*, August 29, 1806.
45. Dunlap, *Rise and Progress of the Arts of Design* 2: 245–6; Edward Biddle and Mantle Fielding, *The Life and Works of Thomas Sully 1783–1872* (Charleston: Garnier & Co., 1969), 8–9.
46. Durang 1, Ch. 38: 76.
47. John W. Francis, *Old New York; or, Reminiscences of the Past Sixty Years* (1857, reprint ed., New York: Benjamin Blom, 1971), 249.
48. Bernard, *Retrospections of America*, 164–7.
49. Joseph Norton Ireland, *Records of the New York Stage* (1866, reprint ed., New York: Benjamin Blom, 1966) 1: 239.
50. Dunlap, *American Theatre* 2: 242–3; *Polyanthos* 4 (December, 1806), 69–71.
51. Odell 2: 283.

Chapter Thirteen

1. Washington Irving, "Theatrics. by William Wizard, Esq." *SALMAGUNDI; or, The Whim-whams and Opinions of Launcelot Langstaff, Esq. and Others.* 6 (March 20, 1807), ed., Bruce I. Granger and Martha Hartzog, vol. 6 of *The Complete Works of Washington Irving* (Boston: Twayne Publishers, 1977), 137–8.
2. Pierre M. Irving, *The Life and Letters of Washington Irving By His Nephew* 1[of 3], vol. 12 of *The Works of Washington Irving*, (1862, reprint ed., New York: AMS Press, 1973), 155–6.
3. Coad and Mims, *American Stage*, 62. See also Dunlap, *American Theatre* 2: 247.
4. Durang 1, Ch. 41: 83.
5. Dunlap, *American Theatre* 2: 245–7.
6. See Laurence Hutton, *Opening Addresses* (1887, reprint ed., New York: Burt Franklin, 1970), 22–6.
7. Durang 1, Ch. 63: 135.
8. Reese Davis James, *Cradle of Culture 1800-1810 The Philadelphia Stage* (Philadelphia, 1957), 21.
9. Durang 1, Ch. 32: 65.
10. Henry Dickinson Stone, *Personal Recollections of the Drama or Theatrical Reminiscences* (1873, reprint ed., New York and London, 1969), 207–8.
11. Wood, *Recollections*, 302–4, 414–15.
12. *Commercial Advertiser*, January 11, 1808. The family record in the frontispiece of the *Bible* Frederic Raoul gave to Mary Grace Cooper as a wedding present [See *Acknowledgements*, 13] makes it apparent that Mary Grace, Cooper's eldest child of his second marriage, kept up with her half-brother, Thomas Hercules Price Cooper. She noted that her father had three children by his first wife, that two died in infancy, and that the eldest, Thomas, became a midshipman in the U.S. Navy, but died "at Pensacola, of yellow fever about 1823 or 24" (when Mary Grace was ten or eleven years old). This primary evidence sets the record straight; until now, in all the various accounts of Cooper's life, scholars have assumed that all three (some say there were only two) of Cooper's children by his first wife, Joanna, died in infancy.
13. Dunlap, *Diary* 2: 399–400.
14. Durang 1, Ch. 63: 135.
15. Ludlow, *Dramatic Life*, 227.
16. Clapp, *Boston Stage*, 94–6. See also: Durang 2, CH. 6: 176: "Cooper's *Iago* was acted like the gentleman of high comedy. He differed from the received mode of playing this gentlemanly villain. There was a suavity about the performance that pleased, as it stamped it with a very correct originality. Cooper's idea of the part should be more generally adopted." J.B. Irving, "Reminiscences of a Tragedian" Parts 3 and 4, September 5 and 12, 1857: Recalling Cooper as having less "stage trick ... than any man I ever saw in the profession."—"His Iago always thought *a very finished piece of acting*, ... in the stern and unbending *in purpose*, the insidious and pliant in manner, the complete, smooth-varnished villain.... Many of his readings struck me as so beautiful and illustrative, that, although I had seen Iago enacted with great felicity on many occasions, *the extent* of the significations of some of the passages never before presented themselves to me. His rapid transitions from deliberating on the fell purpose of Iago to the practical *act* itself, from hate to vengeance, from the *creation* of his agents to the *employing* of them, were all striking and felicitous." *Southern Patriot*, Charleston, January 9, 1838: In the soliloquy beginning "That Cassio loves her,"—"[W]e thought we could perceive in every lineament and change of voice the development of that dark intellect and subtle, plotting spirit of mischief in Iago that balances probabilities of success with the chances of failure, in mentally working out a plan of demoniacal wickedness. It was truly a master piece of acting, the vivid embodyment of deep calculating cunning, sharpened by concentrated hate."
17. Washington Irving, "THEATRICAL INTELLIGENCE. By William Wizard, Esq." *Salmagundi* 14 (September 19, 1807), *Complete Works* (Twayne Publishers) 6: 244–5.
18. Durang 3, Ch. 91: 286; Odell, *New York Stage* 2: 297.
19. James Fennell, *An Apology for the Life of James Fennell* (New York, 1969), 398.
20. Durang 1, Ch. 28: 55.
21. Washington Irving, "BY ANTHONY EVERGREEN, GENT." *Salmagundi* 5 (March 7, 1807), *Complete Works* 6: 126.

22. Washington Irving, *Life of George Washington* (New York: G. P. Putnam & Co., 1857), 4 [of 5]: 475–6.
23. Washington Irving to Joseph Gratz, March 30, 1808, New York, *Letters* (Twayne Publishers) 1: 254.
24. Washington Irving to "Mac," [Richard McCall?] November 18, 1808, New York. See Stanley T. Williams, *Life of Washington Irving* (New York/London, 1935) 1 [of 2]: 101; 405, n. 162.
25. Dunlap, *American Theatre* 2: 256.
26. Willis T. Hanson, Jr., *Early Life of John Howard Payne With Contemporary Letters Heretofore Unpublished* (Printed for the Bibliophile Society in Boston, Cambridge: University Press, 1913), 119–20.
27. Wood, *Recollections*, 127–8.
28. Harrison, *John Howard Payne*, 241.
29. *Mirror of Taste and Dramatic Censor* 1: 3 (March 1810), 231–2. Cooper and Price brought George Joseph Holman to America in 1812.
30. *Mirror of Taste and Dramatic Censor* 1: 5 (May 1810), 420–1.
31. Walter Prichard Eaton, *The Actor's Heritage* (Boston, 1924), 203–4.
32. "Life of Mr. Cooper," *Mirror of Taste and Dramatic Censor* 1: 1 (January 1810), 28–44.
33. Godwin, *Journal, Abinger*, Dep. e. 210 Folio 31 ᵛ.
34. Dunlap, *Cooke* 2: 130–173.
35. Don B. Wilmeth, *George Frederick Cooke Machiavel of the Stage* (Westport, Ct and London, 1980), 255.
36. See Marc Baer, *Theatre and Disorder in Late Georgian London* (Oxford, 1992), 18–36.
37. *Monthly Mirror* 8 (November 1810), 397.
38. Thomas Shepherd Munden, *Memoirs of Joseph Shepherd Munden Comedian* (London, 1844), 179–81.
39. *Monthly Mirror* 8 (October 1810), 315–16.
40. Arnold Hare, *George Frederick Cooke The Actor and the Man* (Great Britain, 1980), 177.
41. Dunlap, *Cooke* 2: 164–5.
42. Don Wilmeth, *George Frederick Cooke*, 258, n. 9.
43. Dunlap, *Diary* 2: 439.
44. Durang 1, Ch. 44: 88.
45. Dunlap, *Diary* 2: 415.
46. Ireland, *Memoir of Cooper*, 37; Dunlap, *Cooke* 2: 179–81.
47. See Doron Green, *A History of the Old Homes on Radcliffe Street* (Bristol, Pa., 1938), 129–30.
48. Cooper to unknown recipient, February 5, 1811, Harvard Theatre Collection, Houghton Library.
49. Cooper to Godwin, March 27, 1811, Ship Magdelen, Longitude 70 west of Greenwich.
50. Cooper to Godwin, April 4, 1811, New York City.
51. Ireland, *Memoir of Cooper*, 37.
52. Washington Irving to Henry Brevoort, May 15, 1811, New York, *Letters* (Twayne Publishers) 1: 318.
53. Dunlap, *Diary* 2: 420–1.
54. Durang 1, Ch. 44: 88–9.
55. Dunlap, *Diary* 2: 416–35.
56. *Ibid.* 2: 446.
57. Dunlap, *Cooke* 2: 331–2.
58. Durang 1, Ch. 44: 89.
59. Dunlap, *Cooke* 2: 343.
60. John Randolph to Cooper, January 16, 1812, George Town, Library of Congress. Anthony Hart Harrigan, *The Wit and Wisdom of John Randolph of Roanoke*, private collection.
61. Durang 1, Ch. 51: 107.

Chapter Fourteen

1. William Winter, "Famous Actors of the Nineteenth Century A Chapter of Theatrical History," *Munsey's Magazine* 35 (April–September, 1906), 351.
2. Elizabeth Tyler Coleman, *Priscilla Cooper Tyler* (Tuscaloosa, Al., 1955), 1–4.
3. John Pintard to his daughter, May 31, 1833, in *Letters from John Pintard to his Daughter Eliza Noel P. Davidson 1816–1833* (New York, 1940–1), 4 [of 4]: 157.
4. *New-York Mirror*, November 2, 1833.
5. Washington Irving to Brevoort, July 8, 1812, New York, *Letters* (Twayne Publishers) 1: 338.
6. George Sidney Hellman, *Washington Irving, Esquire* (New York: A. A. Knopf, 1925), 80.
7. Thomas Cooper to John P. Kemble, December 11, 1811, New York, Folger Shakespeare Library.

8. Durang 3, Ch. 29: 91.
9. Clapp, *Boston Stage*, 134.
10. *The Columbian*, September 24, 1813.
11. *The Columbian*, October 23, 1813.
12. *The Columbian*, November 27, 1813.
13. William Warren, *Journal*, Sunday, September 18, 1814, Channing Pollock Theatre Collection, Howard University.
14. Washington Irving to Brevoort, August? 1814? New York, *Letters* (Twayne Publishers) 1: 366.
15. Washington Irving to Brevoort, December 28, 1815, Birmingham, *Letters* (Twayne Publishers) 1: 430.
16. Durang 1, Ch. 52: 108.
17. Reese Davis James, *Old Drury of Philadelphia A History of the Philadelphia Stage 1800–1835* (1932, reprint ed., New York/London: 1968), 187–8.
18. *Boston Weekly Magazine*, November 30, 1816.
19. *Boston Weekly Magazine*, November 23, 1816. See Joseph T. Buckingham, "*Recollections of a Favorite Actor*," The Boston Book, 205: "Of all his [Cooper's] attempts in comedy, the part of Duke Aranza, in the Honey Moon [John Tobin], was immeasurably the best, and in this part he stood as far above all competition, as he did in Hamlet or Macbeth."
20. *Boston Weekly Magazine*, December 14, 1816.
21. *New-York Evening Post*, June 12, 1817.
22. Odell 2: 58.
23. *New-England Galaxy and Masonic Magazine*, December 31, 1819.
24. *New-England Galaxy and Masonic Magazine*, January 7, 1820.
25. Coleman, *Priscilla*, 11, n. 3.
26. Charles Mathews to Mrs. Mathews, September 12, 1822, Philadelphia., in *The Life and Correspondence of Charles Mathews, The Elder, Comedian. By Mrs. Mathews*, Edmund Yates, ed., (London: Routledge, Warne, and Routledge, 1860), 260–1.
27. Wood, *Recollections*, 388.

Chapter Fifteen

1. Washington Irving to Cooper, September 10, 1819, private collection of the Bristol Riverside Theatre, Bristol, Pa.

2. *New-York Mirror, and Ladies' Literary Gazette*, October 25, 1823.
3. *Boston Commercial Gazette*, December 9, 1819.
4. *New-England Galaxy & Masonic Magazine*, December 31, 1819.
5. *New-York Mirror, and Ladies' Literary Gazette*, September 27, 1823.
6. *New-York Evening Post*, November 18, 1820.
7. *The American*, November 29, 1820.
8. *New-England Galaxy*, November 30, 1820.
9. *New-England Galaxy*, November 24, 1820.
10. Joseph T. Buckingham, *Miscellanies Selected from the Public Journals* (Boston, 1822), 227.
11. *New-England Galaxy*, December 8, 1820.
12. Ludlow, *Dramatic Life*, 233.
13. *The American*, January 4, 1821.
14. *New-York Evening Post*, January 8, 1821.
15. *New-York Evening Post*, January 11 and 12, 1821.
16. J. B. Irving, "Reminiscences of a Tragedian" Part 6, *Home Journal*, December 5, 1857.
17. J.B. Irving, "Dr. Irving's Reminiscences of the Charleston Stage," *South Carolina Historical and Genealogical Magazine* 53: 1(January 1952), 40.
18. Murdoch, *The Stage*, 143–4.
19. Henry L. Pinckney and Abraham Moise, eds., *A Selection from the Miscellaneous Writings of the late Isaac Harby, Esq.* (Charleston, 1829), 268–9. See Harby for his description of Cooper's Coriolanus (278–9): "The proud unbending Patrician, the haughty aristocratic spirit of *Coriolanus*, were admirably adapted for Mr. Cooper's voice and countenance. Indeed, we consider him in this character to be, comparatively, faultless.... In the scene in which *Coriolanus* solicits for the consulship, Mr. Cooper gave a forcible expression of the anti-democratic patrician. He begged, as if he would demand. In the last act, the supplication before the walls of Rome, was a scene we have never seen excelled. The workings of his countenance, the restraint which pride and honour lay upon nature and humanity, were inimitably pourtrayed."

Pointing to "Mr. Cooper's manner of testifying his broken pride and returning tenderness," in the scene "when *Coriolanus* relapses from the tyrant to the man," and his resentment at being called "boy" in the last scene, Harby remarks on "these scenes of high-wrought passion," where he says, "we have often been impressed with the belief that Mr. Cooper exhibits rather than masters the emotion. There is such strength and nature in his manner, on these occasions, that he takes us in spite of the cold dictates of judgment, and hurries us along in the rapidity and glow of his own conceptions." And notices, "In the act of dying, Mr. Cooper very judiciously covered his face with his garment—as Anthony describes Julius Caesar, when he falls—'and in his mantle muffling up his face.'"
20. John Pintard to his daughter, May 29, 1821, New York, *Pintard Letters* 2: 45–6.
21. Don Wilmeth, *George Frederick Cooke*, 278–82.

Chapter Sixteen

1. In 1818 Noah Miller Ludlow with his American Theatrical Commonwealth Company had offered New Orleans one season of theatre in English.
2. *Rider's Digest*, October 15, 1856.
3. Durang 1, Ch. 63: 135.
4. *Louisiana Gazette*, March 23, 1821.
5. *Louisiana Gazette*, March 26, 1821.
6. *Louisiana Gazette*, March 23, 1821.
7. James Rees, *The Dramatic Authors of America* (Philadelphia, 1845), 55.
8. *Ibid.*, 53.
9. Joe Cowell, *Thirty Years Passed Among the Players* (New York, 1844), 60.
10. Green, *Old Homes on Radcliffe Street*, 177; Coleman, *Priscilla*, 12–13. Although Cooper's home at 722 Radcliffe Street was torn down in the 1950s, the home he built for his children is still in use as a private residence. On Radcliffe Street in the twentieth century the Margaret R. Grundy Memorial Library was erected, and an active legitimate theatre, the Bristol Riverside Theatre, developed. At the end of the street near the ferry landing, the King George II Inn is said to be "the oldest operating inn in America—established 1681."
11. Durang 3, Ch. 29: 91.
12. *Louisville Public Advertiser*, May 4, 1822; See John J. Weisert, "The First Decade at Sam Drake's Louisville Theatre," *The Filson Club History Quarterly* 39, 4 (October 1965), 294.
13. Solomon Smith, *Theatrical Management in the West and South for Thirty Years* (1868, reprint ed., New York/ London, 1968), 24.
14. *New-York Mirror, and Ladies' Literary Gazette*, September 20, 1823.
15. Wemyss, *Twenty-Six Years* 1: 75–6.
16. *National Advocate*, September 24, 1823.
17. *Daily National Intelligencer*, February 7–8, 1825.

Chapter Seventeen

1. Doron Green, *A History of Bristol Borough* (Bristol, Pa., 1911), 131–143; Dr. Julius Sobel, "From Bristol to the White House," *Old Bucks County Magazine* 21: 1995, 4.
2. Durang 2, Ch.30: 226.
3. *New-England Galaxy*, March 18, 1825.
4. Durang 2, Ch. 32: 233.
5. Reprinted in *New-England Galaxy*, November 16, 1827.
6. *New-York Enquirer*, November 12, 1827.
7. *New-England Galaxy*, November 16, 1827.
8. Mary Fairlie Cooper to James Fairlie Cooper, January [1828], Bristol, Coleman Papers.
9. Durang 2, Ch. 3: 169.
10. *Morning Herald*, December 18, 1827.
11. *London Age*, December 23, 1827.
12. *London Standard*, December 18, 1827.
13. *Morning Herald*, December 18, 1827.
14. *London Standard*, December 18, 1827.
15. Durang 3, Ch. 29: 91.
16. Ireland, *Memoir of Cooper*, 49. Joseph Norton Ireland, *Mrs. Duff* (Boston, 1882), 87.
17. Godwin, *Journal*, January 21, 23 and March 3, 1828, *Abinger*, Dep. e. 223 Folio 3 ʳ.
18. *Boston Courier*, March 18, 1828, reprinted in *New York Evening Post*, March 20, 1828. Also see Buckingham, *Miscellanies*

Selected from the Public Journals, 226–7: "There is no truth in the suggestion, which is sometimes made, that Mr. Cooper's powers are on the decline, and that his acting is wanting in that spirit and energy, which once made them so attracting. Whoever has seen him from year to year, must have perceived a gradual improvement. His style of acting, it is granted, is very different, in many parts, from that which he has formerly exhibited. But it is all for the better. There is more of natural tenderness in his Hamlet, more of dignity in his Coriolanus, more passion in his Othello, more terror in his Macbeth, than formerly; there is more of philosophical deliberation in all his parts; and he seldom introduces a variation from his former manner, seldom makes a deviation from the beaten track, which antiquity and fashion have consecrated, that has not something, at least, plausible, if not convincing, to offer in its vindication." Citing his delivery of Mark Antony's funeral oration in *Julius Caesar* as "a model of eloquence[,]" he said, "Though always elegant and graceful Mr. Cooper has also improved essentially in declamation.... His gesture is natural and graceful; his utterance, though choked with the rising passion, which is to soften and subdue the Roman rabble, is yet distinct and energetic; and his voice, capable of almost every variety of modulation, never disappoints by running into a false inflexion, or an imperfect cadence."

19. Ireland, *Memoir of Cooper*, 52.
20. Willard, *The Providence Stage*, 114.
21. Ludlow, *Dramatic Life*, 311.
22. Ireland, *Records of the New York Stage* 1: 614.
23. Ludlow, *Dramatic Life*, 319.
24. Holbein, "Shakespeare in Charleston," in Kolin, *Shakespeare in the South*, 93–4.
25. *Louisiana Advertiser*, March 9, 1829.
26. Cooper to Mary Grace Cooper, March 27, 1829, New Orleans, Harvard Theatre Collection, Houghton Library.
27. *Louisiana Advertiser*, March 16, 1829.
28. *Louisiana Advertiser*, March 23, 1829.
29. Mary Fairlie Cooper to James Fairlie Cooper, November 2, [1829], Bristol, *Coleman Papers*.
30. Cooper to James Fairlie Cooper, July 13, 1830, St. John, New Brunswick, *Coleman Papers*.
31. Mary Fairlie Cooper to James Fairlie Cooper, September 5 [1830], Bristol, *Coleman Papers*.
32. Cooper to [?], October 1830, Folger Shakespeare Library.
33. *Evening Post*, October 11, 1830; Mary Fairlie Cooper to James Fairlie Cooper, October 15, 1830, *Coleman Papers*; Robert Tyler, "James Fairlie," in John Schuyler, *Institution of the Society of the Cincinnati Founded by the Officers of the American Army of the Revolution ... from the Transactions of the New York State Society*, (New York, 1886, reprint ed., Chelsea, Mi., 1998), 199–201.
34. Mary Fairlie Cooper to Washington Irving, December 9, 1830, New York, *Coleman Papers*. In 1842, when Priscilla was serving as First Lady for her father-in-law, President John Tyler, after the death of his wife, she welcomed Washington Irving to a White House levee honoring the British novelist Charles Dickens. See Coleman, *Priscilla*, 96–7.
35. Ireland, *Memoir of Cooper*, 55.
36. Durang 3, Ch. 15: 47.
37. Unidentified clipping, July 18, 1831, Harvard Theatre Collection, Houghton Library.
38. Thomas Cooper to Nicholas Biddle, June 30, 1831, Bristol, Harvard Theatre Collection, Houghton Library.
39. Mary Grace Cooper, *Diary*, December 17, 1831, *Coleman Papers*.
40. Washington Irving to his brother Peter Irving, June 21, 1832, Philadelphia, *Letters* 2 (24 of *Complete Works*, Boston: Twayne Publishers, 1979), 707.
41. Ireland, *Records of the New York Stage* 2: 47.
42. Dunlap, *Diary* 3: 642.
43. Cooper to Godwin, June 10, 1802, New York.
44. Cooper to Charles J. Ingersoll, March 19, 1833, Bristol, *Charles Jared Ingersoll Collection*, Historical Society of Pennsylvania.
45. John Pintard to his daughter, March 25 and 27, 1833, New York, *Pintard Letters* 4: 133–4.
46. Thomas Cooper to James Fairlie Cooper, September 5, 1840, Bristol, Harvard Theatre Collection, Houghton Library.
47. Durang 1, Ch. 63: 135; Ch. 62: 134.
48. Murdoch, *The Stage*, 375.

Chapter Eighteen

1. Ireland, *Memoir of Cooper*, 59–60.
2. Dunlap, *Diary* 3: 693.
3. Cooper to Charles Ingersoll, March 31, 1833, Bristol, *Charles Jared Ingersoll Collection*, Historical Society of Pennsylvania.
4. Ireland, *Memoir of Cooper*, 60.
5. Priscilla Cooper to James Fairlie Cooper, undated, *Coleman Papers*.
6. Dunlap, *Diary* 3: 739. In 1837 Mary Fairlie Cooper's second sister, Julia Fairlie, 13 years younger than she and a favorite aunt to the Cooper children, would marry Samuel G. Ogden, a widower whose daughter, Anna Cora Ogden Mowatt Ritchie, followed Priscilla on the stage and wrote *Fashion*, the first successful American play by a woman. See Mrs. Ritchie, *Autobiography of an Actress; or, Eight Years on the Stage* (Boston: Ticknor, Reed, & Fields, 1854).
7. Cooper to Edwin Forrest, October 2, 1833, New York, Harvard Theatre Collection, Houghton Library.
8. *New-York Mirror*, November 2, 1833.
9. Ireland, *Memoir of Cooper*, 61–3. The address was reprinted in *New-York Mirror*, November 16, 1833.
10. *New-York Mirror*, November 23, 1833.
11. Dunlap, *Diary* 3: 754.
12. *New-York Evening Post*, February 17, 1834.
13. Perrine, *op cit.*, *Ladies Home Journal* (October 1904), 4.
14. *New-York Evening Post*, February 18, 1834.
15. Maria Yates Fairlie to Mrs. John V. N. Yates, March 5, 1834, Albany, *Coleman Papers*.
16. *Louisiana Advertiser*, April 2, 1834.
17. *Louisiana Advertiser*, April 10, 1834.
18. *Louisiana Advertiser*, April 14, 1834.
19. *Louisiana Advertiser*, April 19, 1834.
20. Joseph Leach, *Bright Particular Star The Life and Times of Charlotte Cushman* (New Haven and London, 1970), 39–42.
21. Front-page obituary, April 26, 1849, *The Pennsylvanian* 32: 5459.

Epilogue

1. Mary Shelley to Thomas Cooper, August 24, 1836, in *The Letters of Mary Wollstonecraft Shelley*, ed. Betty T. Bennett (Baltimore and London: Johns Hopkins University Press, 1983), 2 [of 3]: 274–5.
2. Mary Shelley to Thomas Cooper, April 6, 1837, author's collection.
3. *Southern Patriot*, January 5, 1838.
4. Coleman, *Priscilla*, 66.
5. Rober Tyler to Priscilla Cooper, author's collection.
6. Ireland, *Memoir of Cooper*, 76; Coleman, *Priscilla*, 63–4.
7. Cooper to Godwin, [n.d.], in reply to a letter from Godwin, December, 1800.
8. Priscilla Cooper Tyler to Mary Grace Raoul, August 15, 1840, Bristol, *Coleman Papers*; Coleman, *Priscilla*, 80.
9. Oliver Perry Chitwood, *John Tyler Champion of the Old South* (New York and London: D. Appleton-Century Co., 1939), 205.
10. Ireland, *Memoir of Cooper*, 78–9.
11. *Bucks County Intelligencer*, May 1, 1849.

Bibliography

Manuscripts

Abinger Papers. Godwin and Shelley manuscripts owned by Lord Abinger on deposit at the Bodleian Library, Oxford University. Microfilm copy: New York Public Library, The Carl H. Pforzheimer Shelley and His Circle Collection, File 15.

Elizabeth Tyler Coleman Papers, 1776–1955. The W. S. Hoole Special Collections Library, The University of Alabama.

Warren, William. *Journal, 1796–1831; Scrapbook of Anna Warren Marble*, Chicago, 1853. Channing Pollock Theatre Collection. Howard University.

Books

Archer, Stephen M. *American Actors and Actresses: A Guide to Information Sources.* Detroit: Gale Research, 1983.

_____. *Junius Brutus Booth Theatrical Prometheus.* Carbondale and Edwardsville: Southern Illinois University Press, 1992.

Baer, Marc. *Theatre and Disorder in Late Georgian London.* Oxford: Clarendon Press, 1992.

Baker, Herschel Clay. *John Philip Kemble.* 1942, reprint ed., Westport, Ct.: Greenwood Press, 1969.

Bennett, Betty T. *Selected Letters of Mary Wollstonecraft Shelley.* 3 vols., Baltimore and London: The Johns Hopkins University Press, 1995.

Bernard, John. *Retrospections of America 1797–1811.* Bayle Bernard, ed., 1887, reprint ed., Laurence Hutton and Brander Matthews, New York/London: Benjamin Blom, 1969.

_____. *Retrospections of the Stage.* 2 vols., London: Henry Colburn & Richard Bentley, 1830.

Blake, Charles. *An Historical Account of the Providence Stage; Being a Paper Read Before the Rhode Island Historical Society, October 25th, 1860. (With Additions).* 1868, reprint ed., New York: Benjamin Blom, 1971.

Boaden, James. *Memoirs of the Life of John Philip Kemble, Esq., Including a History of the Stage, From the Time of Garrick to the Present Period.* 2 vols., 1825, reprint ed., New York: Benjamin Blom, 1969.

Borkat, Roberta F.S., ed. *The Plays of Richard Cumberland.* New York and London: Garland Publishing, Inc., 1982.

Bost, James S. *Monarchs of the Mimic World: The American Theatre of the Eighteenth Century Through the Managers—The Men Who Made It.* Orono: University of Maine Press, 1977.

Buckingham, Joseph T. *Miscellanies Selected from the Public Journals*. Boston: Joseph T. Buckingham, 1822.

———. *Personal Memoirs and Recollections of Editorial Life*. Boston: Ticknor, Reed, and Fields, 1852.

Butsch, Richard. *The Making of American Audiences: From Stage to Television, 1750–1990*. Cambridge, U.K.: Cambridge University Press, 2000.

Cameron, Kenneth Neill, ed. *Shelley and His Circle*. 4 vols., Cambridge: Harvard University Press, 1961.

Campbell, Thomas. *Life of Mrs. Siddons*. 1839, reprint ed., New York: Benjamin Blom, 1972.

Clapp, William W., Jr. *A Record of the Boston Stage*. 1853, reprint ed., New York: Greenwood Press, 1969.

Coad, Oral Sumner. *William Dunlap: A Study of His Life and Works and of His Place in Contemporary Culture*. 1917, reprint ed., New York: Russell & Russell, 1962.

———, and Edwin Mims, Jr. *The American Stage*. Vol. 14 of Ralph Henry Gabriel. *The Pageant of America*. New Haven: Yale University Press, 1929.

Colby, Elbridge, ed. *The Life of Thomas Holcroft Written by Himself; Continued to the Time of His Death from His Diary Notes & Other Papers by William Hazlitt*. 2 vols., 1925, reprint ed., New York: Benjamin Blom, 1968.

Coleman, Elizabeth Tyler. *Priscilla Cooper Tyler*. Tuscaloosa: University of Alabama Press, 1955.

Cone, Carl B. *The English Jacobins Reformers in Late 18th Century England*. New York: Charles Scribner's Sons, 1968.

Cowell, Joe. *Thirty Years Passed Among the Players in England & America: Interspersed with Anecdotes and Reminiscences of a Variety of Persons, directly or indirectly connected with the drama during the Theatrical Life of Joe Cowell, Comedian*. New York: Harper and Bros., 1844.

De Marly, Diana. *Costume on the Stage 1600–1940*. Totowa, N.J.: Barnes and Noble Books, 1982.

Dircks, Richard J. *Richard Cumberland*, in Twayne's *English Authors Series*. Boston: G.K. Hall and Co., 1976.

Donohue, Joseph W., Jr. *Dramatic Character in the English Romantic Age*. Princeton: Princeton University Press, 1970.

Dormon, James H., Jr. *Theater in the Ante Bellum South 1815–1861*. Chapel Hill: University of North Carolina Press, 1967.

Doty, Gresdna. *The Career of Mrs. Anne Brunton Merry in the American Theatre*. Baton Rouge: Louisiana State University Press, 1971.

Downer, Alan Seymour. *The Eminent Tragedian William Charles Macready*. Cambridge: Harvard University Press, 1966.

———, ed. *The Memoir of John Durang, American Actor, 1785–1816*. Pittsburgh: University of Pittsburgh Press, 1966.

Dunlap, William. *Diary of William Dunlap (1766–1839): The Memoirs of a Dramatist, Theatrical Manager, Painter, Critic, Novelist, and Historian*. 3 vols., New York: The New-York Historical Society, 1930.

———. *History of the American Theatre, and Anecdotes of the Principal Actors*. 2 vols., 1832, reprint ed., *improved, incorporating a list of early plays and a narrative of his connection with the Old American Company, 1792–1797, by John Hodgkinson*. 3 vols. in 1, New York: Burt Franklin, 1963.

———. *History of the Rise and Progress of the Arts of Design in the United States*. 3 vols., 1834, reprint ed., New York: Benjamin Blom, 1965.

_____. *The Life of George Frederick Cooke (Late of the Theatre Royal, Covent Garden). Composed Principally from Journals and Other Authentic Documents Left by Mr. Cooke, and the Personal Knowledge of the Author. Comprising Original Anecdotes of His Theatrical Contemporaries, His Opinions on Various Dramatic Writings, &c.* 2 vols., 1815, reprint ed., New York: Benjamin Blom, 1972.

Durham, Weldon B. *American Theatre Companies, 1749–1887.* New York, Westport, Ct., and London: Greenwood Press, 1986.

Eaton, Walter Prichard. *The Actor's Heritage Scenes from the Theatre of Yesterday and the Day Before.* Boston: Atlantic Monthly Press, 1924.

Fennell, James. *An Apology for the Life of James Fennell.* 1814, reprint ed., New York: Benjamin Blom, 1969.

Francis, John W. *Old New York; or, Reminiscences of the Past Sixty Years. Being an Enlarged and Revised Edition of the Anniversary Discourse Delivered Before The New-York Historical Society (November 17, 1857).* 1865, reprint ed., New York: Benjamin Blom, 1971.

Garlick, Kenneth, and Angus Macintyre, ed. *The Diary of Joseph Farington.* 17 vols., New Haven and London: Yale University Press, 1978–84.

Godwin, William. *An Account of the Seminary That Will Be Opened on Monday the Fourth Day of August, at Epsom in Surrey, for the Instruction of Twelve Pupils in the Greek, Latin, French, and English Languages.* 1783, reprinted in *Four Early Pamphlets (1783–84).* Burton R. Pollin, ed. Gainesville, Florida: Scholars Facsimiles and Reprints, 1966.

_____. *An Enquiry Concerning Political Justice and Its Influence on General Virtue and Happiness.* 2 vols., London: G.G. & J. Robinson, 1793; 1796; 1798, reprint ed., New York and Oxford: Woodstock Books, 1992.

Green, Doron. *A History of Bristol Borough.* Camden, N.J.: C.S. Magrath, 1911.

_____. *A History of the Old Homes on Radcliffe Street Bristol, Pennsylvania, Together with a Brief History of Bristol Borough Anciently Known as Buckingham Which Is the Third Oldest Town and Second Chartered Borough in Pennsylvania.* Bristol, Pa., 1938.

Grimsted, David. *Melodrama Unveiled American Theater and Culture 1800–1850.* Chicago and London: University of Chicago Press, 1968.

Griswold, Rufus Wilmot. *The Republican Court, or, American Society in the Days of Washington.* New York: D. Appleton, 1859.

Harby, Isaac. *A Selection from the Miscellaneous Writings of the late Isaac Harby, Esq.* eds. Henry L. Pinckney and Abraham Moise. Charleston: James S. Burges, 1829.

Hare, Arnold. *George Frederick Cooke: The Actor and the Man.* The Society for Theatre Research, 1980.

Harrison, Gabriel. *John Howard Payne, Dramatist, Poet, Actor, and Author of Home, Sweet Home! His Life and Writings.* 1885, reprint ed., New York: Benjamin Blom, 1969.

Henderson, Mary C. *Theatre in America 200 Years of Plays, Players, and Productions.* New York: Harry N. Abrams, 1968.

Hewitt, Barnard. *Theatre U.S.A. 1668 to 1957.* New York, Toronto, and London: McGraw-Hill Book Co., 1959.

Highfill, Philip H., Jr., Kalman A. Burnim, and Edward A. Langhans. *A Biographical Dictionary of Actors, Actresses, Musicians, Dancers, Managers and Other Stage Personnel in London, 1660–1800.* 16 vols., Carbondale and Edwardsville: Southern Illinois University Press, [1973]–c 1993.

Hillebrand, Harold Newcomb. *Edmund Kean*. 1933, reprint ed., New York: AMS Press, Inc., 1966.
Holmes, Richard. *Coleridge Early Visions, 1772–1804*. New York: Pantheon Books, 1989.
Hoole, W. Stanley. *The Ante-Bellum Charleston Theatre*. Tuscaloosa: University of Alabama Press, 1946.
Ireland, Joseph Norton. *A Memoir of the Professional Life of Thomas Abthorpe Cooper*. 1888, reprint ed., New York: Burt Franklin, 1970.
_____. *Mrs. Duff*. Boston: James R. Osgood & Co., 1882.
_____. *Records of the New York Stage from 1750 to 1860*. 2 vols., 1866, reprint ed., New York: Benjamin Blom, 1966.
Irving, Pierre M. *The Life and Letters of Washington Irving by His Nephew*. 4 vols., 1862; 3 vols., 1869, reprint ed., vols. 12–14 of *The Works of Washington Irving*, New York: AMS Press, 1973.
Irving, Washington. *The Complete Works of Washington Irving*. 30 vols., Boston: Twayne Publishers, 1969–89.
James, Reese Davis. *Cradle of Culture 1800–1810 The Philadelphia Stage*. Philadelphia: University of Pennsylvania Press, 1957.
_____. *Old Drury of Philadelphia: A History of the Philadelphia Stage 1800–1835 Including the Diary or Daily Account Book of William Burke Wood, Co-Manager with William Warren of the Chestnut Street Theatre, familiarly known as Old Drury*. 1932. reprint ed., New York / London: Johnson Reprint Corporation, 1968.
Kendall, John S. *The Golden Age of the New Orleans Theater*. Baton Rouge: Louisiana State University Press, 1952.
Kolin, Philip C. *Shakespeare in the South Essays on Performance*. Jackson: University Press of Mississippi, 1983.
Leach, Joseph. *Bright Particular Star: The Life & Times of Charlotte Cushman*. New Haven and London: Yale University Press, 1970.
Levine, Lawrence W. *Highbrow/Lowbrow: The Emergence of Cultural Hierarchy in America*. Cambridge: Harvard University Press, 1988.
Ludlow, Noah Miller. *Dramatic Life as I Found It: A record of personal experience; with an account of the rise and progress of the drama in the West and South, with anecdotes and biographical sketches of the principal actors and actresses who have at times appeared upon the stage in the Mississippi Valley*. 1880, reprint ed., New York: Benjamin Blom, 1966.
Manvell, Roger. *Sarah Siddons Portrait of an Actress*. New York: G.P. Putnam's Sons, 1971.
Marshall, Peter H. *The Anarchist Writings of William Godwin*. London: Freedom Press, 1986.
_____. *William Godwin*. New Haven and London: Yale University Press, 1984.
Matthews, Brander, and Laurence Hutton, eds. *Actors and Actresses of Great Britain and the United States from the Days of David Garrick to the Present Time*. 5 vols., New York: Cassell & Co., 1886.
McConachie, Bruce A. *Melodramatic Formations American Theatre and Society, 1820–1870*. Iowa City: University of Iowa Press, 1992.
Mitchener, Harold, and Carol Mitchener. *Images of America BRISTOL*. Charleston, S.C.: Arcadia Publishing, 2000.
Moody, Richard. *The Astor Place Riot*. Bloomington: Indiana University Press, 1958.
_____. *Edwin Forrest First Star of the American Stage*. New York: Alfred A. Knopf, 1960.

Munden, Thomas Shepherd. *Joseph Shepherd Munden Comedian*. London: Richard Bentley, 1844.
Murdoch, James Edward. *The Stage, or Recollections of Actors and Acting from an Experience of Fifty Years: A Series of Dramatic Sketches*. 1880, reprint ed., New York: Benjamin Blom, 1969.
Nye, Russel Blaine. *1776–1830 The Cultural Life of the New Nation*. 1960, reprint ed., Evanston, New York and London: Harper and Row, 1963.
Oberholtzer, Ellis Paxson. *Philadelphia: A History of the City and Its People; A Record of 225 Years*. 4 vols., Philadelphia and Chicago: J.S. Clarke Pub. Co., 1912.
Odell, George C.D. *Annals of the New York Stage*. 15 vols., 1927–49, reprint ed., New York: AMS Press, 1970.
Paul, C. Kegan. *William Godwin: His Friends and Contemporaries*. 2 vols., 1876, reprint ed., New York: AMS Press, 1970.
Phelps, Henry Pitt. *Players of a Century: A Record of the Albany Stage*. 1880, reprint ed., New York: Benjamin Blom, 1972.
Pintard, John. *Letters from John Pintard to His Daughter Eliza Noel P. Davidson 1816–1833*. 4 vols., New York: New-York Historical Society, 1940–41.
Playfair, Giles. *The Flash of Lightning A Portrait of Edmund Kean*. London: William Kimber, 1983.
Pollock, Thomas Clark. *The Philadelphia Theatre in the Eighteenth Century, Together with the Day Book of the Same Period*. 1933, reprint ed., Westport, Ct.: Greenwood Press, 1968.
Rees, James. *The Dramatic Authors of America*. Philadelphia: G.B. Zieber & Co., 1845.
Rosenfeld, Sybil. *Strolling Players & Drama in the Provinces 1660–1765*. 1939, reprint ed., New York: Octagon Books, 1970.
St. Clair, William. *The Godwins and the Shelleys: The Biography of a Family*. New York and London: W.W. Norton and Co., 1989.
Shattuck, Charles H. *Shakespeare on the American Stage: From the Hallams to Edwin Booth*. 2 vols., Washington, D.C.: Folger Shakespeare Library, 1976.
_____. *The Shakespeare Promptbooks: A Descriptive Catalogue*. Urbana and London: University of Illinois Press, 1965.
Shockley, Martin Staples. *The Richmond Stage 1784–1812*. Charlottesville: University Press of Virginia, 1977.
Smith, Geddeth. *Thomas Abthorpe Cooper: America's Premier Tragedian*. Madison and Teaneck: Fairleigh Dickinson University Press; London: Associated University Presses, 1996.
Smith, Sol[omon]. *Theatrical Management in the West and South for Thirty Years*. 1868, reprint ed., New York and London: Benjamin Blom, 1968.
Smither, Nelle. *A History of the English Theatre in New Orleans*. New York: Benjamin Blom, 1967.
Sprague, Arthur Colby. *Shakespeare and the Actors: The Stage Business in His Plays, (1660–1905)*. 1944, reprint ed., New York: Russell & Russell, Inc., 1963.
Stone, Henry Dickinson. *Personal Recollections of the Drama or Theatrical Reminiscences, embracing sketches of prominent actors and actresses, their chief characteristics, original anecdotes of them, and incidents connected therewith*. 1873, reprint ed., New York: Benjamin Blom, 1969.
Sunstein, Emily W. *A Different Face: The Life of Mary Wollstonecraft*. New York: Harper and Row, 1975.
_____. *Mary Shelley: Romance and Reality*. Boston: Little Brown and Company, 1989.

Taylor, Aline MacKenzie. *Next to Shakespeare Otway's "Venice Preserved" and "The Orphan" and Their History on the London Stage.* Durham: Duke University Press, 1950.

Weigley, Russell, ed. *Philadelphia: A 300-Year History.* New York and London: W.W. Norton and Co., 1982.

Wemyss, Francis Courtney. *Twenty-Six Years of the Life of an Actor and Manager Interspersed with Sketches, Anecdotes, and Opinions of the Professional Merits of the Most Celebrated Actors and Actresses of Our Day.* 2 vols., New York: Burgess, Stringer and Co., 1847.

_____. *Wemyss' Chronology of the American Stage from 1752–1852.* 1852, reprint ed., New York: Benjamin Blom, 1968.

West, Shearer. *The Image of the Actor: Verbal and Visual Representation in the Age of Garrick and Kemble.* New York: St. Martin's Press, 1991.

Willard, George O. *History of the Providence Stage, 1762–1891.* Providence: The Rhode Island News Company, 1891.

Williams, Stanley T. *The Life of Washington Irving.* 2 vols., New York: Oxford University Press/ London: Humphrey Milford, 1935.

_____. *Richard Cumberland: His Life and Dramatic Works.* New Haven: Yale University Press, 1917.

Wilmeth, Don B. *George Frederick Cooke: Machiavel of the Stage.* Westport, Ct. and London: Greenwood Press, 1980.

Wilson, Garff B. *A History of American Acting.* Bloomington and London: Indiana University Press, 1966.

Wingate, Charles Edgar Lewis. *Shakespeare's Heroes on the Stage.* New York and Boston: Thomas Y. Crowell & Company, 1896.

Winter, William. *Other Days Being Chronicles and Memories of the Stage.* New York: Moffat, Yard and Co., 1908.

Wood, William B. *Personal Recollections of the Stage, Embracing Notices of Actors, Authors, and Auditors During a Period of Forty Years.* Philadelphia: Henry Carey Baird, 1855.

Young, William C. *Famous Actors and Actresses on the American Stage: Documents of American Theatre History.* 2 vols., New York and London: R.R. Bowker, 1975.

Articles

Aldrich, Ruth I. "Introduction." To Thomas Holcroft, *The Road to Ruin.* 1892, reprint ed., Lincoln: University of Nebraska Press, 1968.

Buckingham, Joseph T. "Sketch of the Life and Critical Remarks on the Theatrical Performances of Mr. T.A. Cooper." *The Polyanthos* 1 (January, 1806): 72–86.

Carpenter, Stephen Cullen. "Life of Mr. Cooper." *Mirror of Taste and Dramatic Censor* 1: 1 (January, 1810): 28–44; 2 (March, 1810): 223–35.

Durang, Charles. "The Philadelphia Stage from the Year 1749 to the Year 1855, Partly Compiled from the Papers of His Father, the Late John Durang." *Philadelphia Sunday Dispatch*, 1854. Annenberg Rare Book & Manuscript Library, University of Pennsylvania.

Ellis, Joseph J. "William Dunlap: The Dramatist as Benevolent Patriarch." In *After the Revolution: Profiles of Early American Culture*, 113–58. New York and London: W. W. Norton and Company, 1979.

Harbin, Billy J. "Hodgkinson and His Rivals at the Park: The Business of Early Romantic Theatre in America." *Emerson Society Quarterly* 20, 3rd Quarter (1974): 148–69.

Hewitt, Barnard. "'King Stephen' of the Park and Drury Lane." In Joseph W. Donohue, Jr. *The Theatrical Manager in England and America: Player of a Perilous Game: Philip Henslowe, Tate Wilkinson, Stephen Price, Edwin Booth, Charles Wyndham*, 87–141. Princeton: Princeton University Press, 1971.
Irving, John Beaufain. "Reminiscences of a Tragedian. Thomas A. Cooper His Life, Social and Professional, in Charleston, South Carolina." *The Home Journal* (August 1857–January 1858).
Lippman, Monroe. "Stephen Price: The American Theatre's First Commercial Manager." *The Southern Speech Bulletin* 5: 4 (March 1940).
McDermott, Douglas. "The Theatre and Its Audience: changing modes of social organization in the American theatre." In Ron Engle and Tice L.Miller. *The American Stage: Social and Economic Issues from the Colonial Period to the Present*, 6–17. Cambridge and New York: Cambridge University Press, 1993.
Pritner, Calvin L. "William Warren's Financial Arrangements with Traveling Stars—1805–1829." *Theatre Survey* 6: 2 (November, 1965): 83–90.
Rainey, Grace P. "Reminiscences of My Grandfather, Major James Fairlie." Courtesy of Fairlie Maxwell Pasfield, Sarasota, Florida.
Weisert, John J. "The First Decade at Sam Drake's Louisville Theatre." *Filson Club History Quarterly* 39 (October, 1965): 287–310.
Wilmer, Steve. "Federalist and Republican Theatre in the 1790's." *Theatre Symposium* 5 (1997): 78–94.
Wilmeth, Don B. "Checklist of Selected Books on American theatre, 1960–90." In Ron Engle and Tice L. Miller. *The American Stage: Social and Economic Issues from the Colonial Period to the Present*, 290–308. Cambridge and New York: Cambridge University Press, 1993.
Winter, William. "Famous Actors of the Nineteenth Century: A Chapter of Theatrical History." *Munsey's Magazine* 35 (June 1906): 347–59.
Woodbury, Lael J. " The American Theatre's First Star: Thomas Abthorpe Cooper." *The Theatre Annual* 15 (1957–8): 13–14.

Unpublished Dissertations and Theses

Arant, F. "A Biography of the Actor Thomas Abthorpe Cooper 1775–1849." 2 vols., Ph.D. dissertation, University of Minnesota, 1971.
Bearden, James. "A Tabulation of the Stage Performances of Thomas Abthorpe Cooper." Master's thesis, University of Mississippi, 1968.
Duggar, Mary Morgan. "The Theatre in Mobile: 1822–1860." Master's thesis, University of Alabama, 1941.
Jordan, Harold Trice. "Thomas Cooper: A Biographical Chronology." 2 vols., Ph.D. dissertation, Tulane University, 1972.
Leonard, James M. "The Letters of William Duffy, Albany Theatre Manager, 1830–1835." Ph.D. dissertation, Cornell University, 1971.
McKenzie, Ruth Harsha. "Organization, Production, and Management at the Chestnut Street Theatre, Philadelphia from 1791 to 1820." Ph.D. dissertation, Stanford University, 1952.
Miller, Ronnie Richard. "A Treatise on the Relationship of George Frederick Cooke and Thomas Abthorpe Cooper in Connection with Cooke's Arrival in America." Master's thesis, University of Mississippi, 1968.

Schulte, Nancy C. "The Acting Style of Thomas Abthorpe Cooper." Master's thesis, Pennsylvania State University, 1972.
Shank, Theodore. "The Bowery Theatre, 1826–1836." Ph.D. dissertation, Stanford University, 1956.
Woodbury, Lael J. "Styles of Acting in Serious Drama on the Nineteenth Century American Stage." Ph.D. dissertation, University of Illinois, 1954.

Index

Act of Embargo 162
Adams, Abigail 9
Adams, John Quincy 180
Adelphi Club 196
American Company 80–1, 102
American Theatre, New Orleans 199
American Theatre, the Bowery *see* Bowery Theatre
André, Major John 87
Anthony Street Theatre 159, 168, 171
Arnold, Benedict 87
Astor, John Jacob 130

Barnes, Mr. John 180
Barnes, Mrs. John 180, 198
Barrett, Giles 43–4
Barry, Spranger 128, 144, 213 n.19
Battle of New Orleans 160
Beekman, John K. 130
Bell, Mr. (actor 38
Bernard, John 71, 128, 135, 159
Betterton, Thomas 13
Biddle, Nicholas 192
Bingham, Anne (Mrs. William) 76
Blodgett, Samuel 9
Bonaparte, Joseph 156, 181
Bonaparte, Napoleon 121
Booth, Edwin 2
Booth, John Wilkes 2
Booth, Junius Brutus 2, 190, 192; first comes to America 175
Bowery Theatre 188, 197–9, 203
Brevoort, Henry 151, 156, 159–60
Broad Street Theatre 172
Brown, Charles Brockden 94
Buckingham, Joseph T. 186; *Polyanthos* 129, 142
Burke, Edmund 30, 32
Byrne, Mr. & Mrs. Oscar 71

Caldwell, James H. 175–7, 201
Campbell, Mrs. Allan *see* Cooper, Julia
Carpenter, Stephen Cullen 78; *Charleston Courier* 131–2; *Mirror of Taste & Dramatic Censor* 142–4; *Monthly Review & Literary Miscellany of the U.S.* 133
Charleston Theatre 79–80
Chestnut Street Theatre 9, 71, 75–6, 79, 124, 151, 161; burned down & rebuilt 171
Ciceri, Pierre-Luc-Charles (designer) 137
Cincinnati, Society of the 162, 192
City-Hall, NYC 158
Clapp, William 126
Clarissa Harlowe (Samuel Richardson) 31
classical acting style 14, 36
Clinton, Gov. De Witt 162
Coleman, Elizabeth Tyler, vii 2
Coleman, William 103, 139
Coleridge, Samuel Taylor 5, 31, 50
Collins, Mr. (manager) 41–2, 49
Cooke, George Frederick 6, 58, 113–116, 118–119, 157, 174, 184; American debut 150; death 154–5; debut engagement in Philadelphia 151–2; failure in New York benefit 151; first plays Iago in New York 153; marries Mrs. Behn 154
Cooper, Dr. Thomas (Cooper's father) 21–2
Cooper, Elizabeth Priscilla (Cooper's sister) 21, 32, 41, 55–6, 95, 144; description of Cooper as Penruddock, 68–9
Cooper, Grace Mary Rae (Mrs. Thomas, Cooper's mother) 5, 21, 26, 42–3, 81, 95, 120, 159; death 144; husband's death and reduction of circumstances 5, 22, 28; opposition to William Godwin's views 28, 32
Cooper, James Fairlie (Cooper's eldest son by Mary) 159, 184, 191
Cooper, Joanna Johnstone Upton (Cooper's first wife) 90, 108, 116, 122, 214 n.12; death, 139
Cooper, John Robinson (Cooper's brother Jack) 21, 37, 48, 79
Cooper, Julia (Cooper's fourth daughter by Mary) 178; married Allan Campbell, Pres., Harlem Railroad 206
Cooper, Louisa (Cooper's youngest daughter) 178

229

Cooper, Mary Fairlie (Cooper's second wife) 157–9, 161, 164, 165, 181, 184, 191–2, 208 (Ch. 2) n.1; illness and death 192–4; *see also* Fairlie, Mary

Cooper, Mary Grace (Cooper's eldest daughter by Mary) vii 159, 191–2, 214 n. 12; marries Frederic Raoul 134

Cooper, Olivia (Cooper's third daughter by Mary) 178

Cooper, Priscilla (Cooper's second daughter by Mary) 2, 20, 161, 171, 192, 203; marries Robert Tyler 204–6; stage debut 197–201

Cooper, Stephen Decatur (Cooper's second son by Mary) 192

Cooper, Thomas (journalist) 71

Cooper, Thomas Abthorpe: acting style 1, 14–17, 35–6, 58–9, 127, 133–4, 168–70; 217–18 n. 18; adds middle name 71; America, views on 11–12; American debut 74, 210 n 7; attitude toward his guardian Wm. Godwin 11, 17, 29, 31, 81, 83; birth 21, 208 (Ch. 2) n.1; Boston, first appearance in 125–7; breaks with Stockport manager 52–4; breaks with Thos. Wignell 6, 10, 80–5; breaks with Wm. Dunlap 6, 95–6; celebrated return from England in 1804 122–4; charitable acts 194–5; Charleston, first appearance in 131–3; contract with Drury Lane 105, 112–13; Cooke, G. F., meets and receives assistance of 113–16; Cooke, G. F., pursues to arrange American tour for 145–50; Cooper Fund benefits and stage debut of his daughter Priscilla 196–201; death 206; disruption and failure of last appearance in London 184–6; Drury Lane engagement 1803 111–12; effect of mentors' radical politics on career of 17, 54, 61–2, 65, 71; failed venture at Chatham Garden Theatre 189–90; famous recitation of "Alexander's Feast" (John Dryden) 135, 180, 198; "Father of the American Stage" 199; final performance in New York 203; financial difficulties in early career 46–8, 80–3; government appointments 205; heroic ideal 25, 43, 53, 56, 66, 77–8, 80, 96, 103, 127, 165; home in Bristol, Pa. 150, 163–4, 178, 181, 194; home on Park Row 156; imports the Holmans 157–8; independent starring 81, 96, 99, 124, 138–9, 155, 157, 161; introduces *Othello* to Charleston 134; introduces romantic dress for Hamlet in first American performance of 78; John Street Theatre, first appearance at 80; London debut 59–61; managers, views on 97–100; marries Mary Fairlie 157; marries Mrs. Upton 90; meets Mary Fairlie 141; New Orleans, first appearance in 175–7; New York, first appearance in 10, 44, 79; objects to playing Bland in Dunlap's *André* 87–9; offers J. P. Kemble an American tour 157; on Edmund Kean's acting 172–3; original contract with Thos. Wignell 69–70; painted by Gilbert Stuart 38; Park Theatre, first appearance at 85–6; Park Theatre, hires Thomas Sully to paint portraits at 134–6; Park Theatre, last appearance at 193; Park Theatre, management and renovation of 130, 135–8, 140; Park Theatre, resigns management of 161; partnership with Stephen Price 140–1; patriotism of 158; performs in *Othello* with Edwin Forrest 188, 193, 201; personal description 100; Philadelphia debut 76–7; physical description 1, 13–14, 61, 74, 127, 133; physical stamina 48, 103, 135, 138–9; plays Othello to Cooke's Iago 116, 152–4; political views & influence of Wm. Godwin and Thos. Holcroft on 5, 30–3, 44–5, 194; Providence, first appearance in 128; publicity for first Philadelphia benefit 78; recalls Wm. Dunlap to the Park Theatre 130–1; relationship with James Marshal 26, 30, 32–3, 39–40, 42, 48, 69; relationship with Thos. Holcroft 52, 113–14, 118–19; renewal contract with Thos. Wignell 10, 96, 98; resolution of lawsuit with Thos. Wignell 84–5, 96–7; Richmond, first appearance in 131; rivalry with Edmund Kean 171–4, 184; rivalry with James Fennell 77, 79–80, 104; rivalry with John Hodgkinson 83, 88, 92, 95–6, 104; rivalry with John Philip Kemble 97; self-description 17–18, 100; Stephen Kemble fires 39, 185; symbol of the American stage 6; ward of Wm. Godwin 3, 5, 10–11, 22–33; Wm. Godwin and Thos. Holcroft's professional mentoring of 10, 34–5, 41–3, 55–9, 69–70

Cooper, Thomas Abthorpe, compared to: the Booths 139; Charles Mayne Young 160, 183; David Garrick 172; Edmund Kean 127, 139, 168–9, 171–2, 183, 185; George Frederick Cooke 58, 116, 139, 143, 153; James Fennell 77, 79–80, 89–90, 139–40; John Hodgkinson 104; John Moreton 86, 101; John Philip Kemble 58–9, 67, 116, 127, 143, 163, 172; Joseph George Holman 143, 159; Spranger Barry 128; Talma 185; William Charles Macready 171, 182–3, 185

Cooper, Thomas Abthorpe, performances as: Alexander (Nathaniel Lee, *Alexander the Great*) 78, 98–9, 161; Benedick (Shakespeare, *Much Ado About Nothing*) 101, 162, 203–4; Bertram (Charles R. Maturin, *Bertram*) 161–2; Beverly (Edward Moore, *The Gamester*) 130, 134, 137, 152; Brutus (John Howard Payne, *Brutus; or, The Fall of Tarquin*) 142, 167; Cardinal Wolsey (Shakespeare, *King Henry VIII*) 192;

Index

Charles Surface (William Brinsley Sheridan, *School for Scandal*) 140; Columbus (Thomas Morton, *Columbus*) 78; Coriolanus (Shakespeare, *Coriolanus*) 163, 173, 216–17 (Ch. 15) n.19; Damon (John Banim, *Damon and Pythias*) 178, 183; Dionysius (Arthur Murphy, *The Grecian Daughter*) 101; Duke Aranza (John Tobin, *The Honeymoon*) 162, 189, 216 (Ch. 14) n. 19; Frederick (August von Kotzebue, *Lovers' Vows*) 103; George Barnwell (George Lillo, *The London Merchant*) 51–3; Glenalvon (John Home, *Douglas*) 129; Hamlet (Shakespeare, *Hamlet*) 20, 78, 80, 92–3, 101, 105, 111–12, 117, 125, 130, 131–2, 150, 161–2, 170; Horatio (Nicholas Rowe, *The Fair Penitent*) 118; Iago (Shakespeare, *Othello*) 139–40, 153–4, 158, 214 n.16; Jacques (Shakespeare, *As You Like It*) 181; Jaffier (Thomas Otway, *Venice Preserv'd*) 136, 152; King John (Shakespeare, *King John*) 86–7; King Lear (Shakespeare, *King Lear*) 162; Leon (John Fletcher, *Rule a Wife and Have a Wife*) 117, 129, 167; Lothario (Nicholas Rowe, *The Fair Penitent*) 65, 102; Macbeth (Shakespeare, *Macbeth*) 58, 65–6, 68, 76–7, 89, 92, 100–1, 104, 106–8, 112, 118, 122, 132–3, 143, 160, 170, 182, 184–5, 190, 201–2; Macduff (Shakespeare, *Macbeth*) 103–4; Mark Antony (Shakespeare, *Julius Caesar*) 143–4, 203, 217–18 n.18; Mr. Smith (Thomas Holcroft, *The Road to Ruin*) 36–7; Orlando (William Dunlap, *The Robbery*) 94; Osmond (Matthew Gregory Lewis, *The Castle Spectre*) 100; Othello (Shakespeare, *Othello*) 89, 116, 128, 130, 134, 139–140; 152–3, 173, 179; Penruddock (Richard Cumberland, *The Wheel of Fortune*) 20, 66, 74, 80, 124; Pericles (Shakespeare, *Pericles*) 66; Pierre (Thomas Otway, *Venice Preserv'd*) 15–16, 44, 49, 80, 89–90, 118, 158, 190; Pizarro (Kotzebue, *Pizarro*) 101; Richard the Third (Shakespeare, *Richard the Third*) 34, 112, 116–17, 123–4; Romeo (Shakespeare, *Romeo and Juliet*) 20, 87, 93; Serious Father (Thomas Morton, *The Way to Get Married*) 79; Shylock (Shakespeare, *The Merchant of Venice*) 124; Sir John Falstaff (Shakespeare, *Henry IV*) 129–30, 192; Virginius (James Sheridan Knowles, *Virginius*) 167–9, 171; Young Norval (John Home, *Douglas*) 35, 142; Zaphna (Voltaire, *Mahomet the Imposter*) 34
Cooper, Thomas Hercules Price (Cooper's son by his first wife Joanna) 104, 108, 116, 122, 139, 214 n. 12
Cooper, Virginia (Cooper's fifth daughter by Mary) 178

Cooper, William Gaston (Cooper's third son by Mary) 192
Covent Garden, Theatre Royal 5, 10, 20, 42, 46, 47, 59, 71, 97, 99, 105, 113–14, 145, 165
Cowell, Joe 177–8
Cure for the Heart Ache (Mrs. Morton) 20
Cushman, Charlotte 201

Dallas, Mr., (lawyer) 85
Davidson, Eliza 156, 174, 193–4
Davies, Mr. (actor/manager) 46; unfair treatment of Cooper 46–7
Democratic-Republicans 75, 104
Dennie, Joseph 99
Dickinson, Mr. (manager) 126, 146, 173
Dimond, William Wyatt (actor) 68–9
Dorrances, the 163
Dorset, Mr. 55–6
Drury Lane, Theatre Royal 14, 59, 74–5, 104–5, 111, 113–16, 122, 140, 165, 168, 182, 184
Duff, Mary Ann (Mrs. John) 186, 192
Dunlap, William 4, 26, 33, 44, 47, 50, 70, 72, 80, 83–6, 92, 94–6, 106, 114; account of the American engagement of G. F. Cooke 145–52; advises on Cooper Fund benefits and Priscilla Cooper's debut 197–8; 1801 contract with Cooper 102; 1804 contract with Cooper 119–20; first meets Cooper 72; his management fails 125; on Cooper's acting 78–9, 86, 96, 102, 104; on Cooper's decline 193, 196; produces *André* 87–9; produces plays by Kotzebue 90–1; returns to the Park Theatre with Cooper 130–1, 138
Durang, Charles 1, 4, 69, 74, 77–8, 81, 98–9, 103, 135, 138, 150, 152–3, 178, 182, 184, 186, 192, 194
Dwyer, Mr. (actor) 114
Dyson, George 31–2, 38, 48, 50, 52

Early American audience 75–6, 144
Elliston, Robert William 182
Erskine, David Montagu 104
Evening Post 103

Fairlie, Maj. James 141, 156, 157, 159, 162, 194; death 191–2
Fairlie, Louisa (Mary Fairlie's sister) 194
Fairlie, Maria Yates (Mrs. James) 141, 156, 157, 199
Fairlie, Mary 141, 151; *see also* Cooper, Mary Fairlie
Fawcett, Joseph 24, 31
Fay, Theodore S. 179
Federal Street Theatre 130, 186
Federalists 75, 103
Fennell, James 77, 84, 120, 150; competition with Cooper 104, as Jaffier to Cooper's Pierre (Thomas Otway, *Venice Preserv'd*)

89–90; as Richard the Third to Cooper's Richmond 136; as Zanga (Dr. Young, *The Revenge*) 79–80
Forrest, Edwin 2, 175, 186, 188–9; assists with Cooper Fund benefits and Priscilla Cooper's debut 197–201
Fox, Charles James 44–5
Francis, Dr. John W. 135
French Revolution 26, 49, 71

Garrick, David 14, 81, 113, 128, 155
Gielgud, John 13
Gilfert, Charles 159, 172, 188
Godwin, Hannah (Wm. Godwin's sister) 48
Godwin, John (Wm. Godwin's father) 21
Godwin, Mrs. John (Wm. Godwin's mother) 21
Godwin, Mary Jane (Wm. Godwin's second wife) 111
Godwin, William 21, 23–4, 111, 113–15, 150, 186; *An Account of the Seminary* 24–5; *Caleb Williams* 49; death 203; described by Cooper 83; education 21, 23; *An Enquiry Concerning Political Justice* 11, 24, 31, 33, 40–1, 49; guardian of Cooper 3, 5, 10, 22–33; *Notes on Tom Cooper* 27, 33; philosophic and political theory 23–5, 40–1, 49
Goodman's Fields Theatre 81
Gratz, Joseph 141
Greenwich St. Theatre 44, 79
the Grundys 163
the *Guerrière* 158

Hallam, Lewis 72, 87, 104
Hallam, Mrs. Lewis 72
Hamblin, Thomas 190, 198, 203
Hamblin, Mrs. Thomas 190
Harby, Isaac 172–3
Hare, Arnold 149
Harris, Thomas 47, 59, 66, 97–8, 99, 105, 113–15, 147–9, 151, 154, 165
Harrison, Gabriel 142
Harrison, Gen. William Henry 158, 204
Haymarket Theatre 79, 90
Helvétius, Claude Adrien 23
Hewitt, James 140
Hodgkinson, John 72, 79, 80, 83, 84, 87–9, 90, 92; competition with Cooper 94–5, 104; conflict with Mrs. Merry 102–3; departs NYC for Charleston 120; as Faulconbridge to Cooper's King John in *King John* (Shakespeare) 86–7
Hodgkinson, Mrs. John 85, 90, 120
the Hoffmans 156
Holbach, Paul Henri Thiry, baron d' 23
Holcroft, Thomas 3, 24, 26, 39, 47–8, 113–16; acting theory 57–8, 93; arrest & imprisonment 17, 50, 52; *Deaf and Dumb* 113; described by Cooper 83; *The Deserted Daughter* 59, 67, 83; *German Hotel* 32; his plays introduced to America by Cooper 70; *The Road to Ruin* 20, 35, 83, 164; *School for Arrogance* 44, 83, 47; self-imposed exile 113; suicide of his son 27; trial 54, 70; tutelage of Cooper 3, 5, 10, 17–18, 26, 57–9, 61–2
Holland, John Joseph 137–8, 140, 151
Holliday St. Theatre 74
Holman, Agnes 158–9
Holman, Joseph George 42, 46, 67, 78, 97, 99, 113; American engagement 157–9; compared to G.F. Cooke 113
The Home Journal 1
Hoxton Dissenting Academy 21, 23, 25
Hull, Capt. Isaac 158

Inchbald, Elizabeth 5
Incledon, Charles 46
Ingersoll, Charles 193, 196
Ireland, Joseph Norton 2, 66
Irving, Dr. John Beaufain 1, 132, 134
Irving, Peter 104, 119–20, 156
Irving, Washington 3, 137, 140–1, 151, 156, 157, 159–60, 165, 192; on Charles Mayne Young and comparison to Cooper 160; on John Philip Kemble and comparison to Cooper 58–9; speech for Cooper's reopening of the Park Theatre 138; visits the Coopers in Bristol 192–3

Jackson, Andrew 160, 180, 191
James, Reese Davis 138
Jarvis, John 172
Jefferson, Joseph 94, 189
Jefferson, Thomas 89, 121, 156
John St. Theatre 44, 72, 79, 80
Jones, Julia (actress) 139

Kean, Edmund 175, 183, 186; first American tour 165, 168–9, 171–4; London scandal & second American tour 181–2, 184
Kemble, Charles 196–7
Kemble, Fanny 196–7
Kemble, John Philip 58–9, 67, 113, 116, 147, 151, 155; as Penruddock 74; debut 14; declines Cooper's offer of an American tour 157; influence on Cooper 36; leaves Drury Lane for Covent Garden 105, 112; retirement 163
Kemble, Stephen 34–6, 46, 118, 142; Cooper describes acting of 37; fires Cooper 38–40
the Kembles 13, 114
Knowles, James Sheridan 167, 181
Kotzebue, August von 20, 90–1

Lafayette, Marquis de 180
LaMath (actor) 36
Landreth Seed Company, the Landreths 163
Law, Mr. John 12, 20

Index

L'Estrange, Mr. and Mrs. 71
Lewis, Lee (actor) 36
Licensing Act 50, 59
Lincoln, Abraham 2
Liverpool Theatre Royal 146
the Livingstons 156
Ludlow, Noah Miller 124, 139, 171, 189–90

Macklin, Charles 66–7, 113, 211 (Ch. 8) n. 7; comment on Cooper's London debut 67, 86
Macready, William Charles 165, 167–8, 171, 183, 186; first American tour 181–2
the *Magdelen* 150
Marinelli (designer) 137
Marmion, (James Nelson Barker) 154
Marshal, James 24, 26, 30–3, 50, 69, 114–15, 118
Masterman, William (manager) 67
Mathews, Charles 59; visits the Coopers in Bristol 164
Melmoth, Mrs. (actress) 85, 94
Merchant's Hotel, Wall St. 162
Merry, Anne Brunton (Mrs. Robert) 10, 12–13, 20, 71, 74, 79, 83, 138, 169; challenged by John Hodgkinson 102–3; Chestnut St. Theatre, management of 124; death 136; as Elvira (Kotzebue, *Pizarro*) 101; marriage to Thomas Wignell 124; marriage to William Warren 136; as Ophelia 125; recommends Cooper to Thomas Wignell 10
Merry, Robert 10, 17
The Mirror of Taste and Dramatic Censor see Carpenter, Stephen Cullen
Monroe, James 162, 180
Moreton, John 78, 84, 86
Morning Chronicle 104; *see also* Irving, Peter
Morris, George P. 1, 198
Morris, Gouverneur 156
Morse, Mr. (actor) 136
Munden, Joseph Shepherd 61, 147–8
Murdoch, James Edward 58, 172, 195

Newgate Prison 50
Nicholson, William 24

Ogden, David 123–4
Ogden, Henry 156
Old Price Riots 145–6, 155, 177, 185
Olympic Theatre 171

Paine, Robert Treat 139
Paine, Thomas 32, 38, 49
Park Theatre 81–2, 87, 90, 92, 124, 135, 139–40, 150, 158–9, 162, 177, 188–9, 197, 206; burned down and rebuilt 171; Cooper becomes manager 130; Cooper recalls Dunlap 130–1; financial failure of Dunlap's management 125; first opens 84; Stephen Price joins Cooper's management 140
Paulding, James Kirk 156
Payne, John Howard 127, 167, 186; acting debut 141–2; *Thespian Mirror* 129–30, 142
Peale, Rembrandt 78
Perreau, Mr. (husband of Cooper's sister Elizabeth Priscilla) 144
Perry, Commodore 158
Philadelphia as U.S. capital 75, 81
Philadelphia Company 9, 10, 12, 20, 80–1
Pintard, John 156, 174, 193–4
Pitt, William 17, 49–50, 52
Polk, James K. 205
The Polyanthos see Buckingham, Joseph T.
Pope, Mrs. (actress) 61, 116
Portsmouth theatre 41, 49, 97
Powell, Snelling 125–6, 130, 139, 158
Price, Stephen 156–7, 177, 197; joins management of Park Theatre 140–1; manages Drury Lane 182, 184, 186; manages G. F. Cooke's American debut 150–1
Price, Mrs. Stephen 164
Priestley, Joseph 32, 50

Quick, John 46, 61, 67

Randolph, John 154
Raoul, Frederic Sebastian (husband of Cooper's daughter Mary Grace) vii, 134, 214 n. 12
Raoul, Mrs. Frederic *see* Cooper, Mary Grace
Reinagle, Alexander 9, 79, 85
Reveley, Maria 52
Rice, Thomas Dartmouth 196
Richardson, Mr. (Drury Lane) 104
Richmond theatre fire 154
Robinson, Mrs. (actress) 68
Roscoe, William 116
Rousseau, Jean Jacques 23, 25
Rowan, Archibald Hamilton 70

Sansom 71
Schlegel, Friedrich von 135
Scott, Gen. Winfield 162
Shelley, Mary 15, 186, 203; on Thomas Holcroft 27; on William Godwin's treatment of Cooper 27–8
Sheridan, Richard Brinsley 20, 105
Sheridan, Thomas (actor) 14
Siddons, Sarah 14, 59, 66–7; influence on Cooper 34–7, 39
Simpson, Edmund (manager) 161, 197
Sloman, Mrs. (actress) 190–1
Society for Commemorating the Glorious Revolution 26–7, 32
Southey, Robert 50
Steuben, Friedrich Wilhelm, Baron von 141

Stone, Henry Dickinson 138–9
Stuart, Gilbert 38
Sully, Thomas, vii 78, 134–5

Tammany Hall 158
Theatre ban (1778) 75
Theatrical Commonwealth 159
The Thespian Mirror see Payne, John Howard
Thornton, Dr. William 12
Thornton, Mrs. William 12, 20
Tontine Coffee House 154
Treason Trials 54, 113
Twaits, William 128, 159
Twaits, Mrs. William (Elizabeth Westray) 159
Tyler, George Joseph 43–4; Cooper's treatment by 47
Tyler, John 2, 204–5
Tyler, Letitia Christian (Mrs. John) 204–5
Tyler, Robert (eldest son of John Tyler) 2, 204–6
Tyler, Mrs. Robert *see* Cooper, Priscilla

United States' Theatre 6, 10, 12

Van Buren, Martin 191
Venice Preserv'd (Thomas Otway) 12

Walker, John 14
Wallack, Henry 189
Wallack, James William 185, 198
Walnut Street Theatre 171, 175, 192
Warren, William 71–2, 74, 80, 124, 159
Warren, Mrs. William 136; *see also* Merry, Anne Brunton

Warren & Wood 151, 171; *see also* Warren, William; Wood, William B.
Washington, George 76, 87, 89, 93–4
Washington Hall 158
Washington Theatre 20
Webb, Willis 25
Wemyss, Francis Courtney 75–6, 179
West, Benjamin 168
Whitlock, Mr. and Mrs. (Mrs. Siddons' sister) 79
Wignell, Thomas 44, 69–74, 76, 79–83, 106; lawsuit against Cooper 83–5, 95–6, 98; opens first theatre in Washington, D.C. 9–10, 12–13, 18–20; original contract with Cooper 69, 80
Wignell, Mrs. Thomas 124; *see also* Merry, Anne Brunton
Wignell & Reinagle 9, 79, 85; *see also* Wignell, Thomas; Reinagle, Alexander
Wilkinson, Tate 67
Wilmeth, Don B. 145, 149
Wilmot, George 122, 128, 131, 175
Wollstonecraft, Capt. Charles 15, 17
Wollstonecraft, Mary (Wm. Godwin's first wife) 15, 17, 70, 83
Wood, William B. 13, 15, 124, 142, 150, 198; on Cooper 4, 13–14, 17, 38, 51, 71, 74–5, 100, 116
Wood, Mrs. William B. (Juliana Westray) 198
Woods, Mr. (actor) 37–8
Woodworth, Samuel 198
Wrekin, the (London pub) 114

Young, Charles Mayne 118, 160, 165, 183, 194

www.ingramcontent.com/pod-product-compliance
Ingram Content Group UK Ltd.
Pitfield, Milton Keynes, MK11 3LW, UK
UKHW041940140426
5217IPUK00014B/584